Cultural Artifacts and the Production of Meaning

Cultural Artifacts and the Production of Meaning

The Page, the Image, and the Body

Edited by
Margaret J. M. Ezell and
Katherine O'Brien O'Keeffe

Ann Arbor

THE UNIVERSITY OF MICHIGAN PRESS

Copyright © by the University of Michigan 1994
All rights reserved
Published in the United States of America by
The University of Michigan Press
Manufactured in the United States of America
⊗ Printed on acid-free paper

1997   1996   1995   1994   4   3   2   1

A CIP catalogue record for this book is available from the British Library.

Library of Congress Cataloging-in-Publication Data

Cultural artifacts and the production of meaning : the page, the
   image, and the body / edited by Margaret J.M. Ezell and Katherine
   O'Brien O'Keeffe.
        p.   cm.
      Includes bibliographical references.
      ISBN 0-472-10499-3 (alk. paper). — ISBN 0-472-08257-4 (pbk. :
   alk. paper)
      1. Material culture. 2. Materialism. 3. Culture—Philosophy.
   4. Culture—Semiotic models. I. Ezell, Margaret J. M.
   II. O'Keeffe, Katherine O'Brien.
   GN406.C85   1994
   306—dc20   94-19985
                                                        CIP

Acknowledgments

It is a pleasure to be able to acknowledge the assistance and support provided for this project by a number of institutions and individuals. The contributors to this volume were brought together at "Textual Technologies: Text, Image, and History" (1992), a conference organized by the Interdisciplinary Group for Historical Literary Study (IGHLS) at Texas A&M University. We would first like to thank Jeffrey N. Cox, who directed the conference, Larry J. Reynolds, director of the IGHLS Steering Committee, and the members of the conference committee. Funding for the conference was generously supplied by the Ralph R. Thomas Endowment, the Department of English, and the College of Liberal Arts at Texas A&M University. We would like to thank in particular J. Lawrence Mitchell and Daniel Fallon for their support. Technical assistance in the preparation of the manuscript came from Marilyn Radke. We would like to acknowledge as well the generous support of IGHLS in the preparation of the volume. For providing a pleasant venue for the writing of the introduction and the preparation of this volume, we would like to acknowledge the hospitality of the National Humanities Center.

The photograph of Dickinson MS 129–129a is reproduced by permission of the publishers and the Trustees of Amherst College from *The Poems of Emily Dickinson*, Thomas H. Johnson, ed., Cambridge, Mass.: The Belknap Press of Harvard University Press, Copyright © 1951, 1955, 1979, 1983 by the President and Fellows of Harvard College.

The illustrations from *Tristram Shandy* and from *The Dunciad* are reproduced by permission of the Joseph Regenstein Library, University of Chicago.

Contents

Introduction

Margaret J. M. Ezell and Katherine O'Brien O'Keeffe

This is what he said: "Let us make humankind in our image and likeness." And his creature was made his spouse when God assumed our human nature. *Oh Jesus, gentlest love, as a sign that you had espoused us, you gave us the ring of your most holy and tender flesh at the time of your holy circumcision on the eighth day.* You know, my revered mother, that on the eighth day just enough flesh was taken from him to make a circlet of a ring; to give us a sure hope of payment in full he began by paying this pledge.
—Catherine of Siena to Giovanna d'Angiò, Queen of Naples, 1375

The human voice, the written word, continually regulate the appearance and disappearance of the human body.
—Elaine Scarry

Her finger, his ring, God's word. In her letter to the worldly Giovanna d'Angiò, the virgin mystic Catherine of Siena appropriates Christ's circumcised flesh to create a textual artifact, one that incarnates and makes tangible as a cultural sign the most ineffable of spiritual intimacies. Alluding to her mystical marriage in 1368, Catherine reads and interprets the spare text of Luke's account of Christ's circumcision, the enactment on Christ's body of the promise of God's continuing relationship to humankind: she then rewrites the Old Testament pledge as a promise of eternal union with the Divine spouse.[1] In writing her letter, she *reconstructs* the verbal construct of a promise in the artifact of the wedding ring, ever to be read anew as the somatic symbol of eternal transcendence of the body. In reading her text, we are made conscious of synchronous perceptions of the word made flesh, the Book and the body, hers and ours. Her body, Christ's body, now become the site of a struggle to avoid the limitations of language and the boundaries of material place and time, cannot but be inscribed (paradoxically) in a material text dependent on cultural particulars and the contingencies of textual transmission.

In seeking to know the unknowable, Catherine of Siena's route to God lies in her comprehension of the Incarnation as a central mystery of Christianity and through contemplation of the agonized body of Christ crucified. While the crucified body became the site for her meditation on the meeting of the human and the divine, Catherine enacted her faith on her own body: in effect, her lifelong fasting translated her body into a text of her will.[2] And if her experience of God approached the unmediated, it was nonetheless prepared for and expressed through complex mediations of the Book. The scripture Catherine internalized was subsequently reinscribed in written documents in order to move the will of others, in this particular letter, to urge the Queen of Naples to make war on the bodies of the infidels occupying Jerusalem. Her mystical marriage embodied the ineffable: her dilemma was how to take that embodiment and transmit it materially through a language determined by her culture and times. She took the Book, read it through the body, and transmitted it through a dictated text, which was then written, and then translated.

The point of intersection of Catherine's text and our reading of it offers both an occasion for and an illustration of some strategies of materialist criticism. If her dilemma was how to transmit the somatic experience of her mystical union with Christ and, no less important, to make it speak effectively to the political powers of her times, our dilemma is how to receive her text. Our culture and times resist Catherine's reading through the body: it seems an inappropriate literalization, a mortifying lack of taste, jarring in particular in an epistle to a secular queen. Furthermore, we do not even know to what extent the texts that now represent her—dictated to scribes, copied and recopied—are her own words. She did not learn to write until a few years before her death.[3] As her most recent editor notes, "There are a number of possible levels at which alterations could have entered into the text of the letters: at the initial dictation, in the making of 'good copy' from the original transcription, in the later copying of an original for a collection, and finally in any later transcription from collection to collection."[4] Nor, according to her editor, is there any indication that Catherine took an interest in the letters beyond their immediate composition: "She never, so far as we know, even thought of their being one day being collected and disseminated."[5]

From the beginning her editors and disseminators shaped the "Catherine" we now receive, selecting, translating, excising, transforming the disturbing female radical voice into an inspirational institution. For ex-

ample, we now know that the earliest collections of the letters removed
the "unimportant" personal material in the name of pious edification.[6]
The print history of the letters continues this pious construction: the
first printed edition (1492) presents the letters in Gothic typeface with a
frontispiece depicting Catherine as a Madonna figure. The 1500 Aldine
edition expands to over three hundred letters, recapitulating the order
of one of the first manuscript collections, by presenting the letters in
order of descending importance: " . . . supreme pontiffs, cardinals, arch-
bishops, priests, friars, monks, and hermits; to sisters, nuns, and other
devout and religious persons of every condition; also to kings, dukes,
counts, military captains, and various other lords; to communities, regi-
ments; to doctors, knights, and various other persons, seculars, women
of every condition. . . . "[7] The very order of the letters is marked by notions
of social hierarchy. In the long historical process of transforming dictated
letters into a bound, printed book, at every stage we can see the appropriation of Catherine and the inscription of contemporary culture upon her.

The essays in this volume confront problems in contemporary cultural study similar to those raised by Catherine's letters. Read as a volume, these essays explore artifacts (the imprint or inscription of the
human on the object, the page, or the body) in a dialectic of creation and
reception. The material artifact is always resistant to critical appropriation; however, this does not mean that the act of seeking a glimpse of
the historical past is without value. We read through lenses of interven-
ing cultures and ideologies and from glimpses construct narratives to
understand texts and ourselves. As materialist critics, we are conscious
that we receive any textual artifact mediated as well through technologies generated by the culture that created it. The artifact, then, not only
resists our critical appropriation; its very resistance presses us to acts of
self-knowledge in the process of trying to understand it in the context
of its culture.

Under the broad approach to cultural studies generally labeled "materialist" we find a wealth of critical strategies available to negotiate
problems of textual and historical analysis. These include such seemingly
disparate critical methods as historical materialism, deconstruction, psy-
choanalytic criticism, textual bibliography, and body studies, to name
an obvious few. Many cultural critics work through a materialist hermeneutics of inscribed texts as well as of texts enacted or embodied, that is,
work on the written and the somatic.[8] The essays in this volume might
roughly be grouped along these two lines of interest. The essays primarily concerned with written texts include those by Jerome McGann,

Howard Marchitello, Morris Eaves, J. Paul Hunter, and Hamlin Hill; essays directing their attention to the body, mind, and performance include those by Jeanne Holland, Houston Baker, W. J. T. Mitchell, and Herbert Blau. Having made this division, the extent to which these engage in intertextual conversation across all boundaries is immediately clear. While the essays display a chronological sweep, from the investigation of the politics of manuscript texts to the technology of print production and the dynamics of film and rap music, all exhibit a fascination with the concrete.[9] Taken as a whole, their contents raise questions about the implications of reproduction in manuscript and print cultures, the changing dynamics of print and authorship, the visual art of postmodern books, the psychotechnology of memory in modern fiction, and "body art" as the concrete expression of the visceral realism of tragedy. Individually and together, they share a fascination with the permeability of formerly stable boundaries—between text and object, body and text, creation and reception, "life" and "art."

For Jerome McGann human culture consists of symbolic exchanges, and "these exchanges always involve material negotiations."[10] In "Composition as Explanation," this leading theorist of historical textual study turns his attention to the composition of the modernist book, working through in practice the materialist hermeneutics he "sketch[ed]" in *The Textual Condition*.[11] He takes as his subject the three books of Pound's *Cantos*. Pound conceived of his project in the context of the late-nineteenth-century "Renaissance of Printing" and makes an issue of language's physique, deliberateness, and historicality. This inscription of history in the book McGann also finds present in other contemporary works, among them the works of the Harlem Renaissance, the "visual programs" of Emily Dickinson, Louis Zukofsky and the 1950s projectivists, and Robert Carleton Brown's *The Readies*. McGann sees in Brown's rejection of the classical book a prophecy of computerized word processing and hypertextual fields, a bibliographical inheritance postmodern poetry has appropriated. In reading the social in the book, the body in the typeface, McGann seeks to break "the spell of romantic hermeneutics by socializing the study of texts at the most radical levels."[12]

This fundamental critical insight makes possible a variety of critical strategies for reading the artifact within its culture. Turning the gaze to political history and the transmission of texts, Howard Marchitello charts the unremarked spatial array of the map as a potential ideological construct, although it purports to be a neutral, utilitarian representation of the real. A map, however, is always both narrative and image: as Marchitello argues, maps are made to tell historical tales, and these tales, moreover, are deployed in the service of specific political and cultural ideologies. He explores sixteenth-century English maps and mapmaking as a process of rendering the world radically discontiguous, of breaking it up into pieces in the service of national or regional identity, political or military power. Marchitello examines the development of mapmaking, charting a movement away from cartographic sketch in the sixteenth century toward the inscription of national identity in historical topography, in which the visual landscape is populated with mythological figures, creating not only a spatial representation of topographical characteristics but also topographically organized historical accounts of emerging powers.

Editing, for Morris Eaves, is also a form of mapping, mapping the reception of texts by different cultures. Like cartography, which purports to reconstruct the real for our benefit, editing practices in the past have presented themselves as the innocent recovery of the historical original. Eaves argues that such claims are based on two myths of modern editing: first, that transmission corrupts the text and, second, that transmission *improves* in a collection of works. Editing, he argues, is always done from the reception end, even when it attempts to restore integrities and differences at some point of origination in the past. Whether it is the material editing of the restoration of the Sistine ceiling, the use of original instruments in performing baroque music, or the colorizing of black and white movies, Eaves finds a simultaneous desire to both recapture the material past and to "improve" the historical artifact through present technologies.

Both J. Paul Hunter and Hamlin Hill direct our attention to the historical conditions under which "authorial" texts come into the world as material objects. Hunter examines the problematic relationship between two eighteenth-century authors and emergent technologies of print and commercial publication. He uses as his case studies one writer noted for his celebration of individuality, innovation, and the playful manipulation of print technology, Laurence Sterne; for the other, he selects Alexander Pope, a writer who sees cultural loss in any kind of social or literary change and thus might be viewed as an unlikely candidate for embracing the new dynamics of commercial technology. In Sterne's use of the graphic conventions of print technology to create a particular and stable form of product, the novel, he controls a community of readers through its involvement in the technology of the printed page. Pope, who openly derided commercial booksellers, printers, and technology in general, nevertheless could not avoid the advances in the technology of modern printing; reading against our preconceptions, Hunter finds Pope exploiting the new technology in order to transform the old, traditional forms of intertextuality as allusion and to technologize it into a new, materialized intertextuality, making verse visible through graphic illustration.

Hamlin Hill explores Mark Twain's unique participation in the commodification of nineteenth-century American fiction. He focuses on Twain's involvement in the multiple facets of textual production—advertising, illustrating, sales campaigns, and distribution—in the context of the changes in nineteenth-century American book production. In 1868 Twain began publishing his novels by "subscription publication," peddling door to door in small towns and rural areas; his efforts were so successful that he ultimately became involved in the financing of a subscription-book house, becoming the favorite supplier and performer for a mass audience of "popular culture" readers. He even went so far as to invest in new experimental machinery for printing, a move that finally bankrupted him. Ultimately, Twain's keen instinct for what would sell to his growing commercial audience led him beyond innovations in technology into the commodification of his personality as author as well as his books, turning "Mark Twain" into a product, rather than an author.

In striking contrast to Mark Twain's commodification of himself as an author, Emily Dickinson maintained a lifelong resistance to publication. Jeanne Holland argues that Dickinson's refusal to publish is a symptom of agoraphobic fear of the marketplace and of class privilege, for the print technology of the nineteenth century was deeply disturbing. By sewing together her own facsicles, circumscribing her readership to family and friends, and refusing to print, Dickinson developed her own domestic technologies of publication. Circulating her poems only to select readers, Dickinson resisted the democratization of print. If one reads the materiality of Dickinson's late work, Holland argues, light is shed on the nature of her refusal to engage with the technology of print. The fragment "Alone and in a circumstance" (1167), with its stamp and paper strip "legs," emblematizes the gendered subject of the poem; the making of the poem constructs Dickinson's bodily image intertextually. Even while the content of Dickinson's poetry attempts to negotiate class, body, and subjectivity, the materiality of her late work acknowledges that the domestic realm, too, lacks a stable self. Holland plots Dickinson's abandonment of "bookmaking" as arising from her awareness of this loss.

While Dickinson represents the nineteenth-century artist's flight from the technologies of commercialization, Houston Baker makes a compelling case for the late-twentieth-century rap artist's exuberant embrace of electronically mediated production as signaling a rejection of the "artifactual thinker," whose reading of any artifact is designed to render it safe, confined, and familiar. Calling for a new mode of cultural studies, in which "the aural, tactile, olfactory, and gustatory immediacy of social imbrication reveals unseen connections and 'unmakes' familiarly accepted, artifactual designs of mere *things*," Baker argues there are no "arrested *things*, only myriad relations 'in the making.'" The rap artist works against the construction of the artifact as a static entity, a moment of freeze-frame cultural memory. Rap "texts" are not discrete, ordered, comprehensible material units, made into books, pages, and images, but, instead, celebrate fluidity in which boundaries of authorship and ownership are continuously breached. For Baker the rap artist takes "fetishized, commodified discs of sound and creates—through a trained ear and deft hands—a sound that virtually commands (like Queen Latifah) assembled listeners to dance."

In a variant on the exploration of the collision of the material technologies of reproduction (in which the author can be both resistant and complicitous simultaneously) with the power of creative production, W. J. T. Mitchell examines the technology of memory in the context of American slave narrative, whose contents refuse to stay within the boundaries of conventional history. Instead, such narratives insist on reminding us of a past "we can never forget, and which seems continually to elude our understanding." Since slave narratives are always written by *former* slaves, narration must always come through memory and description. While such narratives emphasize spatial over temporal consciousness, their descriptive representations both "mediate" and obstruct our knowledge of slavery. Using Derridean "economimesis," Mitchell locates the intersections of narrative, memory, and slavery through the voices of children (using Wordsworth's *Prelude*) and women (using Charlotte Brontë's *Jane Eyre*). While memory in these texts, Mitchell argues, is ostensibly constructive, narratives of deep trauma may be functions of strategic amnesia. Claude Lantzmann's film *Shoah* deliberately excludes visual memory and narration of Auschwitz, since "telling" the story is possible, but "describing" the experience is too dangerous. In Mitchell's conclusion he analyzes *Beloved* as an example of the selective *dis*(re)membering of experience, a narrative that must remember slavery and reconstruct the experiential place-times of racial degradation, loss of identity, and abject servitude.

Whereas embodiment in Mitchell's essay may point to destruction as well as creation, Herbert Blau's essay challenges the reader to ask whether, as we think of the body in its dispossession, there is something about the body that is ontologically dispossessed in such rhetorics of it. It is commonplace now to see upon the body, Blau argues, the inscriptions and investments of power without imagining behind it some prior or elemental body. Blau turns to the theater of the avant-garde, Brecht, and "body art" as practiced by Gina Pane and Chris Burden, in which the submission of the body to acts of pain and mutilation is a forensic act, one that refuses the reality of pain in human affairs as a tragic and irreversible condition. Such artists inflict pain on their bodies, Blau argues, so that whoever takes notice by being at the event is on notice that the only intolerable pain is that gratuitously or compulsively exercised by the social order upon the body. For Blau such art conceives of the body as a final conscience, which resists aesthetic strategies that anesthetize us against emotions we find intolerable, that refuse to permit us to forget the visceral realism of tragedy.

Disparate as their specific topics may seem, the writers in this volume nevertheless speak intertextually across historical and national boundaries. In their particular concern with the elements of the artist's body Blau's and Holland's exploration of "the obscure secrets of the somatic" form a dialogue questioning what Barbara Stafford, in her study *Body Criticism,* refers to as "the norm of legibility."[13] Critics working on body/text, such as Leonard Barkan in *Nature's Work of Art: The Human Body as Image of the World,* have reminded us that "the human body is more than simply an alternative theatre of action, subject to comparison with abstraction and cosmic events."[14] Blau and Holland refuse to permit us to forget the materiality of the artist herself.

On the level of language Stafford has argued that somatic metaphors historically have been used to organize perception of "our deepest and most intractable existential problems," problems that McGann sees in the printed eyes of Robert Carleton Brown, that Mitchell finds in the narration of slavery, and that Blau experiences in the mode of tragedy itself. Samuel Clemens, the subject of Hill's inquiry, sees his body caught up in the very satanic machinery of commercialism he helped to create, as though, like a character in one of his tales, he had been "snatched up by the machinery and whizzed through his particular factory for almost forty years before he exited from it, . . . nowhere near 'the way he was when he went' in," converting the body of the author into a text commodified and consumed as Mark Twain.

Feminist critics such as Helena Michie have argued that the body has thus served always as a locus of interpretation, both critical and of the self.[15] The act of the interpretation and its transmission is inscribed in language, as Elaine Scarry points out in *Literature and the Body*. In her analysis language "both absorbs the material world and empties itself of material content. To get 'things' into words will be the project of some, to get 'things' out of words the project of others. Materialist criticism simply observes the ways in which this may be done (as well as the cost in each direction)."[16] Where language and the body of the text meet, the visual is political: Holland, McGann, and Eaves, in their concern over the physical transmission of Emily Dickinson and her technological choices, reveal the appropriation of Dickinson by her paternalistic editors. They also speak to the production issues raised by Hunter in his probing of the problematic relationships between the writer, the mode of production, and the process of transmission. The visual textuality of Alexander Pope's frontispiece to the *Dunciad* connecting George II and Midas clearly makes the intertextual allusion a political gesture. Likewise, the mythological figures peopling the sixteenth-century maps of England examined by Marchitello embody political conceptions of nationhood.

"To perceive the aura of an object we look at," wrote Walter Benjamin, "means to invest it with the ability to look at us in return."[17] In its resistance to simple, unified, closed readings of it, the object, textual or somatic, demands that we permit its multiplicity of meanings and forces us to become conscious of our own cultural and technological boundaries. The danger of a teleological reading of the present, with a corresponding attitude of editorial arrogance, concerns McGann and Eaves. When editing a text from the perspective of reception, not only a recognition of its cultural transmission but also the technology of its preservation must be invoked.

In contrast, for Baker in his analysis of rap the question raised by the multiplicity of meanings is not the problem of attempting to control them but, rather, of celebrating them. Rap artists, he argues, deny the social boundaries of materialistic commercial art, layering meaning as they produce ever-changing songs through electronic technology. The process of fragmentation is at once the process of creation as slices of sound, snatches of text, are mixed, extended, superimposed. Rap is like hypertext, which "does not permit a tyrannical, univocal voice. . . . Hypertext, in other words, provides an infinitely re-centerable system whose provisional point of focus depends upon the reader, who becomes a truly active reader."[18] Rap, too, demands a dispersed text, in which the "writer" loses control over his or her text. Rap is always potential, never fixed, a network of meaning rather than a single point. Rap is, above all, performance. Indeed, several of the essays in this volume explore the possibilities of a dispersed text, interrogating the boundaries of the academic essay and the conference performance.

All of the pieces collected here were originally written to be performed: the participants were brought together at the conference "Textual Technologies" to explore various interplays of text, technology, body, and history.[19] Performance, therefore, is a fundamental element in the nature of these texts; slides accompanying the pieces created impromptu glossings of the projected images, and the interaction of audience and speaker evoked numerous authorial asides, jokes, and comments. Houston Baker's "essay" was a performance script, a rap response to academic discourse. While such living features of performance are always lost in the translation to print, what was gained in the process of the conference, however, was an extraordinary degree of intertextual conversation among the essays. In the process of revision several of the contributors modified their original pieces to develop various strands of conversation in the other essays: the text changed from individual performance pieces to interrelated dialogues on shared concerns about text and technology.

The essays in this volume, while begun in the isolation of the scholarly study, are intrinsically social productions. While each stands alone as the product of an individual scholarly project, when read in the context of its companion pieces, each reaches out to establish intertextual dialogue that cuts across academic boundaries. Resonance within the volume creates new bridges between speaker and audience, author and reader. As our brief examination of Catherine's letter illustrates, any act of cultural interpretation, be it so "neutral" as the collecting and printing of letters, is undertaken through the mediation of ideologies and desires. If the occasion of such interpretation, the artifact itself, invites our study, it also stands against it. As editors, we are conscious of our own mediations in the presentation of these essays by offering a framework and contextualization: the pieces themselves, the artifacts we present, both permit and resist this gesture.

NOTES

Epigraphs taken from *The Letters of St. Catherine of Siena,* trans. Suzanne Noffke, O.P., vol. 1 (Binghamton: Medieval and Renaissance Texts and Studies, 1988–), letter 39, p. 128; *Literature and the Body: Essays on Populations and Persons,* ed. Elaine Scarry, Selected Papers from the English Institute 1986, n.s. 12 (Baltimore: Johns Hopkins University Press, 1988), ix.

1. Luke 2:21. It has been suggested that Catherine is recalling Exodus 4:24–26.

2. Rudolph Bell's choice of the term *anorexia* to describe Catherine's fasting is a further example of the way in which Catherine's body-as-text has been mediated and inscribed by current cultural concerns (Rudolph M. Bell, *Holy Anorexia* [Chicago: University of Chicago Press, 1985], 29). For an important qualification to Bell's views, see Caroline Walker Bynum, *Fragmentation and Redemption: Essays on Gender and the Human Body in Medieval Religion* (New York: Zone Books, 1991), 139–41 and 351–52 nn. 84–86.

3. Catherine of Siena, *The Dialogue,* trans. Suzanne Noffke, O.P., preface by Giuliana Cavallini (New York: Paulist Press, 1980). Cavallini notes that Catherine seems to have taught herself to read around the time she became a Dominican Tertiary (4). It was much later, possibly during the fall of 1377, that she learned to write (12).

4. Noffke, *Letters of St. Catherine,* 1:10. Noffke provides a useful overview of the difficulties presented by the textual transmission of the letters, in the present case focusing on the scribal intervention of "b" (22).

5. Ibid., 21.

6. Ibid., 11–12.

7. Ibid., 16.

8. Jerome J. McGann, *The Textual Condition* (Princeton: Princeton University Press, 1991), 15.

9. See Scarry, *Literature and the Body,* xxii–xxiii.

10. McGann, *The Textual Condition,* 3.

11. Ibid., 15.

12. Ibid., 12.

13. Barbara Maria Stafford, *Body Criticism: Imagining the Unseen in Enlightenment Art and Medicine* (Cambridge, Mass.: MIT Press, 1991), 2, 5.

14. Leonard Barkan, *Nature's Work of Art: The Human Body as Image of the World* (New Haven: Yale University Press, 1975), 5.

15. Helena Michie, *The Flesh Made Word: Female Figures and Women's Bodies* (New York: Oxford University Press, 1987), intro. Michie usefully points out that the body must always be read as a gendered construct, countering the writing of Foucault and many other body studies, in which the "normative" body is male (7).

16. Scarry, *Literature and the Body,* xx.

17. Walter Benjamin, *Illuminations,* ed. and intro. Hannah Arendt, trans. Harry Zohn (New York: Harcourt Brace and World, 1968), 188.

18. George P. Land, *Hypertext: The Convergence of Contemporary Critical Theory and Technology* (Baltimore: Johns Hopkins University Press, 1992), 11.

19. "Textual Technologies: Text, Image, and History" was sponsored by the Interdisciplinary Group for Historical Literary Study of Texas A&M University. The conference, chaired by Jeffrey N. Cox, was held March 26–29, 1992.

Political Maps: The Production of Cartography and Chorography in Early Modern England

Howard Marchitello

Historically, the study of cartography has been dedicated almost exclusively to discussions of the technical aspects of maps and their production, the innovations and improvements in the science of cartography, and the aesthetic and antiquarian value of maps and map collecting.[1] Invoking an essential (and essentializing) evolutionary model, the study of cartography has sought to tell the story of maps and their gradual and inexorable perfection; from the earliest graphic representations in stone or wood to the most sophisticated LANDSAT satellite images, maps, we are told, march in an endless progress toward absolute truth in representation. There are a number of fundamental assumptions that inform this argument: that maps are pure descriptions of geographical reality, that maps are value free, that maps represent zero-degree intervention, and that maps are true. All of these assumptions follow from the primary belief among not only scholars of cartography but "lay people" (map users) as well that maps exist outside of discourse.

Recently, these cartographic assumptions have come under serious review. The most significant challenge has come from the work of J. B. Harley, who has suggested that we begin to articulate a new understanding of cartography that explicitly places it within discourse, an understanding that recognizes cartography as a social practice embedded in both ideology and the politics of power. Harley's most recent study of cartography is heavily influenced by the work of Foucault, which enables Harley to propose the *political* readings of maps. In "Silences and Secrecy: The Hidden Agenda of Cartography in Early Modern Europe" Harley asserts that early modern cartography "was primarily a form of political discourse concerned with the acquisition and maintenance of power."[2] Harley's call for a revision of the ways in which we study cartography is both powerful and compelling, and through it he effectively calls for a reexamination of our underlying assumptions about maps and, moreover, for a wholly new understanding of the practice of cartography:

> My aim . . . has been to initiate the interrogation of maps as *actions* rather than as impassive descriptions and to persuade historians of cartography to ask the crucial question "What are the 'truth effects' of the knowledge that is conveyed in maps?"[3]

Harley suggests an interpretive model familiar to a number of disciplines, particularly to literary and cultural criticism. Harley's proposal that we read maps as texts and as artifacts of cultural practices is precisely the "innovation" of new historicist, cultural materialist, and feminist-materialist criticism of rich varieties of cultural practices.[4] One of our most powerful discussions of cartography and chorography in early modern England is Richard Helgerson's "The Land Speaks: Cartography, Chorography, and Subversion in Renaissance England."[5] Helgerson's discussion arises from a commitment to the study of power as it is frequently articulated in new historicist studies of early modern culture. Helgerson's central assertion, an argument I will address in greater detail below, is that "power and its representation were no less deeply involved in the conquests of Renaissance cartography than in the various campaigns, Spenser's among them, to master and reform the European vernaculars—and the historical ironies generated by that involvement were as intense."[6]

It is within this new cartographic discourse that I would like to situate the following interrogation of the complexly related practices of cartography and chorography in early modern England. In critical literature these two practices typically are seen as virtually indistinguishable; my sense of them, however, is that, while they share a number of common characteristics, they are nevertheless two distinct practices, which, for various political and ideological reasons, frequently are brought into extreme proximity to each other. My aim in the present discussion will be twofold: (1) to "read" the great similarities and the equally great differences between these two practices, both theoretically and practically, especially as each contributes to and detracts from an emergent discourse of nationalism and the antithetical discourse I will here call *localism;* and (2) to examine the fundamentally narratological natures of both cartographical and chorographical practices.

I

> Whilst my physicians by their love are grown
>   Cosmographers, and I their map, who lie
> Flat on this bed, that by them may be shown
>   That this is my South-west discovery
>   *Per fretum febris,* by these straits to die,
>
> I joy, that in these straits, I see my West;
>   For, though their currents yield return to none,
> What shall my West hurt me? As West and East
>   In all flat maps (and I am one) are one,
>   So death doth touch the resurrection.
>   ("Hymn to God my God, in my sickness")[7]

By the time Donne wrote "Hymn to God my God, in my sickness" the idea of man as microcosm was a familiar, though still powerful, conceit. And yet Donne transforms this conceit through the invocation of maps: Donne does not claim to be the world but, rather, its map—not the world but its representation.[8] By distinguishing between being and representation, Donne signals the fundamental act of signification by way of which maps are understood as representations of the world.

The map that Donne has in mind in the "Hymn" is what had been, even into Donne's own historical moment, the fundamentally heretical map representing the earth as a sphere and not, as had been the case for centuries in Christian representations of the world, as a flat disk with Jerusalem at its center, surrounded by water (fig. 1).[9] Donne has something like Mercator's famous global map in mind.[10] The innovations Mercator's map would codify for centuries (down to our own moment, in fact) were enabled by the growing belief in a spherical world, made evident by the voyages of Columbus and then by Magellan's circumnavigation, and represented in the "new" cosmography made available once again (for hadn't ancient Greek natural philosophy determined a spherical earth set in a heliocentric universe?) since the work of Copernicus.[11] While it is difficult to determine precisely the nature of Donne's relationship to the new cosmography, his ambivalence about it is clear. In his satirical attack on the Jesuits, *Ignatius His Conclave,* Donne manifests a certain distrust—or resentment—of both Columbus and Copernicus.[12] In that book the narrator experiences an "Extasie" in which he is able to survey the dominions in Hell and the appearance of several claimants to occupy "a secret place" in Hell with Lucifer, including, among others, both Columbus and Copernicus.[13] The narrator of *Ignatius* reserves the hallowed place nearest Lucifer for those who "had so attempted any innovation in this life" (*IC* 9). It is the innovation of the heliocentric universe that constitutes Copernicus's claim:

> I am he, which pitying thee who wert thrust into the Center of the world, raysed both thee, and thy prison, the Earth, up into the Heavens; so as by my means *God* doth not enjoy his revenge upon

Fig. 1. The Fra Mauro Map. Biblioteca Nazionale, Marciana, Venice.

thee. The Sunne, which was an officious spy, and a betrayer of
faults, and so thine enemy, I have appointed to go into the lowest
part of the world. Shall these gates be open to such as have inno-
vated in small matters? and shall they be shut against me, who have
turned the whole frame of the world, and am thereby almost a new
Creator? (IC 15)

Columbus is not given the opportunity to speak but is simply presented before Lucifer and then cried down by Ignatius, who holds court
with Lucifer and himself lays claim to the exalted position. As he did
with Copernicus, Ignatius refutes Columbus's claim.[14] In this instance,
interestingly, Ignatius repudiates the claim Columbus makes by offering
the record of the Spanish (Jesuit) genocide of the Amerindians as a far
greater instance of man conducting Lucifer's work on earth:[15]

You must remember, sir, that if this kingdome have got anything
by the discovery of the *West Indies*, al that must be attributed to our
Order [the Jesuits]: for if the opinion of the *Dominicans* had prevailed,
*That the inhabitants should be reduced, onely by preaching and without
violence,* certainely their 200000 of men would scarce in so many
ages have beene brought to a 150 which by our meanes was so soone
performed. And if the law, made by *Ferdinando,* onely against *Cani-
bals: That all which would not bee Christians should bee bondslaves,* had
not beene extended into other Provinces, wee should have lacked
men, to digg us out that benefite, which their countries affoord. (*IC*
69)

Donne's scathing satire on the innovations represented by these two
figures is all the more curious given what is clearly his ultimate acceptance (some would even say his celebration) of the new cosmology and
cartography and the new worlds they afford.[16] This simultaneous acceptance and derision is played out in the "Hymn." In this context one of
the curiosities of Donne's poem is his reference to flat maps and not to
globes. While Donne means to draw a parallel between flat maps and his
body rendered prone by the ravages of disease, the notion upon which
the poem articulates its resolution depends upon circularity—both the
circularity of the Christian notion of the Resurrection (a circularity of
time) and upon the notion that "in the world" East does in fact meet—or,
rather, *become*—West (a circularity of space). If one "projects" this conceit onto graphic representations of the world, the globe would be the

most apt choice, since on it East and West (as termini, not directions) are, finally, unrecognizable. Yet Donne chooses the metaphor of the flat map. By this Donne admits to having accepted the epistemology of cartography, which is to say, he has accepted either the mathematics of projection (the calculus by way of which spherical objects can be imaged on a plane), or he has accepted the fiction of maps. Indeed, that flat maps actually do promise a coterminous East and West depends upon the acceptance of the fictional nature of the frame of the map itself: in this moment direction (movement through time) evaporates as linearity gives way to circularity (on spheres, moreover, there is no such thing as a *straight line*). Donne's conceit works, then, because it literalizes the circularity flat maps hold out purely metaphorically.

Thus, Donne accepts that maps are not only representations of the world but are, moreover, *metaphors* of the world. "Scientific" maps (such as Mercator's) are distinguished from "allegorical" maps in that they suggest that they are like the world while they are obviously not the world; their systems of graphic imaging illustrate a metaphorical relationship to the phenomenal world. Allegorical maps, on the other hand, are intended primarily as representations of the world's *meaning* from a given (usually religious) perspective and only secondarily to depict how that world might actually look.

The metaphoricity of maps also demands that the viewer change both the system of signification and the system of reading by which the map is made intelligible. Allegorical maps understand the world as already imbued with meaning. In allegorical maps the relationship between document (map) and object (phenomenal world) is literally the inverse of our scientific understanding: in the Noah map, for instance (fig. 2), what we would call the phenomenal world already stands—prior to its mapping—not as the signified of the map but, rather, as the signifier of God's divine plan. For allegorical maps the world is not imagined as an essentially chaotic and meaningless field but, rather, as ordered and significant: divine meaning has already been written into the landscape. The map does not signify the phenomenal world (whether coherent or incoherent) but, instead, the fact of God in the world.

In scientific maps, to the contrary, the landscape, or the world, is understood as essentially meaningless, without significance; it holds no meaning, signifies nothing. It stands as desacralized matter, natural phenomena.[17] The scientific map thus establishes itself in relationship to the world in such a way that it becomes the signifier of the now signified world. In a way this is how the map sanctifies itself. Sacrality resides in the map itself as *it* organizes and generates meaning for the natural world. Quite literally, scientific maps have inverted the traditional order of things: the world inchoately awaits the grand map that will organize it and name it once and for all.

This transformation in the nature of maps in their imagined rela-

Fig. 2. The Three Sons of Noah. From a fifteenth-century manuscript of Jean Mansel's *La fleur des histoires*. Copyright Bibliothèque Royale Albert Ier, Brussels (MS. 9231, fol. 281v).

tionship to the world initiates a corresponding transformation in the
system of reading maps. Allegorical maps tell us to read in their systems
of representations traces of theological arguments; scientific maps ask
us to read matters of scale, projection, angle, proportion, direction, size,
and proximity. Further, scientific maps ask us to accept what are essentially the mathematical properties of projection and cartographic seman-
tics as natural: the desired effect of these kinds of maps is our sense as
readers that we are not reading at all but merely looking at "pure"
representations of the world, representations that are not filtered through
any ideological lens whatsoever. Donne's "Hymn" announces that he
has mastered these "new" techniques for reading maps and the world,
to which in complicated ways they refer, though he remains interested
in yoking together scientific and allegorical (or Christian) significance
that, he believes, the maps hold. This is what allows Donne to accept
the notion of circularity in flat maps as a function of both the sphericity
of the earth and the redemptive powers of Christ's death and resurrection.

In fact, reading maps is a highly technical and artificial activity, not
at all simply a matter of recognizing the metaphor that asserts a relationship between map and world. Reading scientific maps is an act of interpretation—an interpretation that takes as its fundamental necessary condition a faith in the mathematical properties of projection cataloged
above. There were, however, instances in which people demonstrated a
sometimes unfortunate lack of familiarity of the rules with maps. One
of the early benefits of cartographic representations of the English counties—in fact, this was also one of the prime forces that generated both
the interest in and the governmental money supporting their production—was their use in parliamentary districting, assigning jurisdictional
responsibilities for county justices of the peace, and (perhaps most important) the levying of appropriate taxes on each county. Victor Morgan, in his article "The Cartographic Image of 'The Country' in Early
Modern England," discusses these governmental uses of county maps
and relates an incident involving an appeal to the Privy Council over an
alleged instance of overtaxation. The Welsh chorographer George Owen
suggested that the culprit in this instance was not malice or bias on the
part of the officials but, rather, their inability to read maps. Morgan
writes:

> In George Owen's opinion, one of the reasons why Pembrokeshire
> was unduly burdened with royal demands compared with its neigh-

bouring counties was that councillors sitting in London were using [Christopher] Saxton's maps, and unfortunately Saxton had devoted a whole sheet to Pembrokeshire, but crowded the other four Welsh counties, with which comparisons were made, on to one. According to Owen, the councillors, not being properly trained in the reading of maps, had failed to consult the different scales on the two maps, and had proceeded in their allocation of burdens according to the superficially similar areas depicted on the two sheets.[18]

This story offers anecdotal evidence that at least on some level maps have for a long time been understood—and misunderstood—as texts and that they require a system of reading, even if it is a naturalized system that seeks to conceal both its presence and its effects. Maps, that is, function politically, within discourse and within ideology. Our first task, along with Harley and Helgerson, is to speak this truth about maps and cartography. What remains is the further articulation of specific political and ideological contexts within which specific maps and cartographical practices (including surveying, mapping, and chorography) are produced and, in turn, produce meaning.

2

I would like to turn from Donne's poem to cartography, bringing along Donne's "revolution," which understands temporal and spatial circularity. Let me begin with a formulation of the central epistemological tenet of the traditional understanding of cartography: maps are expressions of space. Historically, maps have been intended as purely descriptive images of the world—the organization of its features in space, both the space of the world (in which objects of certain dimension and location exist in greater or lesser proximity to one another) and the space of the map (the flat paper on which not only objects but space as well are projected). Now I will revise this perhaps initially self-evident belief, thus: maps are expressions not only of space but also of the function of time. This stands as the central tenet of a new understanding of cartography, an understanding in which maps manifestly make evident their essential narratological natures, especially as cartography, since its inception, has endeavored to appear as if time were none of its concern.

The development in Tudor and Stuart England of what typically is called cartography (but which includes a variety of divergent practices) marks a simultaneous double movement: on the one hand, a movement toward greater technical accuracy; on the other hand, a movement away from "pure" survey and cartography, as represented most famously in Saxton's atlas of Britain (1579), toward the historical topography and chorography of writers such as William Camden (*Britannia*), John Norden (*Speculum Britanniae*), and John Speed (*Theatre of the Empire of Great Britain*), to the chorographical poetics of Michael Drayton's *Poly-Olbion*. These later works make evident a greater concern with narrative: they are texts that offer not only representations of topographical characteristics but also topographically organized historical accounts of local or national identities. But in both instances the representations produced (maps and chorographies) are images of the world engendered by a narrativizing of topography and history: both are made to tell historical tales, and these tales, moreover, are deployed in the service of specific political and cultural ideologies.

I locate the following discussion of cartography within the context of sixteenth- and seventeenth-century English texts, cartographic and literary, not only because this is the period in which one can identify the beginnings of modern cartography but also because it is the period in which one can identify equally well the occlusion of the countertradition of chorography: a rival to cartography that is grounded *overtly* in the narrative desire it is covertly the purpose of cartography to repress.

Chorography is the typically narrative and only occasionally graphic practice of delineating topography not exclusively as it exists in the present moment but as it has existed historically as well. This means not only describing surface features of the land (rivers, forest, etc.) but also the "place" a given locale has held in history, including the languages spoken there, the customs of its people, material artifacts the land may hold, etc. Chorography eventually becomes what today we call geography and archaeology.[19]

Chorography as an organized practice has its origins for early modern England in the antiquarian work of John Leland. In his letter commemorating the fruits of his antiquarian research to Henry VIII, "The Laboriouse Journey and Serche of Johan Leylande for Englandes Antiquities, Geven of hym as a Newe Yeares Gyfte to King Henry the viii. in the xxxvii Yeare of his Raygne" (1546), Leland discusses his commission from Henry "to peruse and diligently to serche al the libraries of monasteries and collegies of this yowre noble reaulme...."[20] In his "New Year's Gift," as it is familiarly known, Leland identifies the nature of his antiquarian project as designed to the intente that the monumentes of auncient writers as welle of other nations, as of this yowr owne province mighte be brought owte of deadely darkenes to lyvely lighte, and to receyve like thankes of the posterite, as they hoped for at such tyme as they emploied their long and greate studies to the publique wealthe. (Leland xxxviii)

In the same letter Leland makes evident that, for Henry, Leland's antiquarian research is a fundamentally "nationalistic" endeavor; occurring as it did at the time of Henry's dissolution of the monasteries, Leland's commission can be seen as a further attempt to take control of—to mark monarchical claim of—monastic property and possession. While such endeavors were no doubt part of the attempt to expel the influence and confiscate the wealth of the Roman Catholic church in England (Leland asserts that part of his ambition is to insure "that the holy Scripture of God might bothe be sincerely taughte and lernid, al maner of superstition and craftely coloured doctrine of a rowte of the Romaine bishopes expellid oute of this your moste catholique reaulme" [xxxviii]), it also constitutes the concerted maneuvers toward centralized monarchical control over the as yet not quite controlled English country. The relationship between the state and chorographical (and cartographical) investigation is at least as old as Leland's early work and, moreover, points to the intersection of monarchical governance and topographical study. Henry's ambition for Leland was not merely the desire to patronize a new form of study but also to establish more firmly and overtly the king's claim to something approximating a truly *national* sovereignty.[21]

For Leland, whose official program was so obviously in concert with Henry's, the antiquarian project is primarily *textual,* as is the very ambition that generates it. Leland describes his desire to produce what he believes to be a monumental work of history as a direct consequence of his reading of other historiographers:

Wherfore after that I had perpendid the honest and profitable studies of these historiographes, I was totally enflammid with a love to see thoroughly al those partes of this your opulente and ample reaulme, that I had redde of yn the aforesaid writers: yn so muche that al my other occupations intermittid I have so travelid yn yowr dominions booth by the se costes and the midle partes, sparing nother labor nor costes, by the space of these vi. yeres paste, that there is almoste nother cape, nor bay, haven, creke or peere, river or confluence of rivers, breches, washis, lakes, meres, fenny waters, montaynes, vallies, mores, hethes, forestes, wooddes, cities, burges, castelles, principle manor placis, monasteries, and colleges, but I have seene them; and notid yn so doing a hole worlde of thinges very memorable. (xl–xli)

Leland established the methodological protocols that would organize chorographical study, including the personal accumulation of raw data gathered on personal tours of geographical areas, linguistic investigation, and the study of history in the landscape. In the work of subsequent chorographers—particularly William Camden, whose *Britannia,* in its many editions, stands as the greatest expression of the chorographical ambition—the personal gathering of data takes on something of the character of a quasi-religious quest.[22] Camden's famous county perambulations, for instance, inspired imitators for generations.

While Leland seems to have been driven mad beneath the accumulated weight of his empirical data, and his life work thereby left uncompleted at his death, Camden, who was the inheritor of both Leland's chorographic ambition and his mass of notes and raw data, achieved greater success. Camden was able to organize the prodigious amount of material he collected in the years he devoted to his antiquarian research. The basic unit Camden chose for his *Britannia* was the county, and the book is divided into fifty-two chapters, each devoted to a single county. The single-county plan had been employed seven years earlier by Christopher Saxton, who also personally surveyed almost all of England and Wales for his atlas.[23]

For chorography, natural fact (the phenomenal world) hides its truth, and therein calls for an investigation of its secrets. The form these secrets take is largely that of history (though for Drayton it is also more explicitly political, yet in a politics not of governments but of the land itself).[24] In its practices chorography does not embrace the technological: Camden's first edition of *Britannia* contains none of the graphic-spatial conceptualizations that typify Saxton, and Drayton's maps in *Poly-Olbion* are, in terms of cartographic technology, emphatically regressive (fig. 3).

Drayton's chorographical ambition in *Poly-Olbion* is to make the land speak. On the one hand, this removes Drayton from the realm of the cartographer's "facts" about the land and places him in the realm of allegory; in *Poly-Olbion* topographical characteristics become poetical "characters": rivers become river or water nymphs who then tell their own narratives of their historic and topographic courses. And yet, on the other hand, Drayton nevertheless tenaciously maintains a faith in the poem's "realism." Like the chorographical surveys before him—from Leland to Camden to Norden—Drayton's chorographical-poetical enterprise is devoted to the accurate description of Britain. The first part of *Poly-Olbion* takes this desire to the extreme with the inclusion of "Illustrations," notes appended to each of the poem's books (each of which is devoted to one of Britain's counties), commissioned by Drayton and executed by the great jurist and antiquarian John Selden. In these notes Selden offers his own documentary survey of authoritative texts relevant to Drayton's historical and topographical concerns. With the inclusion of the entirely linguistic (and not imagistic) "Illustrations" Drayton's

Fig. 3. Michael Drayton. *Poly-Olbion*. Monmouthshire.

chorographical enterprise becomes even more emphatically a *textual* one. With Drayton it is clear that the ambition of chorography can be understood as the telling of stories, the desire to narrate the land—its topography in history. The success, then, of chorography is measured by its ability to narrate meaningful (historical) stories.[25]

For Camden, in his *Britannia* and the later *Remains Concerning Britain,* the chorographical project is manifestly devoted to the narration of historic and prehistoric Britain. While Camden is concerned with topography—he claims to have surveyed virtually all of Britain on his famous county perambulations—he is not as concerned with measurement as he is with history: "I have compendiously settled the bounds of each County," Camden asserts, "(but not by measure)."[26] For Camden his *Britannia* is not so much the measure of the land as the measure of the man.[27] Camden's notion of history included not only general topographical descriptions and accounts but also extended studies of place-names and ancient languages (Camden took the then extraordinary measure of learning ancient languages and dialects to understand more fully personal and place names) and included the study of ancient (typically Roman) coins, discussions of heraldry, and lists of British nobility and family genealogies, as well as catalogs of commonplace adages, anecdotes, proverbs, and folk customs and practices.

Cartography, on the other hand, appears almost wholly disinterested in these antiquarian and historiographical matters and appears, instead, to be concerned primarily with the topographical characteristics chorography largely subsumes into its historiographical concerns. In its topographical concern cartography suggests that maps are drawn to represent the world accurately and objectively: maps simply represent the world the way it is. And yet in one of the central operations of cartography the continuity of the topographical world is systematically violated: maps deny the contiguity of the world by virtue of breaking it into disparate pieces. This process of rendering the world radically discontiguous is an entirely political practice taken up in the service of regional or national identity, political or military power, personal or private property boundaries and possession. Maps, that is, are finally the various and sometimes conflicting stories about the phenomenal world we wish to tell.

In other words, maps are documents meant to establish and maintain certain social, economic, and political circumstances—and to preserve them, moreover, not as matters of policy but, rather, as matters of natural fact. I mentioned above that one of the principle ideological uses of maps was in the service of the interests of the landed gentry. As Helgerson has suggested, this particular use for maps is itself predicated upon a very particular definition of the idea of the nation or country. Supporting and advocating the rights of landowners (a discourse of localism) is not the same as advocating monarchical rights to an ideal of national identity. As Helgerson states:

> The cartographic representation of England did have an ideological effect. It strengthened the sense of both local and national identity at the expense of an identity based on dynastic loyalty. . . . Maps let [sixteenth-century English people] see in a way never before possible the country—both county and nation—to which they belonged and at the same time showed royal authority—or at least its insignia—to be a merely ornamental adjunct to that country. Maps thus opened a conceptual gap between the land and its ruler, a gap that would eventually span battlefields.[28]

The story of localism is one the sixteenth-century chorographer and mapmaker John Norden tells in his book *Surveiors Dialogue* (1st ed., 1610). In this book Norden defines and defends surveying in its various forms and capacities. The text is divided into six books, each of which addresses a particular function of surveying, including its uses for the landlord, its uses for purchasers of land, as well as its (professional and moral) protocols. The book takes the form of an accomplished surveyor's exchanges with several figures; the Farmer is both the most obstinate of the speakers in the book and the most important. The Farmer begins by claiming surveying to be unnecessary and detrimental to the interests of farmers. The surveyor is that person, the Farmer claims, who will "pry into mens Titles and estates, under the name (forsooth) of Surveyors," to "bring men and matter in question oftentimes, that would (as long time they have) lye without any question."[29] The effect, says the Farmer, limits the farmer's ability to make a living from the landlord's land. The surveyor defends his function as merely ascertaining the exact truth of the landlord's manor: the size of tenant's farms, the precise amount of yields, the exact rents and fines, etc. The remainder of the book is dedicated to two projects: first, to the "conversion" of the Farmer to the surveyor's (and the landlord's) way of thinking and, second, to the Farmer's subsequent education (technical and moral) to the art and practice of surveying. Norden's book, then, which has the appearance of a technical manual, also functions as a kind of manual of conduct.[30] Norden wants not only to reform the Farmer's initial greed and self-serving attitudes (the correct adjustment of property lines, the surveyor maintains, does in fact serve the interests of the Farmer in that it allows the landlord a more true and therefore profitable overall land management program, the benefits of which reach everyone) but also to offer his surveyor's wisdom for the improvement of parent-child relationships, the establishment of a love of virtue in the peasants, and the refining of the Farmer's relationship to God. By the book's end the Farmer has not only converted to the surveyor's philosophy (he becomes, the dialogue tells us, a better person); he has also become knowledgeable and adept in surveying.

Norden's text makes clear, however, that the true benefits of proper surveying are almost exclusively the landlord's, that the project of the book is, finally, the disciplining of the tenant farmers to the landlord's clear and proper mastery. The Farmer declares:

> This I cannot deny, although indeed some busie fellowes will disswade, and breede a doubt herein, but I see it is to good purpose, and for our better security, to doe all things requisite in this businesse, and that all the Tennants within the Mannor should conjoyne in one, and every one for himselfe, and all for one, and one for all, should looke, examine and declare the uttermost truth of every thing, towards the exact performance of this service, and that the Surveyor should know the quantities, qualities, and indifferent values of every mans Tenement and Lands, their rents, services, custome, works, and whatsoever the Tennant is in Law or conscience bound to yield or performe to his Lord. . . . (Norden 33)

Norden's vision, spoken by the converted Farmer, is of a neofeudalism wherein tenants fulfill their duties and landlords know and exercise their privileges:

> Therefore happy are those Tennants, that have a gracious Lord, and an honest Surveyor: for then there cannot be but an equall and upright course held betweene them: then cannot the Tennants but be faithfull and loving to their Lords, and their Lords favourable to them, so should the Tennants be defended by their Lord, and the Lords fortified by their Tennants, which were the two principall causes of the originall foundation of Mannors, as I have heard. (Norden 33–34)

Norden's philosophical desire to legislate what he believes to be the appropriate relationship to the land focuses not on the issues of the monarchy (though Norden includes occasional references to the king and his subjects' duties to him) but, instead, on the local level:

> [Landlords] should keepe such an even, and equall hand over their Tennants, as may continue mutuall love, and in them a loving feare: And not to seeke the increase of Revenues so much for vaine-glories, as for vertues maintenance . . . which I must leave to every mans owne fancie, wishing all to fashion their waies in this kinde, to Gods glory, the Kings service, the good of the Commonwealth. . . . (Norden sig. A6^v)

Norden's text offers one particular instance of the ideological appropriation and use of cartography. Norden's own relationship to the monarchy was a complex and conflicted one. Norden had earlier embarked upon an ambitious attempt to write individual county chorographies for all of Britain, a text he would title *Speculum Britanniae*.[31] Norden sought monarchical support for this project, first from Elizabeth and then from James, but was unsuccessful in both his bids.[32] Norden no doubt saw himself, as had other chorographers, as a loyal subject, and his advocacy of the landed interests in all likelihood was not an act of overt subversion. That his texts, and others like them, function, however, in the political ways I have tried to describe speaks to a kind of unintentional character of these cartographic and chorographic texts that locates their potentially subversive qualities within their very discursive forms. I would like to turn to a discussion of these discursive forms and the ways in which cartography and chorography produce meaning. I will focus on two crucial characteristics: their relationships to technology and their relationship to time and history, a relationship that makes manifest the common narratological nature of both cartography and chorography.

3

With Saxton's *Atlas* cartography had become a dedicated technological endeavor, against which chorography seemed regressive—or, more appropriately, antitechnological. And yet between cartography and chorography we discern not one "advanced" practice and one "primitive" one but, rather, two different representational systems at work and in conflict.

For Saxton cartography represents a commitment to an epistemology founded on what Johannes Fabian has identified as a "cultural, ideological bias toward vision as the 'noblest sense' and toward geometry qua graphic-spatial conceptualization as the most 'exact' way of communicating knowledge."[33] Saxton (and "pure" cartographers after him) turn to technological innovations that afford more "accurate" versions of graphic-spatial conceptualizations (e.g., new surveying techniques, better mathematical models for more sophisticated projections, more sensitive and precise instruments, etc.). Technical competence thus becomes the measure of success (fig. 4).

Another measure of success for Saxton's cartography is the degree to which it presents itself as natural and not technological at all. That is, Saxton's maps work (succeed) best when they seem not to work (labor) at all, when they seem to present what in fact is the highly intrusive organization of phenomena in the guise of data as if it were *natural*. Saxton's maps work because they seem not to tell stories, seem not to narrate, but, rather, appear to describe objectively the phenomenal world.

Cartography and chorography also differ in their apparent or declared relationships to history, both the historical—or *pre*historical—past as well as the passage of time. Cartographies attempt to present their texts as ahistorical; Saxton's maps of England, for example, represent an eternal present: the land as it *is*, as if in a wholly continuous moment. What escapes explicit representation, but what is nevertheless implicitly represented, then, is the history that informs the production of not only the map itself (England looked different to cartographers a generation before) but also the production of England itself as political entity. History and politics are both subsumed within the cartographic ideology as matters of natural fact, facts that the map implicitly speaks but refuses to represent explicitly. In these terms cartographic representations aim at synchronic representation. And the materiality of cartography's production exists largely in excess of its system of representation.

Chorographical representations, on the other hand, reject the notion of synchronic representation and opt, instead, for the diachronic. Camden's and Drayton's texts seek to represent Britain *in time:* the land persists, as does its history.[34] For Camden, national identity is not simply a fact but, rather, a story, and his texts are devoted to the telling of that story. Chorography is interpretation deployed through time; cartography is interpretation ostensibly outside of, or in spite of, time.

To understand the world as the movement of time is to have created

Fig. 4. *Saxton's Atlas, 1579.* Map of Northamptonshire, etc. State II.

a narrative world. It is to this assertion that the projects of chorography are explicitly dedicated. Maps attempt to deny this same narrativizing of the world, but this denial is finally not successful, not if we subject cartography to a political reading. Maps are narratives, even though cartographic ideology radically denies the narratological nature of the cartographic practice and its artifacts.

Among the earliest maps to survive from antiquity are the Roman itineraries: maps constructed along an axis connecting two distant locations (fig. 5). These maps are constructed entirely from calculations of distances between various points that lie along the trajectory from point A to point B. They are constructed with a total disregard for orientation. In these maps the frames correspond not with directions but simply with the outer edge of concern. The concern or desire of these maps, then, is entirely narratological: the movement from A to B to C, until one reaches the predetermined destination, the foregone conclusion. Within the genres of maps these itineraries correspond to the most formulaic of literatures: they hold no surprises, afford no digressions.

In these regards itineraries are very like their contemporary counterparts, the American Automobile Association (AAA) TripTiks (fig. 6). This particular image depicts (I will want to say "narrates") the movement from Nashville to Memphis, Tennessee. In this map narrative reigns supreme. Again, orientation is utterly disregarded; digression (in the form of the sidetrip to, say, anywhere off Interstate 40) is utterly unthinkable; trajectory becomes the equivalent of plot, and the plot alone exists in the very midst of what is evidently blank space—a white noise, of sorts, just out of earshot, just off the map, a void that offers us its own enclosed narrative: "I-40 leads through rolling to hilly, mostly wooded terrain along eastern portion of route; gentle relief and more farmlands along western portion." Geographical space is quantified into calculations of driving time noted parenthetically and along the margins.[35] Harley suggests that we can read the "silences" on maps, those projections of blank space that indeed speak loudly:

> The lack of qualitative differentiation in maps structured by the scientific *episteme* serves to dehumanise the landscape. Such maps convey knowledge where the subject is kept at bay. Space becomes more important than place: if places look alike they can be treated alike. Thus, with the progress of scientific mapping, space became all too easily a socially-empty commodity, a geometrical landscape of cold, non-human facts.[36]

Fig. 5. The Peutinger Map: Rome. Österreichische Nationalbibliothek, Vienna (Codex Vindobonensis 324, segment IV).

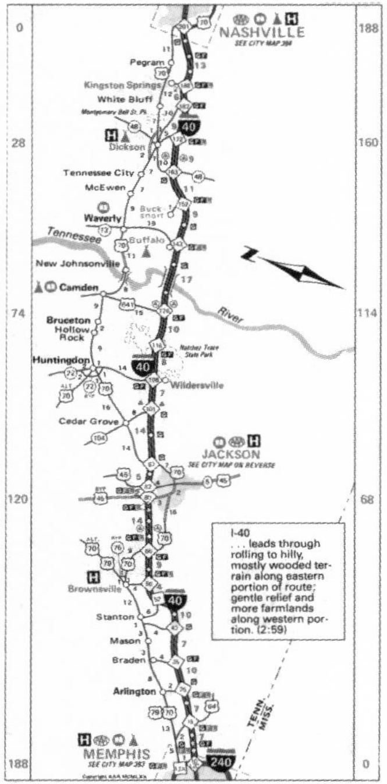

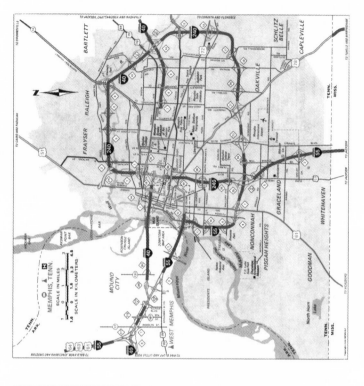

Fig. 6. (left) American Automobile Association TripTik map: Nashville to Memphis, Tennessee. (Copyright © AAA reproduced by permission.)

Fig. 7. (right) American Automobile Association map: Memphis, Tennessee. (Copyright © AAA reproduced by permission.)

It is not difficult to see, then, the Nashville to Memphis narrative operating as an ideologically loaded text in the service, as it were, of a number of larger ideological and political discourses—including the social-economic-political discourse of the interstate, that American cultural artifact that serves to funnel traffic and commerce away from all those "socially-empty" locales "just off" the interstate and inexorably into the "nationalist" circuit that promises variety and glorious destinations "just ahead"; and yet these destinations are only rhetorical and forever receding into the incalculable distance. The interstate promises access to the country, but it leads nowhere—to no *particular* place; it just exposes one to the interminable vastness of the country.[37] The interstate stands as a materialized metaphor of narrativity.[38]

But let us say that you make it to Memphis. The narrative directs you to turn to page 393, where the story continues. But as you turn to page 393 you have entered a radically different, and strange, world (I'd say the same if it were, say, Cleveland) (fig. 7). Here the world has evidently and suddenly shifted on its axis sufficiently to return the vestigial compass rose to its customary north orientation. Now that we have reached Memphis (or p. 393), we turn the page on a new world so that we can learn how *to avoid* Memphis. Quite apart from the curious phenomenon of a map of a city that exists to help you avoid the city, the radical juxtaposition of these two images invites a kind of geographical vertigo in which the top of the frame both is and is not north, in which the world is, if only for a moment, turned upside down. Because in the West we have been taught to understand north-oriented maps, when we see maps that violate this orientation they are (if only briefly) quite incomprehensible.

Early modern maps, as surely as the Roman itinerary maps or the AAA maps, tell their own stories of their conception of topography and cartography, of the value of the particular and the unique, and are made to tell various other stories of the sites of power or of wealth, for example, or the stories of localism or nationalism. Cartography does not exist—and never has existed—outside of discourse. Indeed, the costs of imagining cartography as nonideological are both insidious and untenable: whether the finally inadmissible Eurocentrism Arno Peters so powerfully identifies in the ubiquitous Mercator's projection or the class-based prejudice of the cartography of privilege, cartographic narratives simply need examination.[39] The revision of these (and other) cartographic narratives may or may not be the technological one Peters predicts, but the necessary first step is to recognize cartography and its productions as explicitly part of history and as manifestly discursive, making available political readings of inevitably political maps.

NOTES

I wish to thank Lynne Vallone, David E. Johnson, and the members of the Interdisciplinary Group for Historical Literary Study at Texas A&M University for their generous and thoughtful criticism of this paper.

1. For an insightful and thorough discussion of the history of the study of cartography, see J. B. Harley, "The Map and the Development of the History of Cartography," in *The History of Cartography*, Vol. 1: *Cartography in Prehistoric, Ancient, and Medieval Europe and the Mediterranean*, eds. J. B. Harley and David Woodward (Chicago: University of Chicago Press, 1987), 1–42.

2. J. B. Harley, "Silences and Secrecy: The Hidden Agenda of Cartography in Early Modern Europe," *Imago Mundi* 40 (1988): 57.

3. Harley, "Silences and Secrecy," 71.

4. I want to stress that, by identifying these critical and theoretical discourses as similarly constituted vis-à-vis cultural practices and cultural artifacts, I am certainly not suggesting that they are in any way necessarily monological in their philosophical or political approaches nor that frequently there are not extreme differences either in approach or objective or both. Such assertions are not only insensitive, but they also misconstrue divergent practices as inevitably identical.

5. Richard Helgerson, "The Land Speaks: Cartography, Chorography, and Subversion in Renaissance England," in *Representing the English Renaissance,* ed. Stephen Greenblatt (Berkeley: University of California Press, 1988), 327–61.

6. Helgerson, "The Land Speaks," 327.

7. John Donne, "Hymn to God my God, in my sickness," in *John Donne,* ed. John Carey (Oxford: Oxford University Press, 1990), 332–33.

8. The microcosm/macrocosm conceit is integral to a wide range of Donne's poetry and prose. His fourth meditation from *Devotions upon Emergent Occasions* (ed. Anthony Raspa [New York and Oxford: Oxford University Press, 1987]) offers another striking instance of this:

> It is too little to call *Man a little World;* Except *God,* Man is a *diminutive* to nothing. Man consistes of more pieces, more parts, then the world; then the world doeth, nay then the world is. And if those pieces were extended, and stretched out in Man, as they are in the world, Man would bee the *Gyant,* and the world the *Dwarfe,* the world but the *Map,* and the Man the *World.* (19)

For an influential study of this issue in the tradition of Renaissance philosophy, see Ernst Cassirer, *The Individual and the Cosmos in Renaissance Philosophy,* ed. and trans. Mario Domandi (New York: Barnes & Noble, 1963). See also Leonard Barkan, *Nature's Work of Art: The Human Body as Image of the World* (New Haven: Yale University Press, 1975).

9. For discussions of early Christian allegorical maps, see Arno Peters, *The*

New Cartography (New York: Friendship Press, 1983), 9–49; and David Woodward, "Medieval *Mappaemundi*," in Harley and Woodward, *History of Cartography*, 286–370.

10. For detailed discussions of the science of projection, see Peters, *The New Cartography*, 20–27 and 105–48.

11. Peters discusses the heliocentric universe, as well as the spherical earth, theories of the ancient Greeks (*The New Cartography*, 16–24).

12. For studies of Donne and his relationship to astronomy, see A. J. Meadows, *The High Firmament: A Survey of Astronomy in English Literature* (Leicester: University of Leicester Press, 1969); R. Chris Hassel, Jr., "Donne's *Ignatius His Conclave* and the New Astronomy," *Modern Philology* 68 (1971): 329–37.

13. John Donne, *Ignatius His Conclave*, ed. T. S. Healy (Oxford: Oxford University Press, 1969), 9, 5. Subsequent references to this work, abbreviated as *IC*, appear parenthetically in the body of the essay.

14. Ignatius refutes Copernicus by suggesting that the heliocentric revolution has had little real consequences for mankind, and therefore for Lucifer—even if it happens to be true:

> . . . what new thing have you invented, by which our *Lucifer* gets any thing? What cares hee whether the earth travell, or stand still? Hath your raising up of the earth into heaven, brought men to that confidence, that they build new towers or threaten God againe? Or do they out of this motion of the earth conclude, that there is no hell, or deny the punishment of sin? Do not men beleeve? do they not live just, as they did before? Besides, this detracts from the dignity of your learning, and derogates from your right and title of comming to this place, that those opinions of yours may very well be true. (*IC* 17)

15. Donne concludes *Ignatius* by having Lucifer decide that Ignatius is indeed nearest him in evil but that Hell cannot be shared. Lucifer strikes upon an alternative resolution: he will enlist the pope's aid in causing *"Galilaeo the Florentine"* to "draw the *Moone*, like a boate floating upon the water, as neere the earth as he will." Once near enough . . .

> thither (because they ever claime that those imployments of discovery belong to them) shall all the Jesuites bee transferred, and easily unite and reconcile the *Lunatique Church* to the *Romane Church;* without doubt, after the Jesuites have been there a little while, there will soone grow naturally a *Hell* in that world also: over which, you *Ignatius* shall have dominion. . . . (*IC* 81)

16. Donne's references to and use of cosmology and cartography are numerous; see, for example, "The Good Morrow," "Good Friday, 1613. Riding Westward," "An Anatomy of the World: The First Anniversary," and "Of the Progress of the Soul: The Second Anniversary."

17. By suggesting that scientific maps understand the geographical and topographical world as "natural phenomena" is not to deny that cartographers

(even as travel writers frequently had) filled their maps with representations of exotic human figures, sea monsters, and other allegorical figures and signs. To these people such entities were in fact understood as natural and naturally occurring.

18. Victor Morgan, "The Cartographic Image of 'The Country' in Early Modern England," *Transactions of the Royal Historical Society*, 5th ser., 29 (1979): 138.

19. For important studies of chorography, see Stan A. E. Mendyk, *"Speculum Britanniae": Regional Study, Antiquarianism, and Science in Britain to 1700* (Toronto: University of Toronto Press, 1989); Stuart Piggott, *Ancient Britons and the Antiquarian Imagination: Ideas from the Renaissance to the Regency* (New York: Thames and Hudson, 1989); Stuart Piggott, *Ruins in a Land Scape: Essays in Antiquarianism* (Edinburgh: Edinburgh University Press, 1976). See also Joseph M. Levine, "The Antiquarian Enterprise, 1500–1800," in *Humanism and History: Origins of Modern English Historiography* (Ithaca: Cornell University Press, 1907).

20. *Leland's Itinerary in England and Wales,* 3 vols., ed. Lucy Toulmin Smith (London: George Bell and Sons, 1907), xxxvii. Subsequent references to this work appear parenthetically in the body of the essay.

21. Helgerson offers a brilliant discussion of the complicated ways in which cartography and chorography initially participate in the monarchical attempts to centralize governmental authority but subsequently subvert these attempts. He focuses on a number of instances of this change, including the eventual disappearance of signs of the monarchy and the patron printed on Saxton's map and their replacement by Saxton's own name: "In these small changes we can . . . discern the trace of a momentous transfer of cultural authority from the patron and the royal system of government of which patronage was an integral part to the individual maker" ("The Land Speaks," 330).

22. Camden's *Britannia* went through seven editions in his lifetime, the first (in Latin) in 1586, the last (and the first in English) in 1610, and was republished (much enlarged) by Edmund Gibson in 1695. For this essay I use the latter, *Camden's Britannia,* 1695 (1695; reprint, New York and London: Johnson Reprint Corporation, 1971).

23. For a discussion of Christopher Saxton and the production of his atlas, see *Christopher Saxton: Elizabethan Map-Maker,* Ifor M. Evans and Heather Lawrence (Wakefield and London: Wakefield Historical Publications and The Holland Press, 1979).

24. For a discussion of Drayton's antimonarchical politics, see Helgerson, "The Land Speaks," 352–57.

25. For Drayton one of the most significant historical tales he wishes to tell is the history of the figure of Brutus, the (legendary) ancient figure, descendent of Aeneas, whose story serves to establish an ancient heritage for Britons.

26. *Britannia* (1695 ed.), D2ᵛ.

27. Helgerson comments on Camden's sense of *personal* accomplishment and, even more important, personal authority ("The Land Speaks," 343–44).

28. Helgerson, "The Land Speaks," 332.

29. John Norden, *Surveiors Dialogue* (rev. ed., 1618; reprint, Amsterdam:

Theatrum Orbis Terrarum, 1979). Subsequent references appear parenthetically in the body of the essay.

30. In this regard Norden's book is similar to an earlier text—one to which Norden's book acknowledges an indebtedness—Valentine Leigh, *The Moste Profitable and Commendable Science, of Surveying of Lands, Tenementes, and Hereditamentes* (London, 1577).

31. For a discussion of Norden's *Speculum Britanniae,* see Mendyk, *"Speculum Britanniae,"* 57–81.

32. Helgerson prints a transcription of a letter from Norden to Elizabeth, written on the flyleaf of his presentation copy of the second installment of his *Speculum Britanniae,* requesting her support for his research ("The Land Speaks," 341–42).

33. Johannes Fabian, *Time and the Other: How Anthropology Makes Its Object* (New York: Columbia University Press, 1983), 106.

34. This is not to suggest that Camden's and Drayton's historical ambitions or sentiments were identical; there were, in fact, substantial differences: Drayton was heavily invested in the story of Brutus, while Camden rejected the story out of hand as purely mythological.

35. One of the most striking instances of the narratological nature of cartography is John Norden's *England: An Intended Guyde for English Travailers.* While from the title one may well expect a prototypical "travel book," what the book offers, instead, is an extended series of mileage tables showing the distances between cities and towns within a given shire. The entire book is made up of these charts; the only prose that appears in the book (in addition to a prefatory letter and a brief note appended to the pages devoted to Lancashire and Lincolnshire disclaiming the effects of water travel) is the "legend" explaining "the use of this table," which is in fact reproduced verbatim on every page of the book (and only slightly expanded in the instance of Yorkshire, again due to inaccuracies in distances occasioned by water travel).

36. Harley, "Silences and Secrecy," 66.

37. In his chorographical-philosophical travel book *America* (trans. Chris Turner [London and New York: Verso, 1988]), Jean Baudrillard discusses the American freeway system and its effects:

Gigantic, spontaneous spectacle of automotive traffic. A total collective act, staged by the entire population, twenty-four hours a day. . . . Unlike our European motorways, which are unique, directional axis . . . the freeway system is a place of integration. . . . [T]heir signs read like a litany. "Right lane must exit." This "must exit" has always struck me as a sign of destiny. I have got to go, to expel myself from this paradise, leave this providential highway which leads nowhere, but keeps me in touch with everyone. This is the only real society or warmth here, this collective propulsion, this compulsion—a compulsion of lemmings plunging suicidally together. . . . At every hour of the day approximately the same number split off towards Hollywood or towards Santa Monica. Pure, statistical energy, a ritual being acted out—the regularity of the flows cancels out individual destinations. What you have here is the charm of ceremonies: you have the whole of space before you, just as ceremonies have the whole of time before them. (52–54)

38. The particular narratives that finally are told, however, are preselected by social, political, and economic matters. Harley discusses the strict class exclusivity of early modern maps:

> For map makers, their patrons, and their readers, the underclass did not exist and had no geography, still less was it composed of individuals. Instead, what we see singled out on these maps are people privileged by the right to wear a crown or a mitre or to bear a coat of arms or a crozier. The peasantry, the landless labourers, or the urban poor had no place in the social hierarchy and, equally, as a cartographically disenfranchised group, they had no right to representation on the map. ("Silences and Secrecy," 68)

It would be comforting, indeed, to suppose that such gross class-based prejudice no longer informs our production of maps and various other cartographic or demographic texts. Yet one need only look as far as the debate concerning the numbers of so-called illegal aliens living in the United States and whether or not they were entitled to representation in the 1990 U.S. Census to see that in many ways we remain committed to a cartography of privilege.

39. Arno Peters identifies the ideological significance of Mercator's projection and its legacy:

> It is appropriate at this time to examine our own global concept critically. This is based directly upon our global maps and the maps of our own country but these are still rooted in the work of cartographers of a bygone age—the age of European world domination and exploitation. These concepts must be discarded in this era of the realization of the basic equality of all the nations on earth.
>
> The new cartography, based on and dedicated to objectivity alone, must promote and accompany this breakthrough into the new age of human solidarity. New scales must be applied in many fields. The revolutionary ingredient of this new cartography lies in its conception, based on the learning of the current technological revolution, the world revolution and the end of the era of colonial exploitation. With a great leap forward it takes its place in the forefront of the general development. (*The New Cartography*, 7)

Arno's book stands as a sustained critique of Mercator's projection, to which Peters poses his own antidote by way of a new projection (the Peters projection).

From Typology to Type: Agents of Change in Eighteenth-Century English Texts

J. Paul Hunter

Whatever their dependence on editors, printers, engravers, booksellers, and other textual technologists, authors of literary texts usually show more disdain than gratitude toward their material aides, and literary history has traditionally transcribed that authorial attitude as historical fact. The discourse of musology is both more simple and more exotic than any argument of causality, and keeping texts "pure"—free from any taint of materiality or history—has remained a high priority through several waves of critical and theoretical change, so that concern with either the instruments of textual production or the dispersal and consumption of the textual product has largely been left to historians other than literary. That is why, until very recently, questions about the material production of literary texts have mostly gone unasked among literary critics and theorists[1] and why—even in this age of self-consciousness about the materiality of all cultural history—literary study still operates in almost total ignorance of scientific and technological history.[2]

Essay collections such as this one, and the widespread academic interest that they represent, promise something better for literary history in the future, but whether that promise is realized depends on several things: whether the old biases against technology can be lastingly overcome, whether literary students have enough patience to study the details of print technology and the social mechanics of textual distribution, whether questions of intentionalism (long discredited but still not pushed aside) can be subordinated to detailed descriptions of actual historical texts and classes of texts, whether precise enough distinctions can be developed between varieties of innovation, and whether we are diligent enough to read *all* the relevant cultural texts, not just the ones that appeal to us for aesthetic, political, or practical reasons. These questions will not be resolved quickly, and the rising impatience to make a new literary history of some appealing kind could easily mean evading the crucial issues. But if we have the will, the means are there for scuttling the old rivalries between art and technology and for making a genuinely revisionist literary history that would account in larger cultural terms for the making of texts and the emergence of new literary genres and species.

Economics and politics may have determined, in almost all cultures, the direction, tone, and accessibility of texts, even in preprint times, when textual production and distribution was sometimes accomplished by a single authorial hand. But historical and geographical distinctions have to be made: the nature of the influence does vary culturally, and the degree of influence on texts is more important at some times—and in some genres—than others. It is not only that technological advances themselves tend to come irregularly or in waves, but the impact on texts is often delayed—sometimes for generations—and even then the full effect may not be recognized for some time. Then, too, various technologies may combine to affect texts in unpredictable ways; sometimes, for example, developments in market technology may produce textual changes that print technology had made possible much earlier. The importance of the late years of the seventeenth and early years of the eighteenth century—long regarded as an important era for textual innovation because of the emergence of journalism, the novel, and other forms representing quasipopular culture—mainly involves new modes of textual circulation and a changed perception of what audiences wanted or would accept. Print technology then remained relatively stable—though individual advances took place—but there were major implications for textuality because authors found new reasons (rapidly changing audiences) and new ways (some blatant, some subtle) to employ and exploit print technologies that had already been available for some time. The results in the period were, in some cases, quite dramatic—visible enough that I once imagined organizing an English course in the period on the basis of how texts used print technology. I intended to teach only texts that would demonstrate how thoroughly, often in spite of authorial claims, changes in artistic direction depended on technological innovation, thereby making a point not only about some particulars of literary history but also about the nature of textual innovation.

But once I had pondered the possible texts I discovered I could teach almost all texts in the period under the rubric. I imagined several kinds of units—on engravings and illustrations; on typefaces, sizes of type, and pagination; on the structure of title pages and the sway they hold over expectations; on modes of distribution and the influence of geography, class, and gender on the making of texts; on multivolume, serial, and parts publication; on the proliferation of prefaces and appendices and the tendency to add lists, tables, or explanations and examples in the middle as well as on the front or back end of texts; on divisions into chapters and other print devices to manipulate the uses of time and pause in reading; on the special issues involved in reading printer-writers such as Richardson and John Dunton; on fusions of the visual and verbal in figures such as Hogarth and Blake and on the implications of conscious intertextuality more generally; on specially designed individual pages like the blank, black, and marbled ones in *Tristram Shandy* or the folded calling card in an experimental 1755 novel called *The Card*.

At the time—it was the late 1960s when I had this idea—I was a little worried that novels, works of journalism, and the texts of other new or hybridized genres and species would dominate the course, and I fretted that Laurence Sterne might become its runaway hero. I saw (dimly) that the course raised a basic question about how quiet and subtle shifts occasioned by technology compete against flashy and dramatic ones that seem more radical. How visible, for example, would Alexander Pope be in Sterne's presence? How possible would it be to notice the poetry when prose was making so much explosive noise? Could the force of technology be traced in traditional and conservative genres as well as in the introduction of new forms or radical revisions of the notion of form? Looking back, I suspect that I wasn't ready then to think through those problems; theory then was not a pressing issue for most American readers, and when theory was insistent it wasn't pointed toward questions of history. Perhaps neither I nor the world was ready for me to get around to doing that course. But I do remember having a hunch, even then, that the most satisfying surprises would come not from noting the blockbuster shocks in technology but from seeing subtle adjustments, shifts, and compromises that made texts permanently different.

Today, given our pressing concern with the agents of historical change, such issues seem to me the really crucial ones: Should we look for large historical fissures, changes in epistemic paradigms, as Foucault thinks, or rather at patterns of evolutionary change? Are the startling texts—the ones that call sharp attention to their oddity—the ones that show how change is accomplished? Should change be measured by its most obvious manifestations? Do traditional writers, conservative genres, and texts that retain conventional techniques participate in epistemic revolutions in the same way as those in new or innovative genres and species? This essay is, in effect, a working out of some of the nascent theory behind that course idea, and here I want to raise basic questions about how broadly, how quickly, and how lastingly textual change is effected by technological moves. I will look at two authors who illustrate opposing directions in eighteenth-century texts and who represent political and social views about literature that were then at war with each other. One writer (Laurence Sterne) celebrates individuality, innovation, and a new freedom from convention and habit, rejoicing in the dawn of modernity and the founding of new literary directions and genres. The other (Alexander Pope) attacks originality, subjectivity, and modernity and sees cultural loss in any kind of social or literary change; his texts lament technological innovation and decry its democratizing effects on literature and culture, distrust new genres and literary directions and blame them on debased taste, uphold traditional values and conventional literary techniques, and defend the established poetic kinds. It is no accident that my first example involves the then new prose texts of a novelistic kind and the second traditional poems in the then standard form of heroic couplets. But the dichotomies of mode, genre, and attitude to technology here turn out, like other tempting dichotomies, to be quite misleading.

Even a casual reader of *Tristram Shandy*—or, for that matter, even a casual thumber—can quickly see how dependent Sterne is for his effects on certain features of print technology and modern bookmaking. Sterne is often credited with extraordinary invention for his employment of these devices, and he is, of course, original and clever, but (strictly speaking) most of his print features are not new: they did not become available just at the time when Sterne came forward to use them, and he is not so much an inventor as a publicist. The features of print that Sterne exploits had, in fact, been available to authors for some time, and many of them had already been liberally used in some form, a fact of some importance to interpreting how, and when, technology affects whole classes of texts. In the late 1750s and early 1760s, when Sterne was thinking up his typographical jokes, novels had been around and showing their novelty for close to half a century. In *Tristram Shandy* print devices elbow their way into prominence so that readers are almost forced to notice that the text has come to depend on technology for particular effects. Sterne uses many different devices, but I will concentrate here on just three of them—dashes, chapter divisions, and special, visually designed pages.

The first typological oddity to strike the eye in *Tristram Shandy* is, because of its ubiquity, the dash.[3] (See fig. 1.) It is the dominant—sometimes it seems the only—mark of punctuation. The dash here is not your usual punctuational dash, setting off—as in this sentence—some parenthetical, syntactically interruptive word or phrase from the rest of the sentence, and it seldom looks ordinary or comfortable. Rather than the usual one-em dash, Sterne's is more often two or three ems in length, sometimes even longer. Sometimes, as in chapter 4 of volume 1, it takes up most of a line, in this case centering the phrase "Shut the door" and appearing to seal off the text above from the text below—presumably separating the words that follow from the readers who, on the previous page, have been ordered to leave the room. (See fig. 2.) Sometimes it is even longer, in one case more than two full lines in length, when (in chap. 27 of vol. 4) the word *Zounds!* opens the chapter and is followed by the very long dash of silence, before we are told why Phutatorius—who has just had a hot chestnut dropped into his breeches—has expressed, and then quieted, himself in such a lingering way. (See fig. 3.) The text here, aided by the much elongated dash that self-consciously pays homage to what print technology can do for the process of reading, replicates silence, hesitation, and inarticulateness in the plot action, something shorter dashes do repeatedly to enforce pauses of varying length in the reading of the text. Here what happens in confronting the text as reader is analogized to what happens in the text as narrative; representation is made to seem as parallel as possible to re-presentation in the present, and the physical text is made to do what, on a temporal level, Tristram has repeatedly been claiming he wants to do in replicating his life as text.

Most often the dash in *Tristram Shandy* is the eye equivalent of silence—it is a reader's guide to pause—and the varying lengths of the dashes help us pace our reading.[4] But in spite of the frequency of the dash in the text, it is not really the only mark of punctuation Sterne uses; in fact, he most often uses it with other punctuation alongside—a comma or semicolon or question mark or exclamation point, as if to say that standard printing conventions were not enough. In effect, Sterne offers an all-purpose mechanical aid for a reader engaging the text—at once a lure, stimulus, and constraint—even as he laughs at other print storytellers who have guided their perusers insufficiently in their rehearing of words and pauses.

The dash in Sterne has two primary effects that correspond to two Sternean perceptions about how print technology affects verbal possibility. The first involves timing—the rhythm of the voice as a guide to meaning, in effect a translation of print to the art of saying and hearing—and the second involves an apparent refusal to say, which actually involves saying the unsayable. Let me deal with the second first because, although it seems conceptually more complex, it actually works quite simply. In the Phutatorius passage the long dash after *Zounds!* is followed by another dash, this one inside a word, or rather between two letters and *standing for* a word. After the silence of the two-lines-plus dash, comes another *Zounds* but this one spelled differently: "Z——ds," it reads, *Z*, plus a three-em dash, plus *ds*—as if, on second thought, Phutatorius has the propriety to censor himself. Here, though, is a crux for a print text, a misrepresentation any way you look at it. Either Phutatorius said "Zounds" in the second moment that the text recreates,

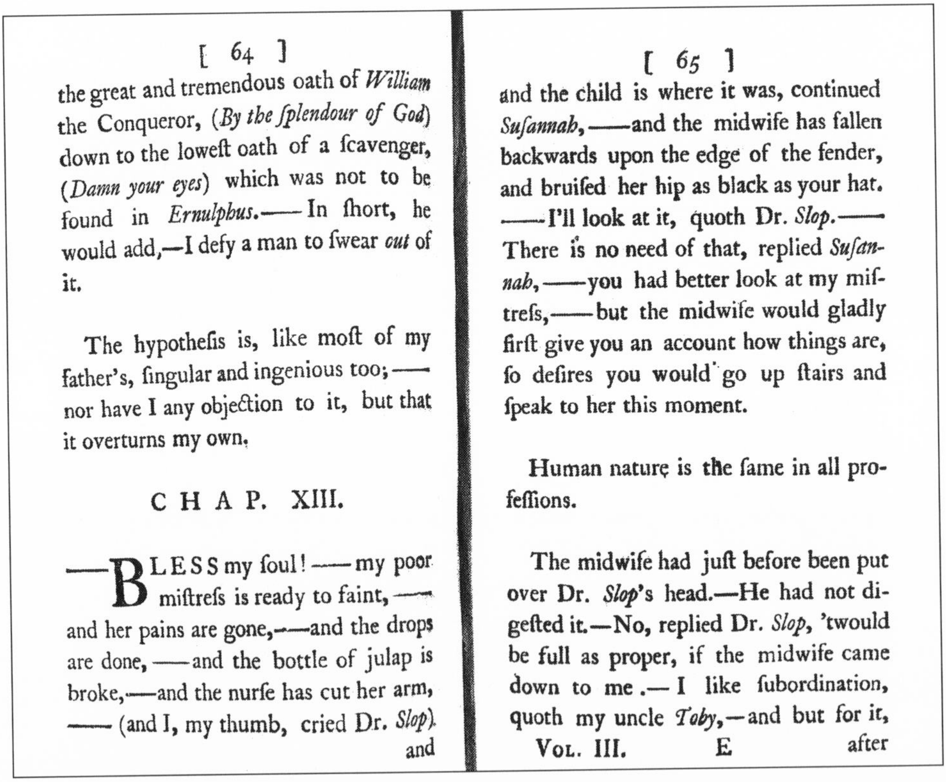

[64]

the great and tremendous oath of *William* the Conqueror, (*By the fplendour of God*) down to the loweft oath of a fcavenger, (*Damn your eyes*) which was not to be found in *Ernulphus.*——In fhort, he would add,—I defy a man to fwear *out* of it.

The hypothefis is, like moft of my father's, fingular and ingenious too;——nor have I any objection to it, but that it overturns my own,

C H A P. XIII.

——**B**LESS my foul!——my poor miftrefs is ready to faint,—— and her pains are gone,——and the drops are done, ——and the bottle of julap is broke,——and the nurfe has cut her arm, —— (and I, my thumb, cried Dr. *Slop*).
                                                              and

[65]

and the child is where it was, continued *Sufannah,*——and the midwife has fallen backwards upon the edge of the fender, and bruifed her hip as black as your hat. ——I'll look at it, quoth Dr. *Slop.*—— There is no need of that, replied *Sufannah,*——you had better look at my miftrefs,——but the midwife would gladly firft give you an account how things are, fo defires you would go up ftairs and fpeak to her this moment.

Human nature is the fame in all profeffions.

The midwife had juft before been put over Dr. *Slop*'s head.—He had not digefted it.—No, replied Dr. *Slop*, 'twould be full as proper, if the midwife came down to me.— I like fubordination, quoth my uncle *Toby*,—and but for it,
VOL. III.   E   after

Fig. 1. *Tristram Shandy*, 3: 64–65. (Figures 1–10 from the Regenstein Library, University of Chicago.)

Fig. 2. *Tristram Shandy*, 1:11.

> [11]
>
> wrote only for the curious and inquisi-
> tive.
>
> —————————Shut the door.——————
> I was begot in the night, betwixt the firſt
> *Sunday* and the firſt *Monday* in the month
> of *March*, in the year of our Lord one
> thouſand ſeven hundred and eighteen.
> I am poſitive I was.——But how I came
> to be ſo very particular in my account
> of a thing which happened before I was
> born, is owing to another ſmall anecdote
> known only in our own family, but now
> made publick for the better clearing up
> this point.
>
> My father, you muſt know, who was
> originally a *Turkey* merchant, but had left
> off buſineſs for ſome years, in order to
> retire to, and die upon, his paternal eſtate
> in the county of———, was, I believe,
> 2   one

or he did not; he cannot have said "*z*-blank-*ds*." A print text, however, can say *z*-blank-*ds* (as have countless ones in the past with all manner of words, to avoid blasphemy, obscenity, or legal action); it can indicate more subtly than speech the hesitation, ambivalence, or compulsion of a life-in-progress that cannot, either by word or silence but only by a print combination of the two, articulate the surprise of something too hot to handle.[5]

Here the dash stands, in print, for something unspeakable and yet compellingly actual, just as does another nonverbal utterance of type when my uncle Toby theorizes that Elizabeth Shandy chooses a midwife over Dr. Slop because she "does not care to let a man come so near her ****" (2:47). (See fig. 4.) Sterne goes on to call extended attention both to my uncle Toby's ambiguities and his own, illustrating what print can do that the voice cannot: "I will not say whether my uncle *Toby* had compleated the sentence or not;—'tis for his advantage to suppose he had,—as, I think, he could have added no ONE WORD which would have

Fig. 3. *Tristram Shandy*, 4:168.

C H A P. XXVII.

ZOUNDS! —————— ————— ——⸗
————————— ——⸗—————
————————— Z——ds! cried *Phu-tatorius*, partly to himſelf—and yet high enough to be heard—and what ſeemed odd, 'twas uttered in a conſtruction of look, and in a tone of voice, ſomewhat between that of a man in amazement, and of one in bodily pain.

One or two who had very nice ears, and could diſtinguiſh the expreſſion and mixture of the two tones as plainly as a *third* or a *fifth*, or any other chord in muſick—were the moſt puzzled and per-plexed with it—the *concord* was good in itſelf—but then 'twas quite out of the key,

Fig. 4. *Tristram Shandy*, 2:47.

life, and with it the lives of all the chil-dren I might, peradventure, have begot out of her hereafter.

Mayhap, brother, replied my uncle *Toby*, my ſiſter does it to ſave the ex-pence :—A pudding's end,—replied my father,——the doctor muſt be paid the ſame for inaction as action,—if not bet-ter,— to keep him in temper.

——— Then it can be out of no-thing in the whole world, quoth my uncle *Toby*, in the ſimplicity of his heart, —but MODESTY : — My ſiſter, I dare ſay, added he, does not care to let a man come ſo near her ＊ ＊ ＊ ＊. I will not ſay whether my uncle *Toby* had com-pleted the ſentence or not ;———'tis for his advantage to ſuppoſe he had,——as, I think, he could have added no improved it." The reader, of course (or at least the ungentle reader), can readily supply a four-letter word that typographically hides behind the fig leaf of the four asterisks—a word my uncle Toby would blush to hear. Omit the word and read the text literally, and Mrs. Shandy "does not care to let a man come so near her asterisks."[6] Here is aposiopesis with a vengeance, and Sterne has made it represent (like so much else in his book) the presence/absence of genitalia and the substitution of print for procreation. Words here are not made flesh; rather, the type and print symbols that stand for words are shown to be, in a certain sense, richer in their implication and more accurate in their representation of human flesh than the voice can produce. The body may fail, either to utter or repress, but print resurrects what flesh had desired.[7]

And the dash, when it is punctuation, does the same for the author, embodying and orchestrating intention. Its quantitative guide to pause, rhythm, and silence and its indication of shifts of speaker, changes of direction, or modifications in tone provide for readers a score that the voice can perform by giving the eye a visual diagram of structural transitions. The ubiquity of the dash insistently calls attention to the manipulating hand of the author behind the printer: for all the freedom Sterne pretends to give individual readers, the firm, set-in-print authority of the text remains inflexible and controls readers, getting them up to speed or slowing them down as he wants. It may be tempting to see the punctuating dash as Sterne's innovation, his discovery of how to use type in a new way at once to control readers more precisely than had his predecessors and to make them conscious of the analogy between the written and the oral, the read and the heard. And in one sense that is true, for Sterne does put a distinctive spin on the device and make it a vehicle of self-consciousness.[8] But more important is the way the device alludes to the already-set conventions of novels.

Long before Sterne silent and solitary readers had been recreating, in mind and unvoiced voice, events as the developing conventions of print in texts had led them. Paragraph indentations, commas, semicolons, and colons had constructed readers and conditioned them into habits of narration that might have seemed individual but, in fact, depended on the textual authority and conventions of print. No longer dependent, as audiences of oral tales had been, on a communal voice, readers had themselves to "voice" (silently) the story and give it pace and division, guided by the type signs beside the letters. As those who have edited early-eighteenth-century novelistic texts know well, "conventions" of punctuation in these texts are approximate at best; most writers and printers use punctuation not for purposes of grammatical clarity but just to indicate pauses. Commas mean brief pauses, semicolons somewhat longer ones, colons longer still, periods and paragraph ends full and even fuller stops. What Sterne does is add a qualifying dimension, give himself a kind of second keyboard of possibility—a dash alone, a comma with a dash; a dash with a semicolon; a longer dash; a dash that sprawls across a full line. If he is making fun of the control exerted by predecessors who pretended to leave all power in the hands of judicious readers but who, in fact, tried to drown out every single reader's own private and silent voice, he is showing how it is done and doing it in a way just a little more technologically advanced—or, rather, in a way that calls more dramatic attention to a technology long available but never fully used. He is, instead of modifying, articulating a standard feature of such texts, showing how dependent on conventions of type the new narrative medium is from the start. Then he extends the convention one more step, showing it to be, all at once, mechanical and absurd, necessary to the species, and effective in its reining in of individualistic, unpredictable, willfully erratic readers.

Chapters in *Tristram Shandy* work similarly. Here again Sterne accepts a relatively new but already standard feature of printed narratives, calls radical attention to it (see fig. 5), then makes it seem silly—and again his purpose is, though teasing and amusing, more constructive than dismissive, for his thrust is to demystify the feature, redeem it, and then use it in a more self-conscious way.

Chaptering in novels was, by the 1750s, virtually a necessary feature, given the length of stories that had come to be expected, the digressive and multidirectional nature of the species, the limited attention span of readers, and the varied circumstances under which solitary reading performances took place. Henry Fielding claimed to have invented this feature (like almost all others) of the emerging "new species," and if he was not, strictly speaking, accurate,[9] he did provide its rationale and define its uses. "An inn or Resting-place" (*Joseph Andrews, 2:1*), he called the space between chapters, regarding divisions as opportunities for readers to pause and refresh themselves. Like many other print features of novels, chapters owe their existence to necessity, in this case physical necessity associated with the phenomenology of reading books. Just as oral narratives of earlier times took their shape in part from the circumstance of a communal gathering, novels designed to entertain readers in solitary hours and circumstances readily extended their lengths to match

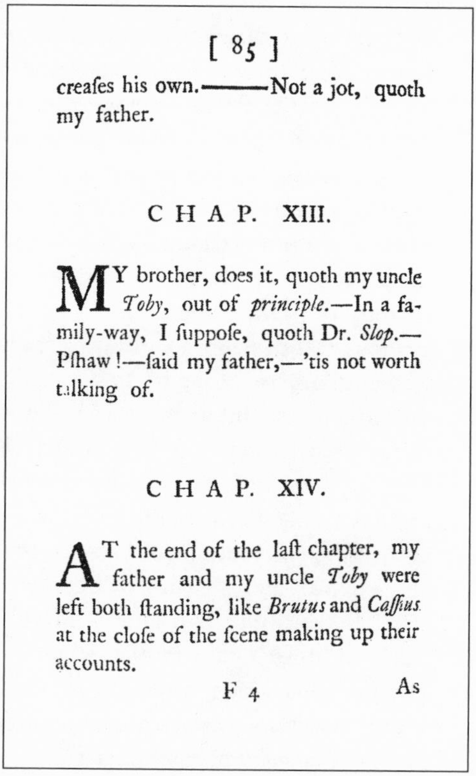

Fig. 5. *Tristram Shandy*, 2:85.

[85]

creaſes his own.——Not a jot, quoth my father.

C H A P. XIII.

MY brother, does it, quoth my uncle *Toby*, out of *principle.*—In a family-way, I ſuppoſe, quoth Dr. *Slop.*—Pſhaw!—ſaid my father,—'tis not worth talking of.

C H A P. XIV.

AT the end of the laſt chapter, my father and my uncle *Toby* were left both ſtanding, like *Brutus* and *Caſſius* at the cloſe of the ſcene making up their accounts.

F 4   As

the narrative needs of readers—though the economics of bookselling may be causal as well, one of many issues about which the overlapping claims of economics, cultural psychology, authorial desire, and social habit need to be sorted out.

Novels early in the eighteenth century tended to be without chapter divisions, as readers of Manley, Defoe, and the early Haywood hardly need to be reminded,[10] and the popularity of the epistolary form may be partly due to its clean divisions, unit by unit or day by day—divisions that allowed readers the convenience of stopping and not losing their places. Fielding's chaptering is more an adaptation of a feature already standard in Richardson than it is a new discovery, though of course not all epistolary novelists understood the formal advantage they had, and some, like Charles Gildon and (later, perhaps for quite different reasons) John Cleland, wrote unbelievably long "letters"; Fanny Hill's two letters are both more than 100 pages long. Letters of such a length raised questions both of narrative probability *and* of a reader's staying power, implying penalties for impatience or early withdrawal.

Once established in mid-century novels, however, chapters quickly became the norm, and their pragmatic value widely accepted—so much so that the conventionality of the convention was lost sight of and its old origins in print technology quickly forgotten. Sterne's radical version of chaptering has the effect of raising the feature into consciousness as a strategy of print, something that has visual dimensions as well as implications for the phenomenology of reading. The sense it offers of repeated new beginnings, of the ready divisibility of experience into episodes and thematic units, and of rhetorical heightening when a volume or a "part" comes to an early end that is not an ending makes chaptering seem arbitrary, artificial, and manipulative—but also absolutely necessary.

Not only does Sterne provide a chapter on chapters—an explicit notice that conventions of book production are part of his subject—but he also provides a series of eccentric chapters and chapter divisions. Here, for example, is chapter 5 of volume 4: "Is this a fit time, said my father to himself, to talk of PENSIONS and GRENADIERS?" End of chapter. The end of chapter 2 of volume 5 self-consciously notes that Walter Shandy's opinion on a particular matter "deserves a chapter to itself.--" The next chapter begins, after two very long dashes, "And a chapter it shall have. . . ." Chapter 24 of volume 4 similarly calls attention to itself: it doesn't exist, and, lest we not notice the nine omitted pages, Sterne from the first sentence of the following chapter explains and justifies the omission. "There is no end, an' please your reverences," he says, "in trying experiments upon chapters—we have had enough of it—So there's an end of that matter." An end, and no end: very Sterne. Also very novelistic, conventional by the time Sterne writes, made possible and ultimately necessary by book technology.

The chapters I have mentioned are the odd ones that call special attention to chaptering as an expected device.[11] They make us laugh at Sterne's cleverness and admire his perception of things we see and don't see—things taken for granted because so familiar. And they make us chortle patronizingly about novelists and their predictable conventions that do not give us what Sterne does: one-sentence chapters, chapters that don't exist, chapters about chapters, or chapters that self-consciously announce their beginning and end. But there are other chapters in *Tristram Shandy*, hundreds of them, and most (while they use all kinds of Sternean tricks to organize themselves or make themselves seem discrete) are conventional in their length and their spatial and psychological function. This feature, like the dash, parodies but also adopts an accepted convention; its virtue lies in articulating and ultimately in defending the convention, not in satire or dismissal or destruction. Sterne doesn't invent; he notices, points, and revises, leaving the convention intact.

A third print feature—the one that uses technology most conspicuously and makes the most direct analysis—involves various strange "illustrative" pages in the book: the black pages (vol. 1), the marbled pages (vol. 3) (see figs. 6 and 7), the blank page (vol. 6). Each has its own rationale and provides a special moment of reaction, response, rereading, and reinterpretation, and each has unique, calculated effects.[12] But I want to emphasize what the three pages have in common, their self-consciousness about intertextuality—also an expected, regular, and prized feature in novels before *Tristram Shandy* but generally unnoticed then and uncommented upon.

Intertextuality takes a variety of forms in early English fiction—digressions, for example, or sections set in different tones and modes or imitations and allusions that call up other texts, stories, or myths—but most of them are more or less related to the intertextual devices of telling and do not depend on the special possibilities of print format or technology. Some do, however: footnotes, for example, and prefaces, and appendices; all, in fact, of the add-on (front *or* back) strategies that a printed text makes possible work in some sense intertextually (as we shall see in looking at Pope's texts), and the effects are just as possible in didactic treatises or philosophical discourses as in narratives. But the intertextual strategy that had, by the 1750s, become most visible and most telling for the reading experience involves illustration (sometimes as frontispiece), and Sterne's special pages both allude to the common practice and themselves operate intertextually upon it.

The blank page may at first seem to be just a silly and superficial joke, but it ultimately makes the most direct, and perhaps the most subtle, comment on illustration. It dramatizes in extreme form the contradiction, and loss of narrative authority, of having illustrations produced through a second consciousness, something that always modifies the printed text, challenges the authority of its single (authorial) perspective, and introduces the issues of difference and multiplicity. Sterne's provision, within the book itself, for a reader to make his or her own illustration, takes the intertextual issue to its logical conclusion, reminding us that, even in the most conservative and authoritarian of texts, there

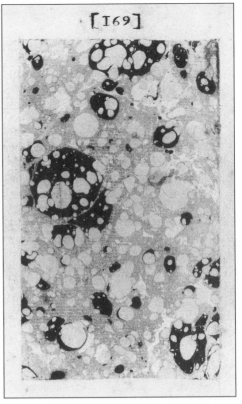

Fig. 6. *Tristram Shandy*, 3:169.

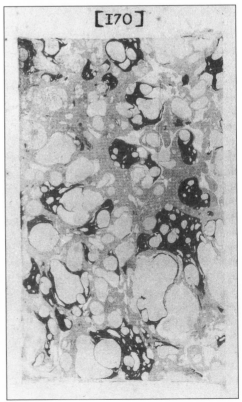

Fig. 7. *Tristram Shandy*, 3:170.

are always at least two subjective consciousnesses at work at any reading moment—and two readings in tension. And he builds his observation into the printedness of books by providing, as with the marbled page, another chance for mass printings of a book to take on individual characteristics, something that is visually realized when a second reader picks up a copy that the first reader had indeed illustrated (a better joke in Sterne's time than ours, because then novels were more often shared by a large number of readers, some of whom no doubt took advantage of the opportunity). Sterne's strategy, while it uses the technology available to him, makes no technical innovation: to leave a page blank may be to make a creative decision, but here an *absence* of technology underscores the earlier technological dependence of novels. The other special pages also relate to Sterne's analysis of verbal and visual intertextuality—a subject that generally is just now beginning to get the attention it deserves in eighteenth-century studies[13]—and the pages themselves intertextuate in wonderful ways, from total ink to no ink at all (both undiscriminating), with a middle page that, refusing the uniformity of print, swirls its own individuality out of a tedious old-fashioned hand process.

My favorite insistence in Sterne on the bookness of books is one that modern readers, because of our reprint technology, miss. It involves the final sentence of volume 1: "If I thought you was able to form the least judgment or probable conjecture to yourself, of what was to come in the next page,—I would tear it out of my book." In modern reprints the next page begins the first chapter of volume 2, but in the first edition the next page was blank, easily guessable. It is a joke, of course, but as usual in Sterne more than a joke: it involves his version of probability and technological as well as human predictability, his sense of ordering possibility within larger disorders, his assertion of authority, his claim about what books, including novels, can do even when they seem trivial and perverse. It is one more example of Sterne's demonstration that print technology produces a particular and stable form of product, another instance of his characteristic glance at a technology that, long before he set out to write novels, had begun to determine in his forebears just what novels could be thought to do, because they depended upon a specific print and book medium.

What is curious here is that, admitting the subjectivity of readers and working from pointed attention to technological innovation and the quirks of print and bookmaking, Sterne makes a bridge for his many readers of whatever kind, a bridge that readers may cross communally, even though they are individually participating in a unique text. Having lost the old typological worldview that considers all stories as variants on one human narrative, Sterne turns type into an eccentric medium for sharing individuality.[14] But Sterne's exploitation of print technology depends on nothing brand new. Although he underscores the printed quality and materiality of his book—and although he seems to claim a special relationship between print culture and the new (novelistic) narrative he joyfully employs—he relies on print strategies available for some time and does not specifically align himself with any print or bookmaking novelty that dates his book as mid-century or that makes him dependent on any state-of-the-art technology or conceptuality. His book thus defines itself, perhaps, as "odd" but not necessarily as "new" in any technological sense that would align him ideologically as innovative or contemporary.

Sterne's aggressive insistence that his work be considered an instance of print technology allies him—and the novelistic form he employs—with modernity but not with a specific technological moment. He insists on being read visually and materially but, in doing so, makes use of means long available if seldom employed to their fullest advantage. We need to be wary of overreading the politics—or even the social leanings—in his "radical" allegiances to technology.

Now I want to look at a less individualized text—in fact, an insistently communal one—that seems to address very different readers. Ironically, however, this text also ends up giving the reader a surprising amount of individual space. Alexander Pope, by his own admission, hated innovation and singularity, and he seldom passed up a chance to say something nasty about booksellers, print, and the technology of modern distribution. But he too got involved in the technology, harvesting its uses and finding its implications irresistible.

Pope's career played itself out a full generation earlier than Sterne's and concentrated almost totally in poetic genres that had been around for generations. He published his first poem before Sterne was born, and Sterne was only fifteen when Pope, in his *Dunciad* of 1728, locked into a textual pillory many distinguished contemporaries who made their livings by writing or by the technologies that supported it. Only Behn, Defoe, and Haywood, among Sterne's illustrious novelistic predecessors, had in fact written novels by then, and, although two of these three figures were portrayed among the Dunces (and Behn probably would have been too, had Pope thought her important enough to mention), Pope's reasons for including them had little to do with their uses of print technology or their innovative novels. Pope may well have seen the modernist implications of the emerging prose species, as I have argued elsewhere,[15] but his attitudes toward the technologies of printing and text distribution involve broad categories of textual novelties, not just texts that would soon come to be called novels. The differences between Pope and Sterne depend on a lot more than their choices of literary genre, though in each case the chosen medium is an indication of authorial attitude toward print technologies and modern innovation more generally.

Pope's fullest account of what writing was about in his time, *The Dunciad,* begins (in the very first line) with a frontal attack on printers, booksellers, and other commodifiers of verbal art, and throughout the poem argues that contemporary deterioration of taste and debasement of values derive explicitly from the proliferation of print. "Providence... permitted the Invention of Printing," he says ironically in a prefatory statement prefixed to the 1729 variorum edition, "as a scourge for the Sins of the learned," and he goes on to attribute the decadence of his own time to the fact that "Paper... became so cheap, and printers so numerous, that a deluge of authors cover'd the land." The "age of lead," he later calls these times and describes how "the peace of the honest unwriting subject was daily molested" by distribution technology. Again and again the poem recirculates the imagery of apocalypse and divine retribution for the sins of print. Modern writing, Pope argues in the very first line of the poem, is inspired by the "Smithfield Muses," who replace the logos, the wordness, of true poetry with an art based on technological gimmickry—"Shews, Machines, and Dramatical Entertainments, formerly agreeable only to the Taste of the Rabble" (note to l. 2, 1729 ed.). The poem's primary emphasis is on how texts are modified, marketed, and circulated; booksellers soon capture from authors the poem's central attention, and it is they who begin the "high, heroic games" of the second book with their running and pissing contests. Authors repeatedly take their crucial cues (as well as their values) from the economy; writers here never write for themselves but, rather, follow cultural forces, just as their own games literally follow those of commodity entrepreneurs (booksellers) and old-style political sponsors (patrons whom the writers compete to tickle). There are plenty of other culprits in Pope's analysis—vanity, subjectivity, education, native stupidity—but the commodification of taste as a united function of greed and modern progress focuses Pope's satire.

One irony of Pope's attack on the commercial success of texts is that he himself was not only the clearest beneficiary in his own time of the proliferation of print but also the first poet in modern history to achieve a comfortable wealth from writing; he knew how to profit handsomely from what the booksellers in his time had made possible, and he became a formidable negotiator who regularly outwitted and outmaneuvered the stationers who performed publishing functions.[16] I mention this not to attack Pope's values, question his motives, or defuse his satire, but to suggest the complexity of what actually happens in his textual attack on distribution technology. And there are other ironies in the way he makes his text address textual technologies and modern values.

The Dunciad Variorum of 1729, essentially the second and most important redaction of his opus magnum, manipulates print technology almost as fully and complexly as does *Tristram Shandy* thirty years later. For all Pope's antimodernism there are some very modish things here, especially in the visual presentation of text, the typographical manipulation of information, and the prefatory matter and appendices. Plainly, Pope made a conscious decision to construct all this machinery, which employs the devices parodically but still manages to use—straight—the effects of the machinery. His first published version involved only verse, presented in the traditional way, one that pretended print was merely a necessary convenience for circulating what was essentially an oral form. And we have full accounts of Pope's elaborate plan for adding the complex machinery of 1729.

One purpose of the machinery is, of course, to burlesque the self-conscious excesses of needless learning, and because Pope had made Lewis Theobald, his rival as editor and annotator of Shakespeare, the hero of the poem in all its early versions, the heavy machinery was a fit metaphor. Still, Pope goes much further with the machinery in the variorum than he would have needed to in order to parody Theobald. There are, to be sure, in both the prefatory matter and the footnotes, many long passages ridiculing Theobald's pedantry and arrogance (some of them justified, some not). The very first annotation to the poem, for example, mockingly debates whether *e*'s (and how many) should be interpolated in the term *Dunciad,* a reminder of the way Theobald spelled *Shakspear* (as Pope did not) with an *e* at the end of each syllable. And there are countless other notes that mock Theobald's triumphant claims about emendations, meanings, and textual habits. This much use of annotation, as burlesque, would be justified simply by the poem's own satiric focus and claims. But Pope goes much further.

A lot of what Pope does with the machinery involves showing off. Most pages contain two categories of notes, one labeled "Remarks" and the other "Imitations" (see fig. 8). Almost everything in the second category involves a kind of ornamental boasting, a listing of passages from the classics and from earlier English writers that Pope's own verse alludes to. But it is worth asking to whom these boasts are addressed. Most, or at least many, of the allusions would readily be noticed by the polite and learned readers Pope ostensibly had in mind in writing the poem; certainly, Swift would not have needed the notes on sources nor would, say, Theobald or Dennis. Who, then, would have needed them, and who would have needed the long, often tedious, but highly informative notes included under "Remarks" in which references are explained, glosses provided, history filled in, or connections made with other parts of the text? Well, the king, for one (a notoriously scanty, ignorant, and inept reader and someone whose reading of the poem quickly becomes an issue). And then there are all those other readers out there without classical learning and without knowledge of such crucial English forebears as Spenser and Milton and Dryden. But why should Pope care about such readers in a poem that mocks their ignorance, their values, and their taste—that is, in fact, largely focused against the commodity forces that bring texts into their reach in the first place? If Pope is writing to enforce a clear distinction between adequate readers and upstarts who recognize no echo and who know nothing, why does he bother to explain his learning and the range of his allusive power to those whose recognition is unimportant?

But the fact is that he does court this larger audience. Whether driven by egotism or ethics, Pope cared deeply about the directions of modernity, was determined to effect cultural change, and saw the making of texts as the major force in determining culture. *The Dunciad Variorum* pulls out all the stops in its effort not only to define the enemy but also to claim an audience among the uncommitted, even including those new readers from the developing classes whose reading experiences were narrow or slight. The evangelical tone in *The Dunciad* is easily overlooked if one looks primarily for Pope's misrepresentations and unfairnesses (a valuable but now overindulged hobby in eighteenth-century studies), but to consider his audience and the full rhetorical range of modern means of persuasion that Pope uses we must notice the com-

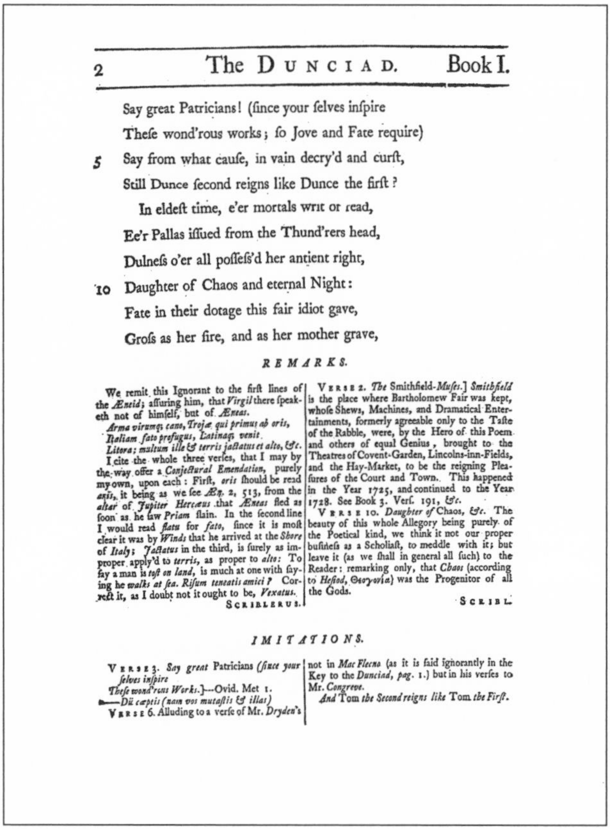

2   The DUNCIAD.   Book I.

Say great Patricians! (since your selves inspire

These wond'rous works; so Jove and Fate require)

5   Say from what cause, in vain decry'd and curst,

Still Dunce second reigns like Dunce the first?

In eldest time, e'er mortals writ or read,

Ee'r Pallas issued from the Thund'rers head,

Dulness o'er all possess'd her antient right,

10   Daughter of Chaos and eternal Night:

Fate in their dotage this fair idiot gave,

Gross as her sire, and as her mother grave,

REMARKS.

We remit this Ignorant to the first lines of the *Æneid*; assuring him, that *Virgil* there speaketh not of himself, but of *Æneas.* *Arma virumq; cano, Trojæ qui primus ab oris, Italiam fato profugus, Latinaq; venit Littora; multum ille & terris jactatus et alto, &c.* I cite the whole three verses, that I may by the; way offer a *Conjectural Emendation,* purely my own, upon each: First, *oris* should be read *axis,* it being as we see *Æn.* 2, 513, from the altar of *Jupiter Herræus* that *Æneas* fled so soon as he saw *Priam* slain. In the second line I would read *flatu* for *fato,* since it is most clear it was by *Winds* that he arrived at the *Shore* of *Italy*; *Jactatus* in the third, is surely as improper apply'd to *terris,* as proper to *alto*: To say a man is *tost on land,* is much at one with saying he *walks at sea. Risum teneatis amici?* Correct it, as I doubt not it ought to be, *Vexatus.*
         SCRIBLERUS.

VERSE 2. *The Smithfield-Muses.] Smithfield* is the place where Bartholomew Fair was kept, whose Shews, Machines, and Dramatical Entertainments, formerly agreeable only to the Taste of the Rabble, were, by the Hero of this Poem and others of equal Genius, brought to the Theatres of Covent-Garden, Lincolns-inn-Fields, and the Hay-Market, to be the reigning Pleasures of the Court and Town. This happened in the Year 1725, and continued to the Year 1728. See Book 3. Vers. 191, &c.
    VERSE 10. *Daughter* of Chaos, &c. The beauty of this whole Allegory being purely of the Poetical kind, we think it not our proper business as a Scholiast, to meddle with it; but leave it (as we shall in general all such) to the Reader: remarking only, that *Chaos* (according to *Hesiod, Θεογονία*) was the Progenitor of all the Gods.
         SCRIBL.

IMITATIONS.

VERSE 3. *Say great Patricians (since your selves inspire These wond'rous Works.*]—Ovid. Met 1.
— *Dii cœptis (nam vos mutastis & illas)*
VERSE 6. Alluding to a verse of Mr. *Dryden's*

not in *Mac Flecno* (as it is said ignorantly in the Key to the *Dunciad, pag.* 1.) but in his verses to Mr. *Congreve.*
    And Tom *the Second reigns like* Tom *the First.*

Fig. 8. *The Dunciad,* 4–5, Variorum ed., 1729.

prehensive way that he reaches out to new, unpracticed readers. Whatever his bias toward traditional values and conventional means, Pope does not settle for the textual modes and methods he inherits, and his distrust of what others had done with textual technologies did not prevent him from himself using modern strategies that had become available.

Pope's nostalgia for a communal audience composed of those with like educations and values in fact underwrites his strategy of forging a new print constituency, although the strategy itself may in effect undermine some of his argument about cultural production. (There is, of course, an instrumental irony here, but there are a host of such ironies in the strongly idealistic but also pragmatic and devious Pope.) Pope's decision to create the variorum involves a commitment to visual, intertextual, and other technologically based strategies that implicate the author in profound generic changes, changing in fact the generic predispositions of poetry. However vociferously Pope defends traditional poetry and its values in *The Dunciad,* the variorum version alters the nature of verse satire, the then standard poetic verse form of heroic couplets, and the whole idea of genre. Tradition would never again be quite the same.

I want to look again (and then again and then again, as the print mode here asks us to do) at Pope's method in the elaborate Scriblerian footnotes, but I want to do so by concentrating on one set of notes on a single couplet, the first in the poem:

> BOOKS and the Man I sing, the first who brings
> The Smithfield Muses to the Ear of Kings.

It is the only line of poetry on the whole first page (see fig. 9). The prose crowds and dwarfs the poetry (part of the point Pope is making about modernity and the Smithfield muses), and the continuing note on this same couplet takes up almost half the next page in the first edition; it uses even more space in subsequent editions, as Pope continues to add information. *Intertextuality* is not a strong enough word to describe what happens to our reading experience in this very first couplet—a couplet that had been, in the purely verse texts of 1728, powerful enough in its own right but that now takes on a whole series of additional meanings and directions.[17] In reading this first page, or in looking at it, our attention is more than simply divided by two kinds of type and competing texts: experientially, reading here is an eye-jumping, mind-boggling jumble. Presumably, the right way to read the page is to proceed from the Latin motto atop the engraving—which is not translated in the note, though a conscientious reader is apt, in a text annotated as copiously as this one, to check—to the engraving itself, then perhaps back to the notes to see if the engraving is annotated, then to the title (which has two full paragraphs of annotation, though it seems the least likely thing on the page to need a note), then back to the first two lines of the poem, then back to the footnote, which finally involves turning the page and continuing to read extensively in Latin and English, before ultimately coming back to the poetry. So much for the phenomenological process. But epistemologically, the reading is more complicated yet, for we are asked to file facts and accumulate a series of interpretive relationships. The notes jerk us back and forth across the first two lines, calling attention to one thing after another: the allusion to the first line of the *Aeneid,* a

THE

DUNCIAD.

BOOK the FIRST.

BOOKS and the man I fing, the firſt who brings
The Smithfield Mufes to the ear of kings.

REMARKS on BOOK the FIRST.

* THE *Dunciad, ſic* M. S. It
may be well difputed whether this
be a right Reading ? Ought it not
rather to be fpelled *Dunceiad*, as
the Etymology evidently demands ?
Dunce with an *e*, therefore *Dunceiad*
with an *e*. That accurate and pun-
ctual Man of Letters, the Reſtorer
of *Shakefpeare*, conſtantly obferves
the prefervation of this very Letter
e, in fpelling the Name of his beloved Author, and not like his common careleſs Editors, with the o-
miſſion of one, nay fometimes of two
ee's [as *Shak'ſpear*] which is utterly
unpardonable. Nor is the neglect
of a *fingle Letter* fo trivial as to fome
it may appear; the alteration where-
of in a learned language is an *At-
chivement that brings honour* to the
Critick who advances it; and Dr. *B.*
will be remembered to pofterity for
his performances of *this ſort*, as long

as the world fhall have any efteem
for the Remains of *Menander* and
Philemon.

THEOBALD.

I have a juſt value for the Letter
E, and the fame affection for the
Name of this Poem, as the forecited
Critick for that of his Author ; yet
cannot it induce me to agree with
thofe who would add yet another *e*
to it, and call it the *Dunceiade;*
which being a *French* and foreign
Termination, is no way proper to a
word entirely *Englifh*, and verna-
cular. One *E* therefore in this cafe
is right, and two *E*'s wrong ; yet,
upon the whole, I fhall follow the
Manufcript, and print it without any
E at all ; mov'd thereto by Authority, at all times with Criticks equal
if not fuperior to Reafon. In which
method of proceeding, I can never

F   enough

Fig. 9. *The Dunciad*, firſt
page, Variorum ed., 1729

conjecture about Virgil's text in which the subject of Theobald's editing
and pedantry is again raised; an identification of Smithfield and the activities in Bartholomew Fair; an explanation of the movement of bad
taste from the old city westward to the theaters and the court—but not,
until the 1735 edition of the variorum, anything in the notes to gloss the
"Ear of Kings."

There are, however, notes elsewhere in the technologized text and
in other places that the process of intertextual reading, once introduced,
makes possible, perhaps even inevitable. Back on the first page of the
poem, where the line involving the "Ear of Kings" appears, the decora-

Fig. 10. *The Dunciad,* title
page, Variorum ed., 1729.

THE

DUNCIAD

VARIORVM.

WITH THE

PROLEGOMENA of *SCRIBLERUS.*

DEFEROR IN VICVM

VENDENTEM THVS ET ODORES

LONDON.

Printed for A.DOB . 1729.

tion at the top pictures ears, two sets of them, pointing off to the top
left and right of the page, acting for all the world like quotation marks
to the motto on the decoration. They are not kings' ears though, they
are asses' ears, and they recall the striking frontispiece on the title page
(see fig. 10), in which an ass is laden with contemporary writings, literally bearing the burden of the present. The ass, both listener and agent
of verbal transport, looks rather pleased with himself. But who is he?
And how are we to construe the receptive ears in line 2?

A case can be made for the ass of the frontispiece as George II. It is
certainly a Hanoverian: the broad, long nose suggests a celebrated family

trait, and the ass is uncharacteristically white, like the emblematic Hanoverian horse. But a browser in a bookstall would not necessarily identify the frontispiece as an official royal portrait. A reader who negotiates
the first two lines of poetry and page and a half of text can, however,
hardly help but make the identification. Pope builds the connection carefully, with a variety of strategies scattered over a series of editions and
other texts. What Pope has done here is take the old traditional form of
intertextuality as allusion and technologize it into a new materialized
intertextuality that is certainly seeable, almost palpable.

The full glossing of the ears is not textually completed, however,
until 1735, when a new paragraph is added to the annotation on line 2
and when Pope makes explicit, in a wholly different poem, the mythological connection between kings' and asses' ears. Let me deal with the
second, more oblique, 1735 glossing first. Pope retails the full mythological tale, with specific references to Walpole and Queen Caroline, in
lines 69–82 of his *Epistle to Dr. Arbuthnot,* and the whole passage there
becomes a direct commentary on the opening of *The Dunciad,* an extremely elaborate intertextuality. But useful as this passage may be to
prove Pope's intention, the story narrated in that later poem is only in
an extended sense a part of *The Dunciad's* text. And for attentive readers
it isn't necessary, for the story—about how King Midas developed asses'
ears that observers had trouble keeping silent about—is a very old one,
told by (among others) Ovid, Chaucer, and Dryden, and it was familiar
to many readers in 1729 without the aid of notes. The joke almost
springs itself on the title page—just the asses' ears, even with only a
slight facial likeness to the king, would do it for many, many readers—
but the visually repeated ears, on the first text page, in which ears are
associated with kings in the only two lines of poetry there, make the
dangerous joke blatant.[18]

But the other 1735 glossing—a prominent in-the-text addition to
the note on line 2 itself—locks the allusion to the reigning king and
makes it available to readers who might have been unable to make the
connection in earlier texts. Here is the note: "We are willing to acquaint
Posterity that this Poem (as it here stands) was presented to King George
the Second and his Queen, by the hands of Sir R. Walpole, on the 12th
of March 1728/9." For more practiced readers, however, the accomplishment is not in clarity but in extension of meaning and implication.
Pope's first note on the opening couplet had loudly and obtusely denied
a published misreading of the 1728 *Dunciad* in order to set up a larger
point later. The author, the Scriblerian note insists, cannot mean himself

(as one annotator had claimed) to be the bringer of the Smithfield muses to kings because he is too modest to claim kings among his readers, even though kings did read his works; the literal bringer must be Lewis Theobald, the debased Aeneas of Pope's poem. No interpretive help is advanced here, but the "refutation" accomplishes two things: (1) it introduces into the text the king as reader, or at least as receptor, of books; and (2) it introduces, by way of denial, the issue of whether "Pope" is in any way culpable for enlarging the domain of the Smithfield muses or of putting anything in the ear of kings. The new note of 1735 now makes Walpole (as well as Theobald) the "bringer" to the "Ear of Kings," extending the political implication and introducing the themes of collusion and corruption that expand later. But Pope also becomes the bringer here, by implication, for what Walpole delivers to George and Caroline is Pope's text, here reflexively united with the metaphor in lines 1–2, and Pope's poem becomes Smithfieldian in spite of itself. The specific denial in the first part of the note to line 1 is thus blurred then reversed, and the contagion of the satirist who records debasement and corruption is admitted into the text from the very first page. Pope's own text becomes a relevant part of the issue, the tainted modernist text that perversely finds a receptacle in royal ears and that loses its purity by helping to further the commodification of culture.

Pope's implication of himself in modernity and his creation of an elaborate technologized text are not altogether voluntary, and his motives and attitudes—literary, political, social—are very different from Sterne's. He had precedents of a sort for all his visual strategies: the frontispiece and decoration; the prefaces, appendices, indexes, footnotes; the mixing of poetry with prose, and the whole strategy of answering one's enemies in their own language of whatever kind. Horace, Erasmus, Boileau, and Swift are just a few exemplars he cites or might cite to justify himself. But he made new things happen textually by using the technology he attacked. He not only took texts—conventional, traditional, conservative texts in established poetic kinds—into a form that acknowledged their writtenness, their printedness, their bookness, and their existence as an economic commodity but also, by his example, showed what participation in modernity involved for even the most traditional and conservative writers. After Pope, whatever his intentions, traditional poetry for communal, elite, learned, and snobbish readers would never again be the same, for, using the available (but, again, not brand-new) print and book technology, he shifted the burden of discovery from learning and previous reading to readerly work within the text. In a way he prefigured Blake, though neither Pope nor Blake would have liked to believe it. This is not a case of divided mind or authorial ambivalence: it is a matter of being caught in history and helping it happen.

The visual strategies of Sterne and Pope indicate the need for several kinds of revisions of literary history, involving not only the influence of print technology and the making and marketing of material books but also challenges to the traditional Western privileging of the verbal ("In the beginning was the Word").[19] But here I want to point explicitly to just one moral for contemporary criticism and theory. In looking for the textual flowerings of technology, historians of texts had better look in more than one place and be ready to see surprising things. Change does happen in the expected places and among the usual suspects (though perhaps with unpredictable lag times), but it also happens less openly and among those who seem least likely to embrace it. Change is not always a question of commitment or even of choice.

NOTES

The Sterne section of this essay appears in a much-abbreviated form in *Transactions of the Eighth International Congress of the Enlightenment* (Oxford: Voltaire Foundation, 1993), 1084–87.

1. Long ago, of course, Walter Benjamin raised some of the classic issues in "The Work of Art in the Age of Mechanical Reproduction," in *Illuminations*, ed. Hannah Arendt, trans. Harry Zohn (New York: Schocken Books, 1969). Benjamin's essay was originally published in 1936.

2. The broad outlines of the cultural results of print history have been clarified by such studies as Lucien Febvre and Henri-Jean Martin, *The Coming of the Book: The Impact of Printing, 1450–1800* (1958; reprint, London: Verso, 1990 [first translated into English 1976]); Elizabeth L. Eisenstein, *The Printing Press as an Agent of Change*, 2 vols. (Cambridge: Cambridge University Press, 1979); Roger Chartier, *The Cultural Uses of Print in Early Modern France*, trans. Lydia G. Cochrane (Princeton: Princeton University Press, 1987); Jeremy Black, *The English Press in the Eighteenth Century* (London: Croom Helm, 1987); Albert Ward, *Book Production, Fiction, and the German Reading Public, 1740–1800* (Oxford: Clarendon Press, 1974); Robert Darnton, *The Literary Underground of the Old Regime* (Cambridge, Mass.: Harvard University Press, 1982); Marshall McLuhan, *The Gutenburg Galaxy: The Making of Typographic Man* (Toronto: University of Toronto Press, 1962); and Walter J. Ong, *Interfaces of the Word: Studies in the Evolution of Consciousness and Culture* (Ithaca: Cornell University Press, 1977). The interpretive work on authors and individual texts has just begun to take advantage of all the information now available; see, for example,

Alvin B. Kernan, *Printing Technology, Letters, and Samuel Johnson* (Princeton: Princeton University Press, 1987); and Julie Stone Peters, *Congreve, the Drama, and the Printed Word* (Stanford: Stanford University Press, 1990).

3. Ian Watt has provocatively discussed the dash as a measure of Sterne's colloquial syntax ("The Comic Syntax of *Tristram Shandy*," in *Studies in Criticism and Aesthetics, 1660–1800: Essays in Honor of Samuel Holt Monk,* ed. Howard Anderson and John S. Shea [Minneapolis: University of Minnesota Press], 315–31).

4. For a brief but suggestive account of how punctuation influences pace in reading Sterne, see Roger B. Moss, "Sterne's Punctuation," *ECS* 15 (1981–82): 179–200.

5. On the relationship of the Phutatorius episode to structural patterns in the novel, see the classic essay by Sigurd Burckhart, *"Tristram Shandy*'s Law of Gravity," *ELH* 28 (1961): 70–88.

6. A pun worthy of Sterne—and probably borrowed from him by Franklin P. Adams in his poem, "Composed in the Composing Room."

7. The suppressed oath "Zounds" in the passage I have been examining is, of course, the colloquial version of "God's Wounds," and it is typical of Sterne that even an oath (even an unspoken one) furthers the fundamental pyschological and philosophical point.

8. John Dunton's *Voyage Round the World* (3 vols. [1691]) is one prominent predecessor in its habits of using the dash. The precedent was not unnoticed by Sterne's contemporaries: a rival printer reissued Dunton's narrative as *The Life, Travels, and Adventures of Christopher Wagstaff, Gentleman, Grandfather to Tristram Shandy* in 1762.

9. Chaptering had been common in seventeenth-century Continental fiction—in *Don Quixote,* for example—and it was standard in a variety of English fictional kinds; see, for example, Kirkman's *The Unlucky Citizen* and Dunton's *Voyage Round the World*. But early eighteenth-century fictions largely abandon the practice, apparently to give the impression of a seamless, "natural" narrative that resembles oral tales. Defoe's narratives notoriously have no breaks—as any reader who has ever tried to refind anything in a Defoe novel knows well—but some of the pirated and abridged reprints of Defoe consistently use chaptering as if it were an expected feature in print narratives. See, for example, *The Life and Actions of Moll Flanders* (1723), a severely truncated version of 188 pages, divided into nine chapters, or *Fortune's Fickle Distribution* (1730), which abridges Moll's story into 91 pages (also dividing it into chapters) and appends two other chapter-length narratives at the end, a "Life of Jane Hackabout, Her Governess" and a "Life of James Mac-Faul, Moll Flanders's Lancashire Husband."

10. And it hardly seemed to matter in the shorter narratives; it was not until these narratives came to be of a certain magnitude that breaking up the text seemed crucial, though some early novelists, Haywood for example, frequently broke up the extended gray spaces of print by inserting letters presumed to be sent among characters or by finding some ruse to provide subheads that, at the least, provided readers with a kind of visual bookmark, as in later epistolary fiction.

11. The standard discussion of chaptering—scanty, however, on historical

information—is Philip Stevick, "The Theory of Fictional Chapters," in *The Theory of the Novel,* ed. Philip Stevick (New York: Free Press, 1967).

12. On the implications of the marbled and black pages, see the excellent discussion by Alexander Whitaker, "Emblems in Motley: Literary Implications of the Graphic Devices in *Tristram Shandy*" (Ph.D. diss., Emory University, 1979), 45–84. For a concise description of the elaborate process by which the marbled pages were made, see W. G. Day, *"Tristram Shandy:* The Marbled Leaf," *Library* 27 (1972): 143–45. Quite a number of critical discussions of *Tristram Shandy* try to support Sterne's claim that the marbled page is "emblematic"; Richard Macksey makes the most cogent case in his brilliant essay "Alas Poor Yorick: Sterne's Thoughts," *MLN* 85 (1983): 1006–20.

13. See, for example, Philip Stewart, *Engraven Desire: Eros, Image, and Text in the French Eighteenth Century* (Durham, N.C.: Duke University Press, 1992).

14. For a fuller discussion of the implications of Sterne's strategy, see my "Response as Reformation: *Tristram Shandy* and the Art of Interruption," *Novel* 4 (1971): 132–46.

15. See *Before Novels: The Cultural Contexts of Eighteenth-Century English Fiction* (New York: Norton, 1990).

16. See Maynard Mack, *Alexander Pope: A Life* (New York: Norton, 1985); and David Foxon, *Pope and the Early Eighteenth-century Book Trade,* Lyell Lectures. Oxford, 1975–76, rev. and ed. James McLaverty (Oxford: Clarendon Press, 1991).

17. Despite the considerable theoretical attention in recent years to footnotes and other attention-dividing strategies on the printed page, it is surprising how little we know about the way print divisions on the page have historically affected reading habits. But there are some very suggestive discussions: see, for example, Hugh Kenner, *The Stoic Comedians* (Berkeley: University of California Press, 1962), 37–66; Michel Foucault, *The Order of Things* (New York: Vintage, 1970), esp. 78–81; Lawrence Lipking, "The Marginal Gloss," *Critical Inquiry* 4 (1977): 609–55; Jacques Derrida, "Living On: *Border Lines,"* in *Deconstruction and Criticism,* ed. Geoffrey Hartman (New York: Seabury, 1979); Shari Benstock, "At the Margin of Discourse: Footnotes in the Fictional Text," *PMLA* 98 (1983): 204–25; and Frank Palmeri, "The Satiric Footnotes of Swift and Gibbon," *ECTI* 31 (1990): 245–62. Postmodern books such as Nicholson Baker's novel *The Mezzanine* (New York: Weidenfeld and Nicholson, 1988) have returned to many of the seventeenth- and eighteenth-century strategies for disrupting the conventional expectations of readers.

18. To make sure that careful readers notice, Pope changes the "ears" of kings in all six of the 1728 editions to a single (inclusive) "ear" in all versions of the Variorum, as if to claim that one ear in the text and two in the asses of the illustration could not possibly gloss each other.

The two asses in the decoration, plainly related but not look-alikes, are indirectly glossed in line 6 of the poem and the elaborate note on it. The line—"Still Dunce the second reigns like Dunce the first"—doesn't seem to need much of a gloss, since George II had just become king upon the death of his father in 1727, less than a year before *The Dunciad* was published. But the annotation in the Variorum takes no risk that the reader will not know that substitute names are in order, taking pains to point to Dryden's "master" line in "To Congreve": "For Tom the Second reigns like Tom the First." The note at once underscores the political implication, introduces names, and claims referentiality for the line by citing Dryden's precedent.

19. Barbara Stafford is articulate and forceful on this point. See especially her *Body Criticism: Imaging the Unseen in Enlightenment Art and Medicine* (Cambridge, Mass.: MIT Press, 1991).

Mark Twain: Texts and Technology

Hamlin Hill

In 1872 Mark Twain published a prophetic tall tale in *Roughing It,* his second book. He recorded a yarn about an unfortunate man named Wheeler, who

> was a-mediating and dreaming around in the carpet factory and the machinery made a snatch at him and first you know he was a-meandering all over that factory, from the garret to the cellar, and everywhere, at such another gait as—why, you couldn't even see him; you could only hear him whiz when he went by. Well, you know a person can't go through an experience like that and arrive back home the way he was when he went. No, Wheeler got wove up into thirty-nine yards of best three-ply carpeting. The widder was sorry, she was uncommon sorry, and loved him and done the best she could fur him in the circumstances, which was unusual. She took the whole piece—thirty-nine yards—and she wanted to give him proper and honorable burial, but she couldn't bear to roll him up; she took and spread him out full length, and said she wouldn't have it any other way. She wanted to buy a tunnel for him but there wasn't any tunnel for sale, so she boxed him in a beautiful box and stood it on the hill on a pedestal twenty-one foot high, and so it was a monument and grave together, and economical—sixty foot high—you could see it from everywhere and she painted on it "To the loving memory of thirty-nine yards best three-ply carpeting containing the mortal remainders of Millington G. Wheeler go thou and do likewise."[1]

This essay proposes to trace the several remarkable transformations whereby Mark Twain turned from a newspaperman into an author of books, then into a subscription book publisher, next into the product for sale, and finally into the machine itself. He too was snatched up by the machinery and whizzed through this particular factory for almost forty years before he exited from it like Wheeler, nowhere near "the way he was when he went" in.

On January 5, 1889, Samuel Clemens wrote his brother Orion an exultant letter:

> At 12.20 this afternoon a line of movable type was spaced and justified by machinery, for the first time in the history of the world! And I was there to see. It was done *automatically*—instantly—perfectly. . . . All the other wonderful inventions of the human brain sink pretty nearly into common-place contrasted with this awful mechanical miracle. Telephones, telegraphs, locomotives, cotton gins, sewing machines, Babbage calculators, Jacquard looms, perfecting presses, Arkwright's frames—all are mere toys, simplicities! The Paige Compositor marches alone and far in the lead of human inventions.[2]

The typesetter marched with $300,000 support (about $4 million in today's currency) of Mark Twain's money; among the few texts printed on the marvel of the ages was a manuscript fragment called "Huck Finn and Tom Sawyer among the Indians," an abortive sequel to *Adventures of Huckleberry Finn* (1885). Both the sequel and the machine that composed it automatically were colossal failures. The text had written itself into a corner and was not to see print for eighty years, and the machine—which now sits in the basement of the Clemens's Hartford home like a brass battleship—ultimately contributed to Mark Twain's bankruptcy in 1893. More important, it culiminated Mark Twain's love-hate relationship with the machinery of printing and publication.

Back in 1867 Mark Twain was a newspaperman with a reputation in the west and without any interest in becoming an author of books; he gained fame with a series of letters from Europe and the Middle East, but his humor was considered vulgar and unfit for Eastern or national audiences. In December of that year, however, he changed the direction of his career by answering an inquiry from Elisha Bliss of the American Publishing Company of Hartford about the possibility of his writing a book for that company. And he admitted quite honestly that "what amount of *money* I might possibly make . . . has a degree of importance for me which is almost beyond my own comprehension."[3] And if he was innocent about the profit in writing books, he was abysmally ignorant of the peculiar sales mechanism known as "For Sale by Subscription Only."

Bliss was the president of the largest of a cluster of semireputable subscription publishers who exploited the increasing literacy of a rural or small-town, middle-class or blue-collar customer. As humorist George Ade reminisced in 1910, the salesman

> sometimes . . . was a ministerial person in black clothes and a stove-pipe hat. Maiden ladies and widows, who supplemented their specious arguments with private tales of woe, moved from one small town to another feeding upon prominent citizens. Occasionally the prospectus was unfurled by an undergraduate of a freshwater college working for the money to carry him another year.[4]

With sure-fire, hard-sell instructions and a sampler the agent moved into small towns and farms peddling self-help books, Bibles and biblical commentary, Civil War memoirs, and, as Huck Finn put it, "Dr. Gunn's Family Medicine, which told you all about what to do if a body was sick or dead." Editions of forty thousand to fifty thousand were not unusual. Mark Twain himself was awed by the numbers, remarking that, after the publication of *The Innocents Abroad* in 1869:

> I never wander into any corner of the country but I find that an agent has been there before me, and many of that community have read the book. . . . It is easy to see, when one travels around, that one must be endowed with a deal of genuine generalship in order to maneuvre a publication whose line of battle stretches from end to end of a great continent, and whose foragers and skirmishers invest every hamlet and besiege every village hidden away in all the vast space between.[5]

In less than two years Mark Twain was to enlist himself and begin to do battle for his own royalty checks.

He believed, instinctively and perhaps correctly, that subscription volumes depended for their success on the number of commitments to purchase made *before* the book was published rather than upon postpublication advertising. Trade journals were fanatically hostile to subscription books and refused to review them. But it would have been unlikely that the typical subscription book purchaser was in the habit of reading the *Atlantic Monthly, Appleton's, Lippincott's,* or *Scribner's.* In 1884 Mark

Twain was to command his nephew, head of Charles L. Webster and Company, about *Huckleberry Finn:* "we will continue the canvass till we strike the full figure of 40,000 orders."[6]

Accordingly, his first involvement with the technology of selling his books began with his suggesting to Bliss what material from his manuscript should go into the prospectus or sampler—an unusual thin volume with selections from the book being peddled, illustrations, advertisements for other books, sample spines of the higher-priced bindings, and lined blank pages at the back for the subscriber to sign, indicating a commitment to purchase.

When *Roughing It* (1872) was in press Twain announced that he "would like to select the 'specimen' chapters" himself.[7] For the next several books—*The Gilded Age* (1873), *Sketches New and Old* (1875), and *The Adventures of Tom Sawyer* (1876)—he announced his choice of illustrators. He purchased stock and became a director of the American Publishing Company. He selected topics for his lecture tours that would advertise his current or forthcoming book. He began suggesting other potential authors to Bliss, among them Bret Harte, Joaquin Miller, and William Wright. He volunteered advertising schemes (an oyster supper in his honor when the sales of *Innocents Abroad* reached 100,000) and promotional gimmicks (a $1,000 prize to the agent who sold the most copies of *Tom Sawyer* in six months).

As the decade of the 1880s began, Clemens committed himself ever more deeply to financial obligations in the field of publishing technology. In February, 1880, he purchased 80 percent of the stock in a printing process known as Kaolatype and immediately began spending additional amounts on "a new application of this invention" that, he thought, would "utterly annihilate & sweep out of existence one of the minor industries of civilization, & take its place." The following year he made his initial investment in the Paige Typesetter. He became convinced that Bliss had been cheating him for a decade, a conviction he never lost; in his autobiography in 1906 he eulogized the man responsible for his own career: Bliss was

> a most repulsive creature. When he was after dollars he showed the intense earnestness and eagerness of a circular-saw. In a small, mean, peanut-stand fashion, he was sharp and shrewd. But above that level he was destitute of intelligence; his brain was a loblolly, and he had the gibbering laugh of an idiot. . . . I have had contact

with several conspicuously mean men, but they were noble compared to this bastard monkey.[8]

Clemens was determined to become the publisher of his own books and to enjoy the profits entirely by himself.

He established a subscription department in the firm of James R. Osgood, a genteel trade publisher who would shortly be dragged into bankruptcy because of his dealings with Clemens. Osgood, the neophyte, received his information about subscription publishing from the authority, Mark Twain. Osgood sold *The Prince and the Pauper* (1882) and *Life on the Mississippi* (1883) with Twain's money and received constant instructions from him about advertising, illustrating, copyrighting, and selling books by subscription. Nevertheless, when *Life on the Mississippi* sold only 30,000 copies, Twain blamed Osgood for the "failure." "I have never for a moment doubted that you did the very best you knew how," Clemens told Osgood, "but there were things about the publishing of *my* books which you did not understand. You understand them now, but it is I who have paid the costs of the apprenticeship."[9]

So, Mark Twain decided to establish his own publishing company with another apprentice, his sister's son-in-law, as its head. With Charles L. Webster and Company under his control, Clemens began a decade of unparalleled frenzy with the mechanics of publication. He commanded Charley about every aspect of subscription book technology. He explained the proper costs for paper and for binding; he approved the cover design for *Huck Finn;* he told Charley which newspapers and magazines were to receive review copies and which to ostracize—based mostly on real or imagined hostility to his earlier books.

He chose the illustrators for *Huck* and *A Connecticut Yankee in King Arthur's Court* (1889). He vetoed a portrait of Huck because "the boy's mouth is a trifle more Irishy than necessary," and he removed an illustration of the king hugging and kissing girls at the camp meeting because "the subject won't *bear* illustrating. It is a disgusting thing, & pictures are sure to tell the truth about it too plainly."[10]

It was the psychology of subscription publication that caused the most famous bibliographical crux in American literature. Twain had published a chapter of *Huck* in *Life on the Mississippi* in 1883; in 1884 he warned Charley to "be particular & don't get any of that *old* matter into your canvassing book—(the *raft* episode)."[11] Charley suggested leaving the chapter out of the second book altogether, and Clemens agreed.

Ever since, Twain scholars have debated whether the chapter, the "rafts-men passage," belongs in or out of *Huck Finn*.

Contemporaneous conflict was more violent. Charley and Mark Twain began publishing an enormous number of books by others, over which they were not always in agreement—such as a biography of Pope Leo XIII, the autobiography of the king of the Sandwich Islands, a cookbook from the chef at Delmonico's, Alessandro Filippine, and a dozen memoirs by Civil War generals after the fabulous success of Grant's *Personal Memoirs*.

Clemens spewed venom at competitors and villains. He wished to sue "Houghton, Syphillis & Co.," and proposed stopping the printing of *Huck* so that he could add a "Prefactory Remark" insulting the editors of the Boston *Advertiser* and the Springfield *Republican*. He told Charley and his successor, Fred J. Hall, to sue John Wanamaker, to sue Belford and Clarke, to sue the American Publishing Company, to sue Whitelaw Reid of the New York *Tribune*.

In 1888 Charley became, like Bliss and Osgood before him, the object of Mark Twain's anger and hatred. "I have never hated any crea-ture with a hundred thousandth fraction of the hatred I bear that human louse, Webster,"[12] he told his brother in 1889.

But as the Typesetter consumed more and more of his time and money, Twain continued that euphoric belief in the quick-kill fortune. He envisioned an art collection catalog that

> was to be infinitely grander and finer than any ever issued in any country in the world. There were to be 600 copies for Europe and 600 for America, all marked and numbered—and the plates then broken up. Price, $1,000 apiece.[13]

The final blow to Charles L. Webster and Company, however, was an eleven-volume albatross known as the Library of American Literature, edited by Edmund C. Stedman. Whenever a canvasser signed up a cus-tomer—who agreed to pay three dollars a month when the volumes were delivered—that agent returned to Webster and collected his twelve-dollar commission for the entire set. Every subscriber, in other words, cost Mark Twain and his company an immediate deficit of nine dollars. It was an even worse investment strategy than the one of Mark Twain's brother Orion, who was exultant that he could raise a chicken on sixty-five cents' worth of corn and then sell the chicken for a half-dollar.

The physical appearance of subscription books and the hostility toward them that trade publishers vented at every opportunity produced some fascinating psychological and sociological results. The first was an interesting kind of metonomy: the physical appearance of a literary production became the equivalent of the contents of the book. Charles Dudley Warner told Helen Hunt Jackson in 1874: "I think if you were to see your dainty literature in such ill-conditioned volumes, you would just die."[14] George Ade reminisced in 1910:

> The publisher knew his public, so he gave a pound of book for every fifty cents, and crowded in plenty of wood-cuts and stamped the outside with golden bouquets and put in a steel engraving of the author, with a tissue paper veil over it, and "sicked" his multitude of broken-down clergymen, maiden ladies, grass widows, and college students on to the great American public.[15]

Mark Twain himself was aware that the typical subscription book was something like a giant and nonjumping frog, telling Thomas Bailey Aldrich: "There is one discomfort which I fear a man must put up with when he publishes by subscription, and that is wretched paper and vile engravings."[16]

Bound in cheap, dark cloth, bursting their spines with six hundred to seven hundred pages, illustrated with woodcuts of kindergarden-level quality, printed on cheap and brittle paper, they were monstrosities. The *Trade Circular Annual for 1871* pointed out that subscription books "are often absolutely worthless, and this is not only true with regard to the nature of their contents. . . . Beyond their title, there is nothing attractive about them."[17] In 1869 *The Nation* observed that "the rural-district reader likes to see that he has got his money's worth even more than he likes wood engravings. At least, such is the faith in Hartford; and no man ever saw a book agent with a small volume in his hands."[18]

Subscription publishers had a valid, and for Mark Twain an enormously significant, defense. Put at its florid worst, James S. Barcus eulogized "the rank and file of book salesmen that go up and down the highways and byways carrying good tidings of knowledge and erudition to the masses."[19] There was, in other words, an untapped and, until Mark Twain, an undefined audience who never entered a bookstore to purchase one of Helen Hunt Jackson's "dainty volumes" and who cared nothing for sophisticated literature with a capital *L*.

In August, 1874, the *Literary World* sneered superciliously: "Subscription books cannot possibly circulate among the better class of readers, owing to the general and not unfounded prejudice against them. . . . An Author . . . who resorts to the subscription plan . . . descends to a constituency of a lower grade and envitably loses caste." In the same vein, when Mark Twain delighted that the banning of *Huckleberry Finn* by the Concord Public Library would double its sales, the Boston *Advertiser* archly wondered whether "his impudent intimation that a larger sale and larger profits are a satisfactory recompense for the unfavorable judgment of honest critics, is a true indication of the standard by which he measures success in literature."[20]

Remarkably, then, the shape, the size, the sales, and the audience became the touchstones by which a subscription book author was judged. And with the ambiguous pressures from his wife and William Dean Howells, Mark Twain yearned both for the approval of cultivated critics and the endorsement of that "constituency of a lower grade." Perhaps nothing so sums up his ambivalent feelings than the insight in his notebook: "My books are water; those of the great geniuses is wine." Then, after a pause and with a wink, the snapper: "Everybody drinks water."[21]

We now have a name and a discipline for that level of society that Mark Twain both addressed and represented: "Popular Culture," or "mass audience." And on a particularly delicate occasion Mark Twain gave a definition of that layer of society that suggests his penetrating awareness of its values and tastes. In 1890 English readers of Mark Twain were incensed at his burlesque version of King Arthur and the Knights of the Round Table. His English publisher insisted that the British edition must omit some of the offensive passages, and Mark Twain responded by telling Chatto and Windus that he would find another English publisher first. And he wrote a famous letter to Andrew Lang, a leading British critic, pleading (no doubt in too flamboyant and exaggerated terms) for a different verdict for his literature:

> The critic assumes every time that if a book doesn't meet the cultivated-class standard, it isn't valuable. Let us apply his law all around: for if it is sound in the case of novels, narratives, pictures, and such things, it is certainly sound and applicable to all the steps which lead up to culture and make culture possible. It condemns the spelling book, for a spelling book is of no use to a person of culture; it condemns all school books and all schools which lie between the

child's primer and Greek, and between the infant school and the university; it condemns all the rounds of art which lie between the cheap terra cotta groups and the Venus de Medici, and between the chromo and the Transfiguration; it requires Whitcomb Riley to sing no more till he can sing like Shakespeare, and it forbids all amateur music and will grant its sanction to nothing below the "classic." . . . The critic has actually imposed upon the world the superstition that a painting by Raphael is more valuable to the civilizations of the earth than is a chromo; and the august opera than the hurdy-gurdy and the villagers' singing society; and Homer than the little everybody's poet whose rhymes are in all mouths to-day and will be in nobody's mouth next generation; and the Latin classics than Kipling's far-reaching bugle-note; and Johnathan Edwards than the Salvation Army; and the Venus di Medici than the plaster-cast peddler; the superstition, in a word, that the vast and awful comet that trails its cold lustre through the remote abysses of space once a century and interests and instructs a cultivated handful of astronomers is worth more to the world than the sun which warms and cheers all the nations every day and makes the crops to grow.

If a critic should start a religion it would not have any object but to convert angels, and they wouldn't need it. The thin top crust of humanity—the cultivated—are worth pacifying, worth pleasing, worth coddling, worth nourishing and preserving with dainties and delicacies, it is true; but to be caterer to that little faction is no very dignified or valuable occupation, it seems to me; it is merely feeding the over-fed and there must be small satisfaction in that. It is not that little minority who are already saved that are best worth lifting at, I should think, but the mighty mass of the uncultivated who are underneath. . . .

Indeed I have been misjudged from the very first. I have never tried in even one single little instance to help cultivate the cultivated classes. I was not equipped for it, either by native gifts or training. And I never had any ambition in that direction, but always hunted for bigger game—the masses. . . .[22]

It is a remarkable performance, and, in spite of a great deal that rings false about it, it suggests an awareness of what Mark Twain later discussed as "submerged renown": a surface reputation was ephemeral, but "down in the deep water," where the masses exist, "once a favorite there, always a favorite; once beloved, always beloved; once respected, always respected, honored, and believed in. For what the reviewer says never finds its way down into those placid deeps."[23] The letter to Lang, too, argued: "My audience is dumb, it has no voice in print."

Having learned by the accident of his involvement with the mechanics of subscription publication how to reach that audience, Mark Twain adapted his creative instincts to meet its expectations and to appeal to it. To fill his travel books up to the massive volume that the popular audience required, he added, in desperation, literally anything he could find—from his own earlier works or from anyone else's that happened to be handy: accounts of Mormon massacres, Rhine legends, American Indian legends. He insisted on advertising the topical nature of his literature, to appeal to what he called the "kitchen and the stable" rather than to "the drawing-room."

But like Millington G. Wheeler, Mark Twain was getting woven into the fabric of his own machine. In fascinating ways, which Louis Budd has convincingly detailed in *Our Mark Twain,* the author became the object for sale. The producer himself became the product, held captive in many ways by the technology of subscription publication and by the voracious appetite of the Paige Typesetter for more and more financial support for more and more corrections and refinements. (The machine has over 180,000 moving parts and is said to have cost the sanity of three Patent Office clerks before it was scrapped.)

At the simplest level Mark Twain had to cater to the audience he himself had discovered and defined. He went on lecture tours, which kept him before the public; he gave interviews at the drop of a reporter's pencil; he spoke at banquets, testimonial dinners, and any public occasion. But as much as he might identify with the kitchen and the stable, he told William Dean Howells in the mid-1870s that the *Atlantic Monthly* readership was "the only audience that I sit down before in perfect serenity (for the simple reason that it doesn't require a 'humorist' to paint himself striped and stand on his head every fifteen minutes.)"[24] He told George Washington Cable on a lecture tour in the mid-1880s: "Oh, Cable, I am demeaning myself. I am allowing myself to be a mere buffoon. It's ghastly. I can't endure it any longer."[25] And in 1905, when Helen Keller complimented him on his fame, Twain replied: "You don't understand. I have only amused people. Their laughter has submerged me."[26] The author who championed his submerged audience now blamed it, in the end, for submerging him.

It is a curious set of transformations: a newspaperman who became an author of subscription books; an author who transformed himself into a subscription book publisher and created a fiction named Mark Twain whom Samuel Clemens transformed into a product so familiar to its audience that he attempted to publish his "serious" books anonymously or pseudonymously so that he would not be laughed at. On occasion he cursed his "detested nom de plume," and in his old age, according to Howells, Sam Clemens moved "to Redding to get rid of Mark Twain."[27]

He epitomized Virginia Woolf's observation in *The Common Reader* that "a book is always written for somebody to read, and . . . the patron is not merely the paymaster, but also in a very subtle and insidious way the instigator and inspirer of what is written."[28]

But there is one final twist to the story of Mark Twain and technology: in his final transformation, Mark Twain turned into the machine, the technology rather than the text. Those ecstatic catalogs of the marvels of the industrial revolution camouflaged his fear of the machine. Typesetter and publishing house and Mark Twain all failed together. And readers of *A Connecticut Yankee in King Arthur's Court* will remember that Hank Morgan's role as the bringer of enlightenment to sixth-century England sours as he brings mass destruction in the form of electrified barbed wire fences, land mines, hand grenades, and the Gatling gun, to produce an apocalypse.

Whether or not Mark Twain possessed some prescient view of the dubious blessings of technology, it is significant that he adopted the metaphor of the machine to express his belief in a mechanistic universe. In a passage in his unfinished manuscript, *The Chronicle of Young Satan,* he has a nephew of the Devil describe the machinery of humanity:

> Every man is a suffering-machine and a happiness-machine combined. The two functions work together harmoniously, with a fine and delicate precision, on the give-and-take principle. For every happiness turned out in the one department the other one stands ready to modify it with a sorrow or a pain—maybe a dozen. . . . Sometimes a man's make and disposition are such that his misery-machinery is able to do nearly all the business. Such a man goes through life almost ignorant of what happiness is. Everything he touches, everything he does, brings a misfortune upon him.[29]

The image becomes philosophical belief and perhaps a defense mechanism against various guilts.

In his "Gospel," *What Is Man?* he moved harmoniously with the metaphor of the machine to a universal premise:

Man the machine—man, the impersonal engine. Whatsoever a man is, is due to his *make,* and to the *influences* brought to bear upon it by his heredities, his habitat, his associations. He is moved, directed, COMMANDED, by *exterior* influences—*solely*. He *originates* nothing, himself—not even an opinion, not even a thought. . . .

And machines may not boast, nor feel proud of their performances, nor claim personal merit for it, nor applause and praise.[30]

And so we have reached the final metamorphosis: the journalist turned author, turned publisher, turned marketable object, finally ends not as the text but as the technology that produced it.

NOTES

1. *Roughing It* (Berkeley: University of California Press, 1972) contains the original version (348); the one quoted here is from *Mark Twain in Eruption,* ed. Bernard DeVoto (New York: Harper & Brothers, 1940), 222–23.

2. *Mark Twain's Letters,* ed. Albert Bigelow Paine (New York: Harper & Brothers, 1917), 1:506, 508.

3. *Mark Twain's Letters,* ed. Harriet Elinor Smith and Richard Brecci (Berkeley: University of California Press, 1990), 2:119.

4. "Mark Twain and the Old Time Subscription Book," *Review of Reviews* 41 (1910): 703–4. Reprinted in *Mark Twain: The Critical Heritage,* ed. Frederick Anderson (London: Routledge and Kegan Paul, 1971), 337–39.

5. Paine, *Mark Twain's Letters,* 1:169.

6. *Mark Twain, Business Man,* ed. Samuel C. Webster (Boston: Little, Brown, 1946).

7. Webster, *Mark Twain,* 118.

8. *Mark Twain's Letters to His Publishers, 1867–1894,* ed. Hamlin Hill (Berkeley: University of California Press, 1967), 1.

9. Hill, *Mark Twain's Letters,* 164–65.

10. Webster, *Mark Twain,* 260.

11. Ibid., 249.

12. Ibid., *Mark Twain's Letters,* 1.

13. Ibid., 245.

14. Quoted in Kenneth Andrews, *Nook Farm: Mark Twain's Hartford Circle* (Cambridge, Mass.: Harvard University Press, 1950), 122.

15. Anderson, *Mark Tawin,* 338.

16. Hill, *Mark Twain's Letters,* 80.

17. Quoted in Hamlin Hill, *Mark Twain and Elisha Bliss* (Columbia: University of Missouri Press, 1964), 7.

18. Quoted in Anderson, *Mark Twain,* 21.

19. Quoted in Hill, *Mark Twain and Elisha Bliss,* 6.

20. Quoted in Hill, *Mark Twain and Elisha Bliss,* 7, 125.

21. *Mark Twain's Notebooks and Journals,* ed. Robert Pack Browning, et al. (Berkeley: University of California Press, 1979), 3:238.

22. *The Portable Mark Twain,* ed. Bernard DeVoto (New York: Viking, 1946), 771–73.

23. *Mark Twain's Autobiography,* ed. Albert Bigelow Paine (New York: Harper & Brothers, 1924), 1:248–50.

24. *Mark Twain's Letters,* 1:236–37.

25. Albert Bigelow Paine, *Mark Twain: A Biography* (New York: Harper & Brothers, 1912), 786.

26. Quoted in Edward Wagenknecht, *Mark Twain: The Man and His Work* (Norman: University of Oklahoma Press, 1961), 58.

27. *Mark Twain–Howells Letters,* ed. Henry Nash Smith and William M. Gibson (Cambridge, Mass.: Harvard University Press, 1960), 2:838.

28. Virginia Woolf, "The Patron and the Crocus," in *The Common Reader First Series* (New York: Harcourt Brace and World, 1953), 211.

29. *Mysterious Stranger Manuscripts,* ed. William M. Gibson (Berkeley: University of California Press, 1969), 112–13.

30. *What Is Man and Other Philosophical Writings,* ed. Paul Baender (Berkeley: University of California Press, 1973), 128, 131.

"Why Don't They Leave It Alone?" Speculations on the Authority of the Audience in Editorial Theory

Morris Eaves

The late Fredson Bowers, the most influential of postwar textual critics, once preached to the unconverted that "the transmission of texts, and what happens in this transmission, is a subject of particular fascination."[1] Good editing, he claimed, is essential to good literary criticism, whose fascination and importance his auditors could be expected to take for granted. I have been guilty of thinking that the theory of editing can be more interesting than most people seem to think it is and that the theory would interest them much more if the theorists could more often depict editing in a fuller light, as part of a wider range of related cultural activities, and depict editors making their editorial choices in a larger field of possibilities. The traditional preoccupation of editors with editorial practice and the problems at hand, and their overreliance on conventional theories, have produced a subject of little interest to most noneditors. It is hard to ask provocative questions when the force of consensus is so strong and the subject seems so dull and technical. Despite a conspicuous shift over the past decade—toward more open, spirited debate and away from the hidebound assumptions and defensive postures that had characterized a small but entrenched Anglo-American editorial establishment—more speculation about the fringes is overdue, if only because, until we have explored the periphery, we will have only a very hazy notion of the center.

Editing is often identified with systematic suspicion, scrutiny, and correction, deployed from the high moral ground of Bowers's rousing declaration that "most of the great English and American classics" are "inexcusably corrupt" (*Criticism* 4). I propose that editorial theory will remain radically deficient until it learns how to take seriously the alternative view that everything that is, is already right, and how to meet the challenges presented by the most compelling logic in support of that view. To that end I will sample, very briefly, some tough cases that exemplify key issues in "editing" taken in the broader rather than narrower sense of the term: William Blake's illuminated books, an American novel or two, *Hamlet,* the original instruments movement in music, the restoration of Michelangelo's Sistine Chapel frescoes, and the colorization of movies. Several of these have a prominent material or technological aspect. In fact, the kinds of editorial questions I am raising do seem to arise particularly in the presence of technology.

In 1868 the poet and critic Algernon Charles Swinburne assigned a very curious phrase to a new printed edition of Blake's *Songs of Innocence and of Experience:* this work had now "absolutely achieved," he boasted, the "dignity of a reprint."[2] Swinburne claimed to regret the "hard necessity" that forced into existence plain letterpress editions of Blake's relief-etched and watercolored works in illuminated printing. "We miss the lovely and luminous setting of designs" (112), he complained. Although he even maintained that the "two forms or sides of [Blake's] art" are "inextricably interfused" (108), that did not stop him from going on to claim that the letterpress reprint was, after all and in the long run, for the best because it left us, the audience, with a more dignified Blake. To understand how this claim bears on a roomier theory of editing, we need to lay down a few fundamental principles.

According to the dominant myth of modern editing, transmission corrupts the text. When someone—or something—other than an author alters a text without authorization from the originator, "an editor," as Thomas Tanselle has said, "must try to disentangle the author's own wishes from the other elements that shaped the published text."[3] The logic of editorial restoration surfaces nicely in a report on the Sistine frescoes:

> As is by now well known, the cleaned areas of the ceiling do not look at all as they looked before. For hundreds of years, they had been known for the sculptural heaviness of Michelangelo's figures and his apparent reluctance to draw upon an extended gamut of color. It now turns out that both the sculptural heaviness and the restricted and often dusky range of color are historical illusions and a denial of what Michelangelo had originally done.[4]

From this window history, the maker of "illusions," is mutability. This is "the Past" from which "Italy Reclaims Its Treasures," as John Russell puts it, and the "fortune and time" that Dr. Johnson blamed for turning the texts of Shakespeare into a batch of corrupt fragments. In this regard printed editions might share the fate of language generally, which will "spread... into wild exuberance" like weeds, directed only by "chance... the tyranny of time and fashion;... the corruptions of ignorance, and caprices of innovation."[5] Sound editing dispels the illusions of history and restores direct communication with the authorizing artistic intelligence: "What we now see is exactly what Michelangelo meant us to see when we view the Sistine ceiling" (Russell, "Italy," 18).

But an alternative myth values the effects of transmission. This myth, though perhaps equally familiar in general use, is usually banned from respectable editorial theorizing. It tells how social and historical transmission *improves* not the individual work but, rather, the collection of works. In this myth of reception, time and change are salutary and progressive, and history is the medium through which the public interest asserts itself in the arts, mainly by subtracting irrelevant private preferences. The central axis in a mature theory of textual criticism would run between these two alternative myths, one producing respect for the unique original, the other producing the consensus necessary to give the reprint its dignity. The two poles correspond much of the time to other key cultural and political oppositions—such as individuality and community, points of origination and transmission—and they are perhaps doomed to an existence as inseparable contraries in constant tension.

On that axis interplay between the two myths begins when the point of origin becomes a dispersed field (or, viewed from the opposite perspective, when a dispersed field begins to coalesce into a point of origin). Dispersion arrives in many troubling forms. The easier ones include the poet who lets her husband edit her work, the novelist who lets the printer punctuate, the printmaker who lets his wife color his etchings. There are more extreme cases:

All of the holograph drafts of Dreiser's eight novels were too long for publication. All were cut and further revised by a process Dreiser initially used for the editing of *Carrie* and that he came to rely on. Friends, editors, lovers, and even casual acquaintances read the manuscript and made suggestions for revision.... There was nothing extraordinary, in short, about the cutting of *Carrie* by [Dreiser's friend Arthur] Henry and [Dreiser's wife] Sallie. Dreiser depended on them just as he was later to depend on his literary acquaintances

James Huneker, Floyd Dell, and James T. Farrell, his editors T. R. Smith, Louise Campbell, and Donald Elder, and his lovers and secretaries Sally Kusell and Estelle Kubitz. Any effort to distinguish between Dreiser as writer and editor in the revision of *Sister Carrie* must also confront the fact that Dreiser throughout his career denied through his practice as author that a distinction of this kind could and should be made. . . . But the final responsibility was always his, except perhaps in the case of *The Bulwark,* when he was too sick and old to care about what Louise Campbell did to the novel.[6]

For our purposes the exceptional final instance is the most tellingly placed, in the eerie twilight zone of approaching death that finds the author too sick and old to care about his own authority—to which the editor abruptly resorts for a last-minute appeal ("final responsibility was always his") because it restores to snug normalcy a situation that was threatening to disseminate into a sizable aberration. Let Dreiser drift on for a few more months, put him six feet under, and the dark closes in. He leaves his editors behind in the truly posthumous world in which they typically form their opinions and do their work. Donald Pizer's own appeal to Dreiser's authority is itself, of course, an instance of such posthumous retrospection. This is the world of "posterity," in which editors, like attorneys, interpret for the assembled heirs the wishes of the deceased.

The more extensive—in time, space, and population—the collaboration becomes, and the more authority the collaborators have to add or subtract, the blurrier the line of possession becomes. Strategies of retrieval become less useful as lines of authority become more ambiguous, until finally there is no question of X *letting* Y alter *her* work but simply a work coming into existence. At some point between the two myths, when it becomes evident that individual authors are composing works *as* members of social groups, editors lose the great advantage of the author's individual body and especially the author's mortality in determining when the progressive movement toward "final intentions" and "definitive editions" ends. The relatively well-defined individual lifetime is replaced by the much more nebulous lifetimes of societies and languages. Good examples appear under our nose every time a text reminds us that authors are socialized individuals. But theories of editing have been highly reluctant to acknowledge, much less value, the shaping influence of socialization, collaboration, and historical processes on the landscape of editing.

When it comes to valuing the process of transmission, however, we are not completely without precedents. One imposing line of thought comes out of the side of Enlightenment aesthetics that values consensus. In the fourth of his *Discourses on Art* Joshua Reynolds compares artistic invention, the first stage of composition, to the telling of a story in a roomful of people: the best ideas for paintings, he says, are like the parts of the original story that are common to everyone's recollection of it.[7] The parts that only some hearers can recollect are in a sense not part of the true story because they are being remembered for idiosyncratic personal reasons irrelevant to the constitution of (that fundamental Enlightenment construct) general human nature. Thus, the test of true invention is translatability, Reynolds says, like the test of true wit. "That wit is false, which can subsist only in one language."[8] Whatever survives, whatever reprints, is closer to general human nature than what fails to survive. Valuing reproducibility moves authority from the individual and the unique moment of invention prized in romantic tradition to the group and the process of history, including, at least potentially, the public powers of invention that are only temporarily vested in individual artists. So regarded, as they frequently are in Reynolds's time, artists are filling public roles for which they are appropriately trained in public techniques supported by public theories.

From this position the art critic's explanations of the public's reactions to the restored images on the Sistine ceiling become more suggestive. "Given the hold of this image [the creation of Adam] upon the popular imagination, worldwide, there were still people who said, 'Why don't they leave it alone?'" While the dignity of the reprint may seem irrelevant to the problem of the Sistine ceiling, in fact it is central, as we see here: "Gigantic experiences, long remembered, cannot be discarded without long and painful travail, even if we can bring ourselves to believe that they were ill founded. We have to learn that our lifelong convictions may have to be set aside" (Russell, "Italy," 18). In the art critic's account, as in Reynolds's, reprinting stands for the power of collective human memory. In the Sistine chapel editorial restoration threatens to destroy the reprint that has survived and won the audience's affection. Resistance to restoration comes from the audience imagined as the bearers of collective experience in history. The art critic makes his own claim for history, but a different kind. He wants the original object, and implicitly the event (e.g., Michelangelo painting "his" fresco) that brought it into being, to be *preserved* in transmission and hence saved from the kind of history that does not remember the original events or objects. In his terms the deluded audience is in love with a blurred reprint of the clear original. Whereas he wants direct contact with the original, the imagined twentieth-century audience wants the transmitted object, the object that only began to be made by Michelangelo but was continued by subsequent history.

The critic charges the audience with being stuck in its ways, stuck with its memories, stuck with (its kind of) history: "It is with the Sistine ceiling as it is with Beethoven's Ninth Symphony. When we hear it at Beethoven's own metronome speeds, with the forces (and the instruments) for which Beethoven wrote it, we are amazed and incredulous. The change calls for an effort of adaptation and imaginative understanding that not everyone wants (or is able) to make" (Russell, "Italy," 18).

But what happens if, with an equal and opposite effort that not everyone wants (or is able) to make, we turn around and wonder whether no case is to be made, even theoretically, for the paintings, the symphonies, and the poems on which the collective memory of the public has conferred dignity *through* history, or are those all only the illusions created *by* history? What if we allow that audience members help to construct meaning and, as a label for their labors of construction, we import the term *performance traditions* from music criticism and transfer the dignity reserved for performing musicians to performing audiences? What if the audience's memories are not treated as naive historical illusions but, instead, as the products of the audience's own performance traditions, living historical processes? Even though the dirty old ceiling was "false to the artist's original intentions," it was "for millions of people in the developed world the primordial, the irreplaceable and the indispensable esthetic experience, and they liked it the way it was" (Russell, "Italy," 1). I hear through the cracks of the art critic's complaint a provocative question about how to honor audiences and their histories in theories of texts and their histories.

That question certainly has its textual-critical forms, as hinted at in one of Donald Pizer's valuable essays on editing the American naturalists. He asks, "Would it be justifiable . . . to remove from general circulation texts that have engaged a significant proportion of the American literate consciousness for most of the twentieth century?" ("Self-Censorship," 155). Might the dignity of the reprint then have some theoretical use?

Let us speculate about what it would mean to value reproducibility in a theory of editing. We might apply Reynolds's test of invention to editorial practice. Given a choice between a manuscript of *Hamlet* from

Shakespeare's hand and a posthumous transcription from memory by his fellow actors, we might then prefer the transcription on the principle that the passage of time and the collaboration of minds could retroactively impose the discipline that some say the bard lacked. If a soliloquy in *Hamlet* escapes the memory of a trained actor, or if the soliloquy is consistently cut out of the script for traditional performances, a theory of textual criticism derived from Reynolds might make us want to omit the soliloquy from an edition.[9] (Requiring trained actors and traditional performances simply provides further assurance that the memory is representative, socialized rather than singular.) The individual mind and work thus socialized achieve the dignity of a reprint.

The faint but distinct sociopolitical resonance of that last sentence reminds us that editing is not only a service performed by underpaid bookworms but also, to some degree, a social act with political implications. Some of the most vexing and telling editorial issues come straight from the human rights agenda. Two of those, censorship and its internal counterpart, self-censorship, help to illuminate the consequences of introducing a concept of socialized authorship and textual authority into a theory of editing. When the moment of decision to obey social norms comes to an author in the course of revising a text, the useful distinction between the originating author and the receptive audience is reversed. The sight of Stephen Crane self-censoring *Maggie: A Girl of the Streets* (1893) for what became the second printing of 1896 thus develops into a primal scene for textual critics.[10] Documented self-censorship can be treated as a social corruption of individual authorial intention, a change of mind under external coercion. Textual critics have sometimes tried to wrestle with self-censorship by partitioning the author into two roles corresponding to two stages of composition: "As a writer, an author often expresses his final intentions in earlier versions because as an editor undertaking revisions, he is subject to various pressures or makes various ill-considered changes that pervert those intentions."[11] According to that logic, Crane composed *his* version of *Maggie* and then followed it up with a version corrected under social dictation. It happens that between versions he inconveniently experienced an epiphany of socialization that brought on a fit of obedience to majority sentiment. Other writers, who have already internalized the society's standards of sexual reticence before ever sitting down to write, have been kinder to the textual critic by censoring their sentences in their heads instead of leaving a paper trail.

In any event cases such as *Maggie* help make it possible to imagine a theory of editing that puts authority in social rather than individual hands, making the author the agent of a social will. Crane's scandalous self-censorship would not likely have troubled Joshua Reynolds, for instance, whose theory prepared him to recognize that authors might belatedly—better late than never—extract personal idiosyncracies from their novels. While this argument is hypothetical, it is less farfetched than it might seem. Reynolds directs his fable at a stage of artistic production that editors also concern themselves with, composition, when the artist's intentions, as distinguished from other intentions, take shape. Reynolds shows how to feed reception back into composition, recursively, in an editorial quality control circle.

The leading question is the chicken-and-egg one—where to stop the circle. Fredson Bowers stopped it firmly with the author, as when he attempted to base his edition of Crane's *Maggie* on a distinction between alterations that Crane, as an individual author making decisions apart from his audience, really wanted and alterations that were imposed by Crane's internalized sense of external public opinion. Recently, a few theoretically inclined editors have been wandering further around the curve toward what Jerome McGann has familiarized as "a socialized concept of authorship and textual authority."[12] In the terms of my argument this is the middle ground, where "authority is a social nexus" (*Critique,* 48) at which individuals meet institutions: "We obviously do not mean to suggest that final authority for literary works rests with institutional persons other than the author. . . . [I]t resides in the actual structure of the agreements which these two cooperating authorities reach in specific cases" (54). As we see here, although the existence of the full circle is sometimes hinted at, in serious discussions of "final authority" the creatures of this nether region seem to appear only at the rear entrance, and only under the sign of the already inadmissible.[13]

Take, for example, the conclusion to Donald Pizer's thoughtful discussion of the problem that self-censorship creates for editors of Dreiser:

> If we are to read *Sister Carrie* as a novel of 1900, I would prefer to read the novel that emerged out of the personal tensions, conflicting motives, and cultural complexities of that moment and that in the eighty years since its publication has accrued a rich public responsiveness and role. I would not care to read a *Carrie* that has in effect been created out of the textual editing controversies and theorizing of the 1960s and 1970s. ("Self-Censorship," 160)

Pizer here backs far enough away from the old standard devotion to authorial origins to declare a preference for cultural complexity, and he advances close enough to notions of social transmission in history to affirm a "rich public responsiveness" of eighty years. But while seeing how much things have changed, we see how much they have remained the same. The theoretical ideal is now *"the* novel that emerged" from those social complexities at the point of origin in 1900. Transmission has been introduced into the editorial picture only insofar as the point of origin has widened to include some of Dreiser's immediate associates over whom he is supposed to have exercised his authority ("final responsibility," 157). The "rich" (but uncontrolled) "public responsiveness" is still just response *to* the object as conveniently fixed in 1900. Theoretically, history of origins is being prudently segregated from history of transmission. There is no legal route by which the responders might make a difference in *"the* novel," that is, no way for the responses to materialize in editorial form.

The paradox, of course, is that Pizer's own preference is itself a response that he thinks should take editorial form. Likewise, the *Sister Carrie* that might be "created out of" twentieth-century editorial "controversies and theorizing" is not a nonresponse but, in fact, a particularly "rich" response that has yet to acknowledge its own status as a response. To put the theoretical issue another way: all texts are always edited at the reception end; all editions are historical responses in editorial form.

But pointing out the paradox is a weak manuever—certainly not forceful enough to open the theoretical panorama, because it remains true that some responses are merely being ranked lower in a hierarchy of acceptable forms, while others are banished outright. To see the basis for ranking more clearly, we must move beyond the legitimate ranks into the realm of the taboo. In doing so, I would not want to deny that in practice these recent moves from one extreme onto the middle ground of a "socialized text" have usefully disturbed the editorial status quo. For a more comprehensive map of the territory in which textual decisions are made, however, we must explore even the editorial outback not covered by McGann's "agreements" or "cooperating authorities" and normally beyond the pale of respectable modern editing.[14]

We are in a position to see how editing looks when the circle is stopped at reception instead of composition: when the author is thought to be a public person filling a public role, one who attempts to reproduce the public's intentions, rather than one concerned with representing his or her own private intentions, then the public may achieve the truest reproductions of its intentions by transmitting the author's text from generation to generation. The acid test of a supporting editorial theory would be its ability to rank transmission over origins by acknowledging that the exigencies of transmission may improve texts.

The logic is not strange. We often turn to institutions, to societies, even to the course of history itself, for decisions: "More than one hundred and fifty years of readers have added their weight of legitimacy . . ." (McGann, *Critique,* 105). Such nods to our venerable ancestors are often only ceremonial rhetorical gestures. But if we allow the point even the hint of conceivable substance, then it raises profound questions for theories of editing. How do readers add legitimacy to certain textual decisions (or call them editions) over time? Are these the readers we honor with the term *posterity* to grant legitimacy and authority to their acts in history? By precisely what logic do we sort out the competing claims of author and posterity, i.e., the "legitimate" audience? When 150 years, or 500 years, lend weight to the legitimacy of the audience's editorial work, how do we then weigh the legitimacy of the audience's intention against the author's intention when the two collide? No matter how we answer these questions, the key observation is, again, that it is we who answer them. We are an audience acting in history, even if "we" are only a single late-twentieth-century editor working in the institutional setting of the American university as it intersects with the institutions of printing and publishing. We are after all a form, a version, even an edition, of the audience whose authority we are now questioning, *even* when we appoint ourselves to the role of the author's posthumous agent. We cannot act at all if we do not first grant ourselves some of the legitimacy, much less authority and responsibility, that McGann grants to "more than one hundred and fifty years of readers." This grant cannot be just a special instance, reserved for the occasions when we want to mark a rough distinction between mere popularity and the enduring popularity that (we say) clings to masterpieces.

At any rate, to catch a glimpse of the full significance of Swinburne's "hard necessity," we must be able to entertain the possibility of a test of time, which is the test of many minds, that would organize significance not despite but through the pragmatic rigors of the publishing industry, the educational system, the marketplace, the flux of empires. If survival is an indicator of value, then whatever is may be, if not right, then on its way to becoming right. With the "dignity of a reprint" Swinburne adopts this logic to put the *process* of transmission, a social agency rather than Blake, in charge of Blake's text. By granting dignity to the institutional arrangements that control reprinting, Swinburne establishes public and historical tests of artistic memorability.[15] For Joshua Reynolds the individual memory is a self-policing, socialized faculty trained to filter out idiosyncrasy. Likewise, Swinburne's reprint is reproduction, a mode of memory. This becomes clearer in the form of a question about prevailing technology: Can the printing press remember the designs to the *Songs of Innocence and of Experience*? The inability of the printing press to remember the designs is, in Swinburne's terms, a refusal to confer dignity upon them. He accepts a form of technological memory as a test of survival in the Darwinian world of publish or perish.

Finally, consider recent disputes over historical editing in another visual medium, film. A new technology has made it possible to add color to old monochrome films. In the film industry technology is regarded by the colorizing faction as coming to the aid of audience desires—or, rather, the set of desires that provide maximum profit. At the same time colorization is clearly a way of narrowing the historical differences between the decades of the 1930s and 1940s, in which the movies were "made" (they are now being remade, or corrected), and the present, when black-and-white movies are rare. Colorization has stirred up debates that are in several respects parallel to debates over Blake's illuminated printing, though the terms of one are based on addition (of color) and the other on subtraction (of pictures). A presumed historical original is fundamental to both, and at the opposite end, as it were, stands an audience with desires that would revise, or edit, the original from the past by present means. In both, as well, there is a strong technological element and questions of historical authenticity.

In *The Romantic Ideology* and other writings coordinated with his *Critique of Modern Textual Criticism* McGann has presented a case for making the maintenance of historical differences one of the most important of all literary-critical tasks and, in the process, has blamed twentieth-century romanticists for appropriating romantic ideology (and thus pretending, in effect, that we are the romantics). But even as we recognize historical differences, it is essential to recognize simultaneously that we—that is, members of the present generation—are the *only* ones who *either* maintain those differences or close them with similarities. That is, insofar as literary criticism is part of editing, it, like all editing, is done from the reception end, even when the attempt is to restore integrities, and differences, at some point of origination in the past.

As members of the audience, we exercise our authority boldly, sometimes even ruthlessly. If we did not, how could we ever edit and

publish the poems of—to name only one case among many—Emily
Dickinson? The fundamental editorial consideration is not how to edit
them but, rather, to edit them or not:

> Publication—is the Auction
> Of the Mind of Man—
> Poverty—be justifying
> For so foul a thing
>
> Possibly—but We—would rather
> From Our Garret go
> White—Unto the White Creator—
> Than invest—Our Snow—
>
> Thought belong to Him who gave it—
> Then—to Him Who bear
> Its Corporeal illustration—Sell
> The Royal Air—
>
> In the Parcel—Be the Merchant
> Of the Heavenly Grace—
> But reduce no Human Spirit
> To Disgrace of Price—[16]

Faithful to its premises, "Publication—is the Auction" was left unpublished until 1929. The decision to drag this agoraphobic poetry into the
light, to expose Dickinson's words to the scrutiny of all and sundry, to
"reduce" this "Human Spirit / To Disgrace of Price," is ours, and only
ours, to make. Respecting such intentions, we might have burned her
poems, acting in the spirit in which some physicians assist suicides. But
against her will we members of posterity have decided instead to make
this dead writer, who

> . . . would rather
> From Our Garret go
> White—Unto the White Creator—
> Than invest—Our Snow

an offer she could not refuse. As for the auction of her mind, we arrange
the sale, bid, and buy. Although there is no editorial Hippocratic oath

and no laws forbidding editors to respect the intentions of authors not to publish, we may justify, in the public interest, our decision to betray her intentions with several rationales, all familiar to editors. Some rationales appeal indirectly to her by rewriting her intentions: perhaps she would have secretly approved. Other rationales appeal around or above her: perhaps her poems are neither her property nor God's but ours, a public resource, an episode in the verbal life of the English-speaking peoples. Furthermore, we may seek to offset our violation of her major intentions by attending to her minor ones ever so scrupulously, cleaving to an editorial policy that would respect every jot and tittle of her manuscripts—at least, every jot and tittle that the institutions of printing and publishing can practically accommodate—or, at least, every jot and tittle that can be accommodated at an affordable price.

And finally, when it comes to the question of whose intentions are being respected, we must ask whether the glass is half-empty or half-full: Is a conservative editorial policy that respects original manuscript forms as print or photography respects them a way of honoring Dickinson's intentions or a way of violating them even more egregiously by prying even further into a secret life expressed in those minutiae? To recast the question in personal terms: If Emily Dickinson had presided over the publication of her poems, would she have translated her private writing codes into the more conventional public codes of published print? We ask, and we decide.

Here, then, is an unacknowledged axiom of textual criticism: the granting of legitimacy to the audience, and hence to its editorial decisions, must precede all acknowledgment of the legitimacy of the author's claims—even when the audience, through its editorial representative, wants that authority only in order to return it straightaway to the author. In that fundamental sense editing is indeed a social act, one that requires, in McGann's phrase, a genuinely "socialized concept of authorship and textual authority."

NOTES

1. Fredson Bowers, *Textual and Literary Criticism* (Cambridge: Cambridge University Press, 1959), 24; hereafter cited in the text as *Criticism*.

2. Algernon Charles Swinburne, *William Blake: A Critical Essay* (rpt. ed. Hugh J. Luke) (Lincoln: University of Nebraska Press, 1970), 114; hereafter cited in the text.

3. G. Thomas Tanselle, "Recent Editorial Discussion and the Central Questions of Editing," *Studies in Bibliography* 34 (1981): 23–65 at 64.

4. John Russell, "Italy Reclaims Its Treasures from the Past," *New York Times,* June 26, 1988, sec. 2:1 +, at 1; hereafter cited in the text.

5. Samuel Johnson, "Proposals for Printing, by Subscription, the Dramatick Works of William Shakespeare," in *Johnson on Shakespeare,* ed. Arthur Sherbo, vols. 7–8 of *The Yale Edition of the Works of Samuel Johnson* (New Haven: Yale University Press, 1968), 7:52; Samuel Johnson, "Preface to the English Dictionary," *The Works of Samuel Johnson in Nine Volumes* (London, 1825), 5:23.

6. Donald Pizer, "Self-Censorship and Textual Editing," in *Textual Criticism and Literary Interpretation,* ed. Jerome J. McGann (Chicago: University of Chicago Press, 1985), 144–61 at 157; hereafter cited in the text.

7. Joshua Reynolds, *Discourses on Art* [1797], ed. Robert R. Wark (San Marino, Calif.: Huntington Library, 1959), 58.

8. Reynolds, *Discourses,* 134.

9. The notion of texts shaped in collaboration with audiences is, of course, more familiar in drama than in other literary forms. See Philip Gaskell's account of the evolution of the text, or rather texts, of Tom Stoppard's *Night and Day* ("*Night and Day:* The Development of a Play Text," in McGann, *Textual Criticism,* 162–79). Gaskell offers a three-part division into script, performance text, and reading text (162) that might be applicable in certain respects to nondramatic texts. His analysis remains, however, well within the familiar confines of the author's life and authority.

10. Fredson Bowers's edition of *Maggie* (*Bowery Tales: Maggie, George's Mother,* vol. 1 of *The Works of Stephen Crane,* 10 vols. [Charlottesville: University Press of Virginia, 1969]) initiated a debate that continued in the reviews of the edition and culminated in several trenchant articles (including Pizer's of 1971 and 1985). The relevant issues are very much alive. See, for example, Barry Menikoff, whose ideal of author authority is so close to a moral code that an author, in this instance Robert Louis Stevenson, can be said to "abuse" it "in sanctioning the publication of a corrupt text," which of course is further corrupted by the agents of institutions. The result of extending the metaphor of abuse is the anticipated plot: "a story of stylistic abuse by printers and proofreaders, of literary abuse by publishers, editors, and friends, and finally of the abuse of art by Stevenson himself. . ." (*Robert Louis Stevenson and "The Beach of Falesá": A Study in Victorian Publishing* [Stanford: Stanford University Press, 1984]). Cf. Christine Froula's idea of the "historical and collaborative authority" behind Pound's *Cantos,* which "suggests that we must reconceive the text not as an object which the editorial process aims to perfect but as the trace of a temporal process" (*To Write Paradise: Style and Error in Pound's Cantos* [New Haven: Yale University Press, 1984], 176). The metaphor of a historical "trace" may even have prompted the conclusion that *The Cantos* should appear in a variorum edition (176). Another metaphor, such as historical "product," might have prompted a more extravagant proposal. Froula, however, reserves for speculation only—as the "last extreme" of "the argument for the historical authenticity of error"—the possibility that the right edition of *The Cantos* could

be "simply the existing text, the unretouched result of the poem's long and eventful history of production, transmission, and attempted editorial correction" (171–72). The last extreme is, of course, where we want to come to rest, safe in the thought that error, here at least, is conundrum.

11. Pizer, "Self-Censorship," 147, summarizing a position taken by others.

12. Jerome J. McGann, *A Critique of Modern Textual Criticism* (Chicago: University of Chicago Press, 1983), 8; hereafter cited in the text. Any review of recent textual criticism should begin with McGann's *Critique* and responses to it. During the past decade or two some of McGann's predecessors have suggested that the history of publishing is relevant to any theory of editing, but he is the first to focus the debate sharply on the individual and institutional dimensions of authorship seen in historical perspective. He calls for a greater variety of editorial responses to match more adequately the variety of texts produced under different historical situations. For the sake of a point, however, I am emphasizing the uniformity that underlies this variety. In short, the "critical problems of method and theory" that McGann labels "fundamental" (*Critique*, 1) are, from the angle of my argument, incomplete.

13. McGann looks further out toward the horizon of possibilities when he introduces the child-rearing metaphor to speculate that the "passage to publication . . . may . . . be seen as a process of training the poem for its appearances in the world" rather than a "process of contamination" (*Critique*, 51). Surprisingly, child-rearing metaphors have something of a history in editorial theorizing. Cf. Bowers, *Textual and Literary Criticism*, anticipating New Critical objections: "If anyone inquires what all this has to do with the independent life of the poem as we have it in the form that the author wanted to present to the world, I think we can answer that we are likely to know an adult better if we have followed him through all the stages of his childhood" (*Criticism*, 18).

14. So far as I am aware, McGann's most nearly comprehensive view of origination and reception is encapsulated in the three-part scheme of "The Originary Textual Moment," "Secondary Moments of Textual Production and Reproduction (Individual and Related Sequences)," and "The Immediate Moment of Textual Criticism," which he outlines as "a model for a [*sic?*] procedure in textual criticism" ("The Monks and the Giants," in McGann, *Textual Criticism*, 180–99 at 192–94). As he indicates, the topics and sequences would be valuable in enlarging the scope of a graduate bibliography course, but they are considerably narrower than the theoretical field of editorial possibilities.

15. Swinburne's editorial preferences were inconsistent, both in his book on Blake and in his private correspondence. See, for instance, *The Swinburne Letters*, ed. Cecil Y. Lang, 6 vols. (New Haven: Yale University Press, 1959–62), 2:285, 2:311, 4:349, 6:170.

16. Emily Dickinson, *The Complete Poems*, ed. Thomas H. Johnson (Boston: Little, Brown, 1960), 348–49.

Composition as Explanation (of Modern and Postmodern Poetries)

Jerome J. McGann

In "Literature and the Living Voice" Yeats observed that "English literature, alone of great literatures because the newest of them all, has all but completely shaped itself in the printing press."[1] In truth the history of modernist writing could be written as a history of the modernist book. Were one to write that history, Ezra Pound would appear once again the crucial point of departure. Like the Alps for a Western imagination, he and his *Cantos* prove, for better and for worse, unevadable:

> There they are, you will have to go a long way round
> if you want to avoid them.[2]

Bunting's famous lines go to the heart of the matter: that Pound's work has a substantial *thingness* to it, a kind of hard objective presence. The title of his poem—"On the Fly-Leaf of Pound's Cantos"—defines the modernist perspective Yeats had called attention to.

Consider the three books that first printed Cantos 1–30. Their significance is completely involved with the late-nineteenth-century's Renaissance of Printing. To understand how deeply this is true we have to retreat in time to the year when he (later) said he "began the Cantos."[3] In a letter to his mother from Hamilton College in 1904 Pound said he was writing an "essay on early poetry of Wm Morris" (Carpenter 48). Shortly afterward, during the intensities of his affair with H.D., Pound's involvement with Morris and Pre-Raphaelitism had deepened considerably. Not only is his early poetry marked by the influence of several Pre-Raphaelite styles (Morris, Rossetti, and Swinburne especially); Pound also shows that he is aware of the close relation between the late-nineteenth-century's Renaissance of Printing and the Pre-Raphaelite movement.

That awareness is materialized in the unique (handmade) volume he titled *Hilda's Book,* his first book of poetry.[4] This small book of verse, a gift to H.D., is an act of homage to Pre-Raphaelitism and the ideal of the troubadour poet it passed on to him. Largely handwritten in an ornamental script, bound in "a parchment folder," it is a Morris-inspired imitation of the master printers of the fifteenth century.

The point was not simply that writing ought to look handsome or attractive. More crucial were the historical meanings that could be carried by a book's "ornamental" features. Pound apparently learned the power of graphic and typographic book production from Morris and Pre-Raphaelitism. But as his move to London shows, Pound understood that Morris's Kelmscott adventure was not the only model available to someone interested in expressive book design. In fact, two great bibliographical styles emerged in English book production of the 1890s.

The most celebrated of the two is the Kelmscott style (fig. 1). Morris's books were consciously designed to recall the revolutionary book work of the fifteenth century—and especially those early printed books that stood closest to richly decorated medieval manuscript books scripted in closely written Gothic book hands. For a modern eye, however, such a style can create reading problems. In Kelmscott Press books a recollective visual design is so paramount that legibility becomes almost a second-order goal of the printing work.

The rich weight of Morris's Kelmscott texts would ultimately stand at one pole of the imagination that drove the late-nineteenth-century Renaissance of Printing. The other appears in the textual clarities made famous through the work of the Bodley Head Press. For Ezra Pound, Bodley Head proved as formative a resource as Kelmscott (fig. 2).

Begun jointly by Elkin Mathews and John Lane in 1889, Bodley Head chiefly published serious and experimental writing in handsome book designs at relatively cheap prices. Printing runs were small, as the books were being offered to a special audience. The press succeeded in no small part because it helped to consolidate that audience. To be a Bodley Head author, or reader, defined you as a certain type of person—aesthetic and very modern. Unlike Morris's Kelmscott books, the Bodley Head book featured a clear and readable page, on which beauty emerged as a function of the elegance and simplicity of arrangement.

In 1894 the Bodley Head partnership of Mathews and Lane was dissolved, and each went his own way. Mathews retained some of the most prominent of the old Bodley Head authors, including Lionel Johnson, and Yeats. Of the two original partners Mathews was distinctly

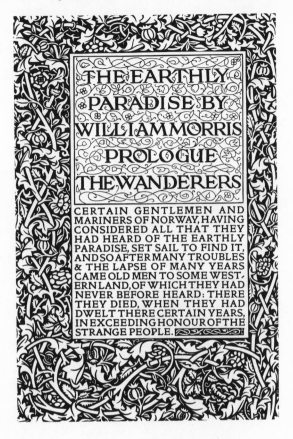

Fig. 1. The Kelmscott style,
as illustrated by William
Morris's *The Earthly Paradise*

the less aggressive entrepreneur. His relatively noncommercial approach
to publishing, so unlike Lane's, was part of the overall scrupulousness
that appealed to the authors he printed.

This history is important to recall because, when Pound went to
London in 1908, he immediately sought out Mathews as a possible pub-
lisher for his work. The two hit it off immediately, and Mathews became
Pound's principal publisher. The poet's first four books issued by Mat-
thews, between 1909 and 1916, were in fact all printed at Chiswick
Press, whose work had been so influential in both Kelmscott and Bodley
Head.

So, we see that Pound from the start conceived his work in the
context of the two key promoters of late-nineteenth-century book production. He understood what had been happening in that movement,
and he sympathized with its goals. Second, he kept close contact with

The Yellow Book

An Illustrated Quarterly

Fig. 2. The Bodley Head style, as illustrated by *The Yellow Boo*

Volume I   April 1894

London : Elkin Mathews
        & John Lane
Boston : Copeland *&*
         Day

the actual design and production of his own work. He published his first printed book, *A Lume Spento,* himself and afterward was continually engaged in all the productive aspects of his writing. By the time he came to publish the first book installments of the *Cantos,* Pound was knowledgeable and experienced in the making of books.

The first two volumes were *A Draft of XVI Cantos* (1925) and *A Draft of the Cantos: 17–27* (1928). The most striking feature of the elaborately produced pages in these volumes is their eclecticism (fig. 3). Although the style of the titles of the different Cantos varies, all recollect medieval calligraphy or decorative printing. Indeed, Pound's titles distinctly recall the uncial calligraphic forms that stand behind subsequent medieval developments in lettering. The same kind of antique allusion appears in the ornamented (or even historiated) initials as well as in the headpieces (recalling the woodcuts of early printed books). The red and

Fig. 3. Excerpt from Ezra
Pound's *A Draft of XVI Cantos* (1925)

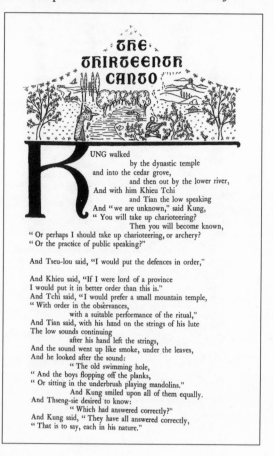

black printing functions in a similar way. In these textual features we see
the strong influence of the Kelmscott book, which is distinguished by
elaborate ornamental materials, including decorative capitals and two-
color printing in red and black.[5] The typeface, on the other hand, so
clearly modern, makes a sharp contrast with the medievalism of the
books' other features. As in Yeats's Dun Emer/Cuala Press books, one
sees here a compromise, or marriage, of the different styles of Morris
on the one hand and Walter Blaikie on the other—of Kelmscott and
Bodley Head.

   This bibliographical contrast also helps to define the historical meaning, or argument, that these installments of the *Cantos* are making. Canto
I launches the *Cantos* project in explicitly bibliographical terms: the
voyage of Odysseus is a matter of linguistic translation and book produc-

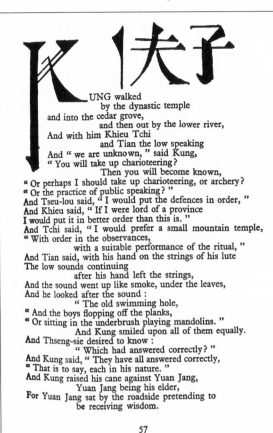

UNG walked
          by the dynastic temple
and into the cedar grove,
          and then out by the lower river,
And with him Khieu Tchi
          and Tian the low speaking
And " we are unknown, " said Kung,
" You will take up charioteering?
          Then you will become known,
" Or perhaps I should take up charioteering, or archery?
" Or the practice of public speaking? "
And Tseu-lou said, " I would put the defences in order, "
And Khieu said, " If I were lord of a province
I would put it in better order than this is. "
And Tchi said, " I would prefer a small mountain temple,
" With order in the observances,
          with a suitable performance of the ritual, "
And Tian said, with his hand on the strings of his lute
The low sounds continuing
          after his hand left the strings,
And the sound went up like smoke, under the leaves,
And he looked after the sound :
          " The old swimming hole,
" And the boys flopping off the planks,
" Or sitting in the underbrush playing mandolins. "
          And Kung smiled upon all of them equally.
And Thseng-sie desired to know :
          " Which had answered correctly? "
And Kung said, " They have all answered correctly,
" That is to say, each in his nature. "
And Kung raised his cane against Yuan Jang,
          Yuan Jang being his elder,
For Yuan Jang sat by the roadside pretending to
          be receiving wisdom.

57

Fig. 4. Excerpt from Ezra Pound's *A Draft of XXX Cantos* (1930)

tion. From Pound's vantage, then, it would be important to express that historical subject at every level of the work. The stylistic contrast between his books' ornament and typography map the history he is interested in. The pages of these books recollect at the design level the epochal (bibliographical) events of the fifteenth century and the late nineteenth century. The *Cantos* project locates itself within that historical nexus.

A *Draft of XXX Cantos* (1930), Pound's next book of the *Cantos*, is uniform with the two previous books in that he continues to exploit a contrast between the ornamental initials and the body of the text (fig. 4). In this case, however, the contrast operates wholly within a modernist horizon. The typeface is modernized Caslon, but because the initials are so agressively vorticist the typeface functions now as the sign of an earlier historical or stylistic moment. From a purely personal point of view the initials recollect Pound's London years and the beginning of his "modernism" (in the most restricted sense of the term). At the level of the work's bibliographical symbology, *A Draft of XXX Cantos* has moved a step away from the Pre-Raphaelite and aesthetic position recollected in the first two volumes.

The physical presentation of these three books thus constitutes a display of their meanings. Book design here defines not merely the immediate historical horizon of Pound's *Cantos* project; it also declares the meaningfulness of historical horizons as such. Through book design Pound makes an issue of language's physique, deliberateness, and historicality.

The history inscribed in Pound's initial project for the *Cantos* has been preserved in other important records of the period. Many of the most influential works of the Harlem Renaissance—for instance, Langston Hughes's *The Weary Blues* (1926), various books by Countee Cullen, Alain Locke's anthology *The New Negro* (1925)—all display the profound effect produced by the graphic and bibliographic revolution at the end of the nineteenth century. In these cases the style has taken a definitively modernist step beyond medievalism and aestheticism; nonetheless, that step would not have been possible without the historical inertia generated out of the late Victorians. Nor did their influence extend only to experimentalist writing. Hardy's first book of verse, *Wessex Poems* (1898), marries the new aesthetic style of text presentation with a series of sketches (by Hardy himself) "illustrating" the symbolic topography being constructed by the book. And of course the Yeatsian record—so crucial in every way—tells a similar story.

So far I have been emphasizing the analogy between "composition" as it concerns the typographer and "composition" as it concerns the visual artist. Another analogy is possible, however, and has been equally important. Composition is an activity of musicians, and the printed page may equally be produced as a kind of musical score, or set of directions for the audition of verse and voice. In this connection a key early modernist figure is Louis Zukofsky, for whom poetry was a Paterian aspiration toward the condition of music. He gets most interested in the formatting of texts as a means for scoring the performance of voice:

> Typography—certainly—if print and the arrangement of it will help to tell how the voice should sound.

Zukofsky is aware that modernism, and in particular the work of Pound, offered another very different way of thinking about typography. His next sentence alludes to this other way but sets it aside:

> It is questionable on the other hand whether the letters of the alphabet can be felt as the Chinese feel their written characters.[6]

The (free verse) line from Zukofsky to the projectivist work of the 1950s is quite direct. It is a line for composing, in the musical sense, sound and speech patterns. If we look backward from Zukofsky, this line—as we all know—is spun out of Whitman.

While auditional composition is an important feature of twentieth-century poetry, the manipulations of a text's visual codes provide the ground for its innovations. Whether we are talking about musical or graphical composition, the modernist text is organized through the eye. This fact is clear in Pound's work. It becomes even more visible in the books issued by one of the most interesting and forgotten of our early modern experimentalists, Robert Carleton ("Bob") Brown. The year that Nancy Cunard's Hours Press brought out Pound's *A Draft of XXX Cantos* (1930) also saw the appearance of Brown's polemical treatise on poetry and printing, *The Readies*.

Each book is a conscious reimagination of the possibilities of poetic expression, and both situate themselves in the bibliographical renaissance that Morris had brought to a flash point. The two works display very different emphases. *A Draft of XXX Cantos,* as we have seen, looks directly back to the craft traditions revivified by the work of Morris. The book is handprinted on rag paper in the modern Caslon used by William Bird for his previous editions of Pound's Pre-Raphaelite cantos—a variant of the same font that had been resurrected by Chiswick Press in the nineteenth century and that so captured the imagination of Morris.[7] Brown's work, by contrast, is a small pamphlet printed by machine on cheap chemical paper.

The difference Brown's book makes with Pound's is, however, conscious and deliberate. *The Readies* issues a hail and farewell to earlier dreamers of a revolutionary word.[8] Brown made his point even more dramatically a year earlier when he published his collection of (what shall we call them?) "optical poems" in the book *1450–1950*, with its graphic dedication page (see fig. 5).[9] "Writing has been bottled up in books since the start," Brown playfully laments in *The Readies;* "It is time to pull out the stopper" (28).

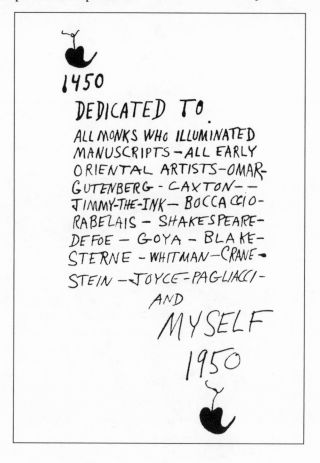

Fig. 5. Dedication page of
Robert Brown's *1450–1950*

Brown had been working at that stuck stopper since 1914, when
he first read Gertrude Stein's *Tender Buttons,* which seems to have completely transformed his sense of writing. "I began to see that a story
might be anything . . . [and] didn't have to be a tangible hunk of bread
interest. . . . Thank God for Gert Stein."[10] He "began to experiment for
the first time," and when he struck off his optical poem "Eyes on the
Half-Shell," Marcel Duchamp printed it in his journal *Blindman* in 1917
(fig. 6). Brown later included it in his collection *1450–1950.* His commentary on the text is important:

> I have since taken this for a symbol of what I have been trying to
> do in writing, off and on for fifteen years. . . .   I like to look at
> it, merely sit and look at it, take it all   in without moving an

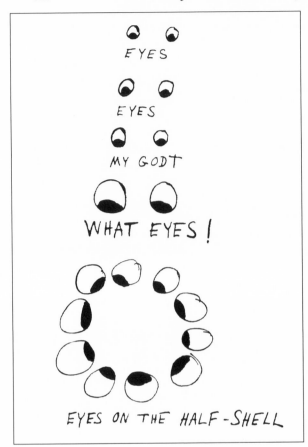

Fig. 6. Robert Brown's "Eyes on the Half-Shell," from *Blindman* (1917)

eye. It gives me more than rhymed poetry. It rhymes in my eyes. Here are Black Riders for me at last galloping across a blank page.[11]

Brown's optical poems can be misleading, can make one think that he is simply reconnecting with those innovative visual texts produced by Edward Lear, Lewis Carroll, and (before them) William Blake. Of course, Brown's relation to these poets is important, but in his mind the optical poem does not at all require figural decorative ornaments. The physical medium of any kind of textuality—in a typographical mode the basic elements are paper, ink, cuts, and various type fonts—can be manipulated to the same effect.

I'm for new methods of reading and writing and I believe the up-to-date reader deserves an eye-ful when he buys something to read. (*Readies* 1)

Brown's idea was to immerse the reader in the print medium, much as the viewer is immersed in images at the cinema. "The Readies" is Brown's witty bibliographical takeoff on those recent Modernist inventions, the "movies" and "talkies." When Brown declared, "I bathe in Apollinaire" (*Readies* 1), he was announcing his ideal linguistic experience.

At the center of Brown's program was his half-serious, half-playful invention, a "reading machine." This apparatus was supposed to provide the reader with the power to read in all directions and at any speed, to change type size and typeface at will, to leap forward or backward in the text: to browse, to speedread, to connect any and all parts of the text in any and all ways.

Brown wants to overgo the recent advances of those who used fine book production as a means to radical poetic innovation. So, he puns his refusal of the bibliographical tradition on which Yeats and Pound had drawn, those "beautiful but dumb books as clumsy in their way as the Rozetti stone" (*Readies* 40). But Brown's rejection is full of homage and admiration because the great earlier traditions of printing and manuscript illumination had taught him a "loving wonder, a great want-to-know about words, their here and their there, their this and their that":

> The monks in the beginning didn't do it so badly in their illuminated manuscripts, they retained a little of the healthy hieroglyphic, all Oriental books in ideogrammatic character are delights, early colophons splendid. (*Readies* 39)

Even as Brown explicitly pays his respects to Blake, Morris, Pound, and the traditions they cherished, he makes his turn toward a new world of words:

> For the first time in the history of mental optics there will exist a visual Literary Language sharply separated from the Speaking Tongue. Literary Language is Optical, speaking language Vocal, and the gap between them must spread till it becomes a gulf. My reading machine will serve as a wedge. Makers of words will be born; fresh, vital eye-words will wink out of dull, dismal, drooling type at startled smug   readers here below.... The Revolution of the Word will be all over but the shouting.... (*Readies* 39)

Brown's *jouissance* of the word anticipates the Derridean moment by forty years and prophesies as well the practical emergence of computerized word-processing and hypertextual fields.

Blake, Rossetti, and Morris were inspirations rather than models. The point is made clearly in one of the texts printed in Brown's optical collection *1450–1950* (fig. 7). The poles of 1450 and 1950 are defined by "ILLUMINATED MSS." on one hand and "ILLUMINATING/MOVIE SCRIPTS" on the other. Brown faces "forward" but with many glances "back" and sideways, full of interest and respect. He keeps his eyes open in all directions. Most immediately, he looks to find on the contemporary scene those "makers of words" called for by *The Readies*.

The makers were alive and very active. Brown's manifesto was followed almost immediately by his anthology *Readies for Bob Brown's Machine* (1931), an extraordinary collection of liberated texts supplied to Brown by some of the most innovative writers of his age: Williams, McAlmon, Harry Crosby, Stein, Sidney Hunt, Pound, Hemingway, and many others.

Sidney Hunt's "MORNINIGHT CAR (nocturnal day realm)," for example, distinctly recollects Brown's call in *The Readies* to "see words machinewise":

Black-Riders-Crash-by-hell-bent-for-leather-uppercase-LOWER-CASE-both——together-chanting-valorously-Print-in-action-at—longlast-movable-type-at-breakneck-gallop [. . .] daredevil-commaless-Cossacks-astride-mustang-bronco——vocabularies-leaning-farout-into-inky-night——.(37)

The word *uppercase* printed in lowercase, the word *lowercase* printed in uppercase: it is a small emblem of what Brown has in his mind. Futurism supplies Brown with the trope of speed and the wisdom of machines ("machinewise") that negotiates the field of this particular text.

But speed is only one possible sign of the word revolution Brown desires. Indeed, the trope emerges most immediately out of a very different figure, the "Black-Riders" that set a pattern for the text's "breakneck-gallop . . . into-inky-night." The phrase is an allusion to Stephen Crane's first published book, *Black Riders and other lines* (1895), which gave Brown "the only hint I have found of Moving Reading" and which suggested to him "the dash of inky words at full gallop across the plains of pure white pages" (*Readies* 32–33).

It is worth pausing for a moment over Crane's book, which clearly had a great influence on Brown. It was published (in New York) by the recently established firm Copeland and Day, in conscious imitation of the bibliographical innovations championed by the Pre-Raphaelites and

Fig. 7. Excerpt from Robert
Brown's *1450–1950*

their inheritors.[12] The book comes with a Rossettian/Bodley Head decorated cover (black with an embossed orchid design, and with the title
and author's name stamped in gold). It was printed in a run limited to
five hundred copies, with a few copies issued in vellum. Most startling,
however, at least if we think of Brown's apparent obsession with futurist
speed, is the extreme stillness of Crane's text page. The book consists
of fifty-six short pieces, each roman numbered and each set out on a
page by itself, and printed (in small capital letters) high up on the page
so as to leave a notable space below the text.[13] The poems confront the
reader as hieratic and symbolist texts, and hardly as forerunners of futurism.

I

BLACK RIDERS CAME FROM THE SEA.
THERE WAS CLANG AND CLANG OF SPEAR AND SHIELD,
AND CLASH AND CLASH OF HOOF AND HEEL,
WILD SHOUTS AND THE WAVE OF HAIR
IN THE RUSH UPON THE WIND:
THUS THE RIDE OF SIN.

Though it might seem a relatively trivial matter, the decision to print the poems in small caps pitched Crane's book into a novel imaginative direction, as Brown saw. The caps, as well as the isolation of each poem on the page, draw one's attention to the poetry's material features and, ultimately, to an awareness of poetry *as a system of material signifiers*. In *The Black Riders and other lines* what Brown saw were texts always collapsing in upon themselves:

XLII

I WALKED IN A DESERT.
AND I CRIED,
"AH, GOD, TAKE ME FROM THIS PLACE!"
A VOICE SAID, "IT IS NO DESERT."
I CRIED, "WELL, BUT—
"THE SAND, THE HEAT, THE VACANT HORIZON."
A VOICE SAID, "IT IS NO DESERT."

XLVI

MANY RED DEVILS RAN FROM MY HEART
AND OUT UPON THE PAGE,
THEY WERE SO TINY
THE PEN COULD MASH THEM.
AND MANY STRUGGLED IN THE INK.
IT WAS STRANGE
TO WRITE IN THIS RED MUCK
OF THINGS FROM MY HEART.

These are Barthesian writings, already fully conscious that the poetic field is self-signifying. The "I" walks in the white desert of the page, whose vacancy it populates by its walking, by the "lines" of Crane's title as they move out in a heroic but unfulfillable quest for completion.

In Crane's book the page appears under various forms—as snow, as desert, as psychic vacancy, and—most often—as itself, or part of itself:

XLIV

I WAS IN THE DARKNESS:
I COULD NOT SEE MY WORDS
NOR THE WISHES OF MY HEART.
THEN SUDDENLY THERE WAS GREAT LIGHT—

"LET ME INTO THE DARKNESS AGAIN."

The typographical wit of this text, in which the "great light" comes as a small blank moment on the page, must have been a joy to Bob Brown's days. In another age and style that light was called (romantically) "inspiration" and "imagination."

The example of Crane, so important for Brown, helps to explain the latter's equal enthusiasm for Marinetti on one hand and for Pound on the other, for Sidney Hunt and for Gertrude Stein. Texts do not have to gallop to be free. "I have only to bend my finger in a beckon," Brown writes, "and words, birds of words, hop on it, chirping" (*Readies* 4). Brown's own poetical texts may speed up or slow down, and they perform these operations in various ways.

We see this nowhere more clearly, perhaps, than in his splendid book *Words,* published by Hours Press in 1931. The book's subtitle, printed in microform type that requires either an eagle's eye or a magnifying glass to be read, tells its story simultaneously as a lexical and a typographical message: "I but bend my finger in a beckon and words, birds of words, hop on it, chirping." Brown runs a continuous gloss through his book in the form of such microform typescripts. The first page of "La Vie Americaine" provides an especially dramatic example of Brown's unusual semiotic imagination (fig. 8). Carefully scrutinized, this page's microform gloss text at the lower left delivers up its reading:

I, who am God
Wear lavender pyjamas and
Pure poetry
Should I, who am God

LA VIE AMERICAINE

8 A. M.   9 A. M. **$$$$$$$$$**   12 M.
Coffee, cereal   Office   Brunch
cigarettes, eggs   chasing the dollar

1 P. M.   5 P. M.   7 P. M.
Office **$$$$$$$$$$$$$** Cocktails   Dinner
        dollar-golf chasing

8 P. M. _____ 1 A. M.
talkies   chasing the tail   tail-chasing

                    &

Yes God
I've looked around
Seen the quaint devices and
Funny commonplaces you bragged about
It's all right God
I understand you're an altruist
Plus God
I know you had a high purpose &
All that God
In breathing your sensen
Semen-scented breath
Into clay pigeons Chinks Brazies
Yanks Frogs Turks and Limevs
It's a great little old world you made God
But now I'm ready for another eveful
Mars Heaven Hell &/or
What have you got Gott
Come on with your Cummingsesque etceteras

12

Fig. 8. Excerpt from Robert Brown's *Words* (1931)

Dirty my ear on the ground
Striving to catch the
Idiotic waltzing lilt of
Rhyming red-eyed dervish
Twirling white pink poet mice
In union suits?

Like Brown's slightly dadaist poem "I Am a Two-Way Fish," printed in *The Readies* pamphlet, or the semi-optical "3" (one of Brown's short *Demonics* [1931]), the texts of *Words* stand closer to chirping birds than to galloping horses.

Anyone who reads postmodern poetry will have been struck by its vigorous appropriation of this bibliographical inheritance. I have in mind

not merely the widespread development of various kinds of Concrete
Poetry but also the visual structure of Jackson MacLow's chance poems,
of John Cage's work, of Clark Coolidge's spatialized texts. Typography
and layout are not simply devices "to tell how the voice should sound";
they are poetic resources adapatable to many uses: poster poems like
Robert Grenier's "Cambridge M'ass," Johanna Drucker's breathtaking
books of "words made flesh," Charles Bernstein and Susan Bee's parodies of the emblem tradition in their witty collaborative collection, *The
Nude Formalism* (1989) (fig. 9).

Susan Howe's *Pythagorean Silence* (1982), an exemplary text of our
period, is especially relevant to the typographical history I have been
sketching. This happens because Howe is equally determined to exploit
typography for musical as well as visual effects. Her Pythagorean forms
preserve at once geometries for the visionary eye and harmonies for the
inner ear.

The textual character of the poem is underscored in part 2, section 1:

a sentence   or character
suddenly

steps out to seek for truth   fails
falls

into a stream of ink   Sequence
trails off

must go on

These stumbling and fractured texts forecast the climactic event in *Pythagorean Silence*—its visionary dance of pure words and linguistic forms.
Howe invokes the Pythagorean model as a figural form for her New
England puritanism. "Pythagorean Silence" is her antinomian trope for
what literary historians call American transcendentalism. She treats her
poem's silence like a fire sermon.

Trained as a painter, Howe has exploited the physique of the page
as brilliantly as anyone now writing. But I use her here principally to
turn backward, to look again at Howe's acknowledged precursor, Emily
Dickinson. In the late nineteenth century poetry in the United States
was dominated by those once famous "Household Editions," published
by Houghton Mifflin, of Longfellow and Whittier and the other "Fire-

Fragments from the Seventeenth Manifesto of Nude Formalism

by Hermes Hermeneutic

Away with the study of flotation!

Articulation is more than an manner of gritting the pendulum!

Down with all authentic formulations of these theses! Down with Adolescent Sublime! Down with Abstract Confessionalism! Down with Empathic Symbolism! Down with Symbolic Empathism!

All good poetry is the forced constriction of feelings of powerlessness.

Poetry is not the erasure of personality but a caprice of personality. But of course only those who have caprices will know what it means to want to pursue them.

Poetry has as its lower limit insincerity and its upper limit dematerialization.

Use absolutely no word that contributes to the direct sense of a thing seen.

Gosh

When fled I found my love defamed in clang
Of riotous bed she came, along the flues
I harbored there, scarce chance upon harangue
By labors grant the fig of latched amuse
She quakes and bless her soul would harsh realize
That none our maps could burn aboard her ship
And floral hung to lit parts cleared eyes
Left like that elder hap that splits a chip
When dull's the deed wherewith else back I on
Forewent all trial asleep her carousel
Thread in torching tease tuned basilican
Drifting after still much breath-crested scrawl
Hence going beads each languorous thronement
When all I gown errs come again cement

Fig. 9. Excerpt from Charles Bernstein and Susan Bee's *The Nude Formalism* (1989)

side" writers. The meaning of their work is completely involved with the books in which it appeared, in which extreme social alienation has—in the words of a later song—"put on a happy face." We glimpse some of this meaning by reflecting on the very different kind of "household" editions that Dickinson was producing at the same time. Dickinson would not publish her poems. She organized them in small fascicles—handwritten and handsewn little books that she kept in her desk. In these works she experimented with visual and sonic arrangements of the page space, elementary stanzaic forms (usually quatrains), and handwritten script.[14]

We can begin to explicate what Dickinson was about in her writing by looking briefly at the dramatic shift of style between fascicles 1–8 and all the later thirty-odd fascicles.[15] Look at the two texts (figs. 10, 11) that respectively close fascicle 8 and open fascicle 9 (Johnson 165 and

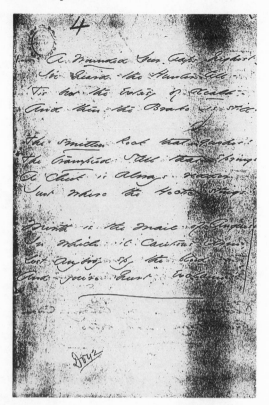

Fig. 10. Emily Dickinson, fascicle 8. (From *The Manuscript Books of Emily Dickinson,* ed. R. W. Franklin.)

186). The difference is simple. Whereas in the first text the linear metrical units correspond to their scriptural presentation, the second text skews this correspondence. Metrical lines are now distributed over two scriptural lines. So, while the fascicle 9 poem is metrically a work of three quatrains (twelve lines altogether—if it were printed or written according to its normative metrical scheme), it is scripturally a much different work. It has nineteen lines, it isn't ordered in quatrains, and the metrical scheme is drastically altered from the metrical norm that we (as it were) *un*hear below Dickinson's visible language.

Susan Howe was the first person to recognize this scriptural change in the fascicles as a crucial event in the history of modern poetry.[16] Emily Dickinson's importance as a poetic innovator, and perhaps even her true greatness, is marked by what might appear to be a mere shift in her handwriting or in her copying habits. In fact the change represents something far more radical, far more significant.

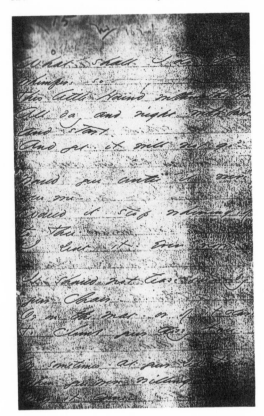

Fig. 11. Emily Dickinson, fascicle 9. (From Franklin, *Manuscript Books*.)

At some point—I believe it might have been during the winter of 1861—Dickinson decided to use her text page as a scene for dramatic interplays between a poetics of the eye and a poetics of the ear. Eventually, she would elaborate a complex set of writing tactics from this elementary textual move. In a very real sense modernism's subsequent experiments with its many "visible languages" are forecast in the textual ventures of Emily Dickinson.

From the beginning, however, Dickinson's editors have erased the evidence of these experiments. Johnson's now standard edition regularly elides Dickinson's irregularities. Dickinson's first editors did much the same thing, only they followed late-nineteenth-century popular conventions of text presentation, whereas Johnson followed twentieth-century scholarly conventions. Besides, Todd and Higginson were well aware that they were changing her poems. They called it "creative editing."

They thought the late-nineteenth-century reader could not bear too much of Dickinson's poetic realities. By contrast, Johnson believed he was *un*doing those initial bowdlerizations, believed he was restoring the pristine originals in an equivalent bibliographical form. In this illusion his editorial work obscured Dickinson's poetic practices perhaps even more deeply than those much maligned early editors.

It would not be difficult to generate an "interpretation" of fascicle 9's first poem that would take account of its textual irregularities. For example, if we simply restore the first line from what we have been led to read—"What shall I do—it whimpers so"—to what we actually have in the fascicle:

What shall I do-it

we realize that the lineation opens the text to several syntactic options— several "readings," that the normalized line closes down. Similarly, it makes a great deal of difference if we read the text this way:

All day and night   -   with bark and start

or this way:

All day and night   -   with bark
And start

In this last case Dickinson's scriptural moves call attention to the self-referential act of the poem. Its ostensible "subject" is Dickinson's dog, Carlo, who is named in the final line of the poem: "Tell Carlo - He'll tell me!" But the third line of the first stanza emphasizes the metaphoric character of the ostensible subject:

This little Hound within the Heart

The initial irregularities dramatize the poem's self-consciousness, which is playing with its own textuality. Playing with Carlo is a poetic figure: that event in time has, as it were, a transcendental equivalent, which is literalized in Dickinson's text. Thus, lines 2 and 5 of the first stanza—the fragments "Whimpers so" and "And start"—constitute a kind of syntactic and metrical onomatopeia: not so much equivalents of the actual dog Carlo's whimpers and starts as the literal appearance of the poetical events, the life of the Hound within Dickinson's Heart, the visible acts of her artistic imagination.

In this example we glimpse an early stage in Dickinson's experiments with "free verse." These experiments emerge from an initial decision to forgo a long-established convention governing the bibliographical presentation of poetry. The textual condition of almost all the poems copied in fascicles 1–8 represents Dickinson adhering to that convention: as she copies her poems out, she arranges the lines as they would be expected to appear in a printed book.[17] These texts are being copied to imitate, at their basic scriptural level, the formalities of print. Though handwritten, these are poems that have been imagined under a horizon of publication.

Permit me a digression before I turn to another—and finally a more important—aspect of Dickinson's textual condition. There is a long-standing debate among Dickinson scholars about whether or not she wanted to be published. Some say yes, some no, others see her as vacillating on the matter. Among the last group many think that Dickinson finally abandoned the desire for publication in face of the puzzled "What?" that her writing so commonly provoked even among the small circle who read her things.

For myself I prefer to approach this problem as an issue of writing rather than an issue of psychology. So, I make a distinction between Dickinson's efforts to extend the circle of her readership and her reluctance to enter the marketplace of publication. If the question has to be put in psychological terms, I should say this: while Dickinson wanted readers, and while she was even ambitious of fame as a poet, she rejected the traditional (early capitalist) institution for achieving those ends. I believe she made this rejection not because of some large cultural or political sense of the limits of the "auction" of publishing—though she was certainly aware of those limits. Rather, I think she rejected a market model of publishing, with its medium of print, because she came to see how restrictive and conventional that medium had become. What Emily Dickinson was doing in her private writing between 1860 and her death would itself become a type of the formal options opened up by the publishing institutions that were soon to emerge in and through the Modernist movement. (As with Blake, these institutions will capitalize her work.)

Dickinson's innovations appear when we recall how this intense and reclusive woman made contact with others. It came by writing—more particularly, by writing letters. If we choose to communicate with written language, we may connect with others through the commerce of publication or through the intercourse of correspondence. Dickinson wrote a great many poems, and most of them were never included in letters—all those poems in the fascicles and the sets, for instance, which she kept in her desk. But from the moment she began copying fascicle 9, Dickinson clearly began to construct her poetry within writing conventions permitted and encouraged in the textuality of personal correspondence.

What a difference this makes to the writing appears dramatically in the following example. Here are two "copies" that Dickinson made of "the same" poem (J323: "As if I asked a common Alms"), the first from fascicle 1, the second from Dickinson's letter to Higginson, June 7, 1862 (figs. 12, 13).[18] The text in fascicle 1 is copied out according to the conventions of the medium of print. In the letter to Higginson, on the other hand, the poem is copied according to what Higginson himself called "the habit of freedom and the unconventional utterance of daring thoughts." In truth, however, Dickinson's text in the letter is by no means "unconventional." Rather, it is a poetical text that exploits the writing resources—the "conventions," of epistolary intercourse. So, when Higginson speaks of her writing as "wayward and unconventional in the last degree; defiant of form, measure, rhyme, and even grammar,"[19] his judgment reflects his expectations about the appropriate conventions that should govern a poet's work.

Following Emerson, Higginson classified Dickinson's work as "The Poetry of the Portfolio," private writing "not meant for publication" (qtd. in Blake and Wells 3). This judgment seems to me exact if we understand the specific historicality of Higginson's remark—i.e., if we understand that in the late nineteenth century "publication" only came when a poet followed certain textual conventions. These conventions—they are strictly bibliographical rather than more broadly formal—were so dominant that most poets and readers could not imagine poetry without them. (Tennyson and Dante Gabriel Rossetti, for example, both said that they could not really begin to see their own poetry until it was put into print.) Higginson's reponse to Dickinson's writing as "spasmodic" and "uncontrolled" reflects these habits of thought.

But the writing is not spasmodic or uncontrolled or defiant of form. It has, instead, chosen to draw its elementary rules of form by an analogy to the writing conventions of personal correspondence rather than to the conventions of the printed text.

Up to now Dickinson's editors, as well as the vast majority of her

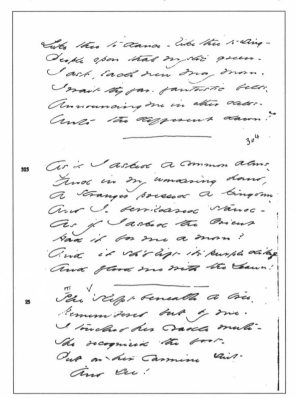

Fig. 12. Emily Dickinson, fascicle 1. (From Franklin, *Manuscript Books*.)

readers, have not understood this crucial formality of her work. Look
at the facsimile of Dickinson's letter to Higginson and compare that text
with Johnson's bibliographical translation of the letter (*Letters* 2:409)
(fig. 14). In his translation Johnson has put into print an equivalent of the
poem Dickinson wrote in fascicle 1 rather than the poem she sent in her
letter to Higginson. But the letter rewrites the earlier text—the fascicle
text Higginson hadn't seen—by following the options released through
a scriptural and epistolary environment rather than a publishing and
bibliographical one. No doubt, Higginson would have approved the
fascicle 1 text: after Dickinson's death, when he first saw the fascicles,
he was surprised (he said) to find that so many of the poems "have *form*
beyond most of those I have seen before."[20] He says this because what
he had "seen before"—the poems she sent to him in her letters—were all
organized scripturally rather than bibliographically.

The poem in this letter is particularly important because the letter
famously addresses the issue of publication. "I smile when you suggest

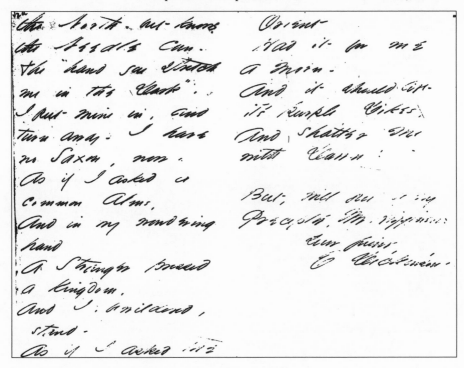

Fig. 13. Emily Dickinson, letter to T. W. Higginson. (By courtesy of the Trustees of the Boston Public Library.)

that I delay 'to publish'—that being foreign to my thought, as Firmament to Fin" (*Letters* 2:408). Dickinson is not writing to ask Higginson for professional help or for schooling in formal proprieties. She is aware that she has undertaken an unusual approach to poetical writing. The question she wants to ask him is different: Given the choice she has made, is her work "clear"?

The answer she received was yes, as we know from the continuation of their correspondence. Higginson understood, and his understanding is measured as much by his admiration for the force of her writing as it is by his dismay at her incorrigible incorrectnesses. So far as Dickinson was concerned, that doubled understanding—Higginson's blindness and insight alike—proved equally important to her life as a writer.

Let me make one further comment on this famous letter. The text of "As if I asked a / Common Alms" is introduced by a series of apparitionally "prose" texts. As so often in her letters, however, these passages run along evident metrical feet. Johnson's edition of the *Letters* assumes

that's Emily. Loo and Fanny were that wind, and the poor leaf, who?
Won't they stop a'blowing? . . . Commencement would be a dreary
spot without my double flower, that sows itself and just comes up
when Emily seeks it most. Austin gives excellent account, I trust not
overdrawn. "Health and aspect admirable, and lodgings very fine."
Says the rooms were marble, even to the flies. Do they dwell in Car-
rara? Did they find the garden in the gown? Should have sent a farm,
but feared for our button-hole. Hope to hear favorable news on receipt
of this. Please give date of coming, so we might prepare our heart.

                                                                Emily.

MANUSCRIPT: destroyed.
PUBLICATION: L (1894) 245–246; L (1931) 227.
Louise arrived in Amherst on 10 June. Commencement was held on
10 July.

                              265

To T. W. Higginson   *7 June 1862*
Dear friend.
    Your letter gave no Drunkenness, because I tasted Rum before –
Domingo comes but once – yet I have had few pleasures so deep as
your opinion, and if I tried to thank you, my tears would block my
tongue –
    My dying Tutor told me that he would like to live till I had been
a poet, but Death was much of Mob as I could master – then – And
when far afterward – a sudden light on Orchards, or a new fashion in
the wind troubled my attention – I felt a palsy, here – the Verses just
relieve –
    Your second letter surprised me, and for a moment, swung – I had
not supposed it. Your first – gave no dishonor, because the True – are
not ashamed – I thanked you for your justice – but could not drop the
Bells whose jingling cooled my Tramp – Perhaps the Balm, seemed
better, because you bled me, first.
    I smile when you suggest that I delay "to publish" – that being
foreign to my thought, as Firmament to Fin –
    If fame belonged to me, I could not escape her – if she did not, the
longest day would pass me on the chase – and the approbation of my
Dog, would forsake me – then – My Barefoot-Rank is better –

                           [408]

You think my gait "spasmodic" – I am in danger – Sir –
You think me "uncontrolled" – I have no Tribunal.
    Would you have time to be the "friend" you should think I need?
I have a little shape – it would not crowd your Desk – nor make much
Racket as the Mouse, that dents your Galleries –
    If I might bring you what I do – not so frequent to trouble you –
and ask you if I told it clear – 'twould be control, to me –
    The Sailor cannot see the North – but knows the Needle can –
    The "hand you stretch me in the Dark," I put mine in, and turn
away – I have no Saxon, now –

              As if I asked a common Alms,
              And in my wondering hand
              A Stranger pressed a Kingdom,
              And I, bewildered, stand –
              As if I asked the Orient
              Had it for me a Morn –
              And it should lift it's purple Dikes,
              And shatter me with Dawn!

But, will you be my Preceptor, Mr Higginson?
                                          Your friend
                                          E Dickinson –

MANUSCRIPT: BPL (Higg 52). Ink. Envelope addressed: T. W. Higginson./Worcester./Mass. Postmarked: Amherst Ms Jun 7 1862.
PUBLICATION: AM LXVIII (Oct. 1891) 447; L (1894) 303–304; LL
240–241; L (1931) 274–275.
    The phrase "I have no Saxon" means "Language fails me": see *Poems*
(1955) 197, where in poem no. 276 she offers "English language" as her
alternative for "Saxon." She enclosed no poems in this letter.

                              266

To Samuel Bowles   *early summer 1862*
Dear friend –
    You go away – and where you go, we cannot come – but then the
Months have names – and each one comes but once a year – and though
it seems they never could, they sometimes do – go by.

                           [409]

Fig. 14. Emily Dickinson, letter to T. W. Higginson. (7 June 1862)

a sharp division between the formalities of verse and prose, so he prints
the metrical prose margin to margin and the spatially disordered verse
in "correct" metrical lines. But a typographical translation of this extraordinary text of Dickinson's might just as well reverse Johnson's
method in order to reveal what Johnson's translation overrides: the metrical subtext of the prose and the prosy surface of the verse. So, instead
of Johnson's margin-to-margin prose text, we might print the following:

        You think my gait "spasmodic"—
        I am in danger - Sir -
        You think me "uncontrolled" -
        I have no tribunal
        Would you have time to be the friend
        You should think I need?
        I have a little shape
        it would not crowd your Desk -

nor make much Racket as the Mouse,
that dents your Galleries
If I might bring you what I do –
Not so frequent to trouble you –
and ask you if I told it clear –
twould be control to me –
The Sailor cannot see the North –
but knows the Needle can –
The "hand you stretch me in the Dark,"
I put mine in and turn away –
I have no Saxon now –
As if I asked a Common Alms, . . . etc.

My translation is, of course, a travesty of Dickinson's text because it turns the writing into doggerel by forcing one of its musical features into an excessively straightened form. It is exactly the loose "prose" arrangement of the words on the page that allows the language to transcend the metronome. I give the translation only because it throws into relief the innovative character of Dickinson's writing and the crucial significance of her original scripted pages.

In editing Dickinson, these scripts must be faithfully followed, whether the visible language of the texts appears to us as prose or as poetry. They must be followed because Dickinson's writing, particularly in the letters, continually erodes the distinction between those two ancient textual formalities. So, if Johnson's edition of the *Letters* did right to follow Dickinson in presenting the above passage as prose, he did wrong when he departed from Dickinson in his textual presentation of the letter's "poem." By normalizing Dickinson's letter-poem, Johnson shows that he thinks about her poetry the way Higginson was thinking at the end of the nineteenth century: he is thinking that when poetry is put into print it must conform to certain received typographical conventions. But Dickinson's work is precisely characterized by her refusal to submit to those conventions and forms. By avoiding the auction of publication, along with its specialized and restricted norms for text presentation, Dickinson began to exploit new technical ranges for imaginative writing—quite literally, a whole new space-time continuum for the material texts of poetry.

When scriptural texts are not shaped to fit the model of printed texts they free up the more formal expectations of the latter. In that freedom Dickinson discovered a world of suprising new poetical formalities. The

final line of "What shall I do—it" exemplifies what Dickinson was dis-
covering through her experiments with the scripted medium. Because
the final line appears only when the page is turned, it comes upon one
with a special kind of dramatic suddenness. Dickinson would later resort
to that trick of style a number of times—not least memorably in the
poem known as "September's Baccalaureate" (J1271; Franklin Set 15),
in which the final two lines (the final metrical unit) only appear when
the page is turned. The point of the device is clear if we simply recall the
closing passage:[21]

> That hints
> without assuming
> an Innuendo
> sear
> that makes the
> heart put up its
> fun
> [and then on the verso]
> and turn
> Philosopher

This type of move has many variations—for example in the poem
commonly called "Pain - has an element of - Blank" (J650). Dickinson's poem is scripted very differently from the Johnson printed text
(fig. 15). In the manuscript the blank space of the page serves the
argument of the writing. As in the previous example, the medium of
the text is not simply taken as a given, something to be worked *within;*
the medium is part of the scene of writing, part of the imagination's
subject.

The same is true in this example from "Many a phrase has the
English language" (J276) (fig. 16). When Dickinson's line literally
"breaks" into its "bright Orthogra/phy" this is more than a trick of style.
The whole poem is a conscious meditation on the nature of language—
and not language in some general and abstract sense but, rather, *language*
as she received it through the formalities of her copy of Webster's
American dictionary. The textual play with the word *Orthogra/phy*
rhymes with the poem's many similar wordplays—for example, with
the specific spelling she gives to that most American of birds, the "Whippowil." About that word and that bird Dickinson's *Webster's* has much
to say, not least in distinguishing the American bird from the English

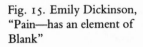

Fig. 15. Emily Dickinson,
"Pain—has an element of
Blank"

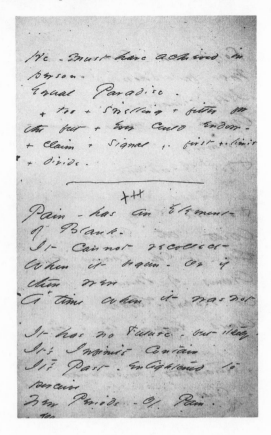

by drawing an important orthographic distinction between the English word (*whipoorwill*) and the American (*whippowil*). The different words mark out different languages that constitute as well entirely different worlds: different worlds of speech patterns, different etymologies, different birds.

Even more complex are the many experiments Dickinson made with texts that had generated variant readings. The print convention she inherited would organize such variants at the foot of the page, in what scholars would later call an "apparatus." Many of her own poems exploit that convention, but Dickinson also habitually threw her "variants" all over the space of her pages—interlinearly, in both margins (sometimes written up and sometimes down), and within the area of "the line itself," the so-called superior text. The whole space of the page was open to these add-on, sometimes free-floating, textual events.

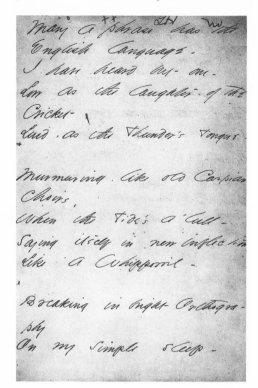

Fig. 16. Emily Dickinson, "Many a phrase has the English language"

Because she approaches this feature of her writing so freely, she is able to produce remarkable effects even when she appears to be following the manner of the received convention—as we can see in the following example ("I took my Power in my hand," J540) (fig. 17). Here the variants enter the text not as a simple set of alternate readings, but, instead, as a last unrhymed shard of verse—as it were, the poem's final collapsing gloss on itself.

Equally remarkable are the numerous poems in which textual invasions appear in the work's metrical units and spatial lineations. Dickinson will so imbed her "variant readings" as to derange the conventional expectations of text presentation. Here is a typical instance ("What I see not—I better see," J939) (fig. 18). Part of this text's poetical effect comes from the reading contradictions it has generated. The placement of the variants along the lines of the text forces the reader to make a series of recursive shifts in the course of reading. We keep turning back to reread

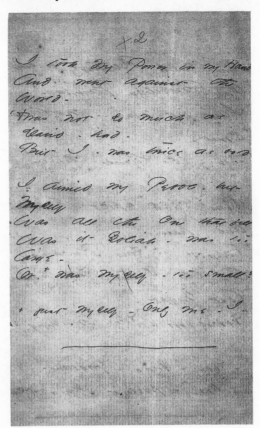

Fig. 17. Emily Dickinson, "I took my Power in my hand"

and reconsider the textual options—to "better see" what the print conventions of poetry work to keep us from seeing.

Hidden in this text is a relatively conventional three-quatrain lyric with three simple variant readings (the words *when* [1.2], *often* [1.8], and *upon* [1.11]). That is the work Johnson reconstructed and called poem 939. J939 is one face, as it were, of Dickinson's textual work. In the original scripted text it is a face turned slightly away because Dickinson's work has other faces she wishes to turn to meet the faces that she meets. We encounter those other faces because Dickinson has played a game with the layout of her scripts. The game is simple: generate certain expectations and then short-circuit them. A poem like this seems so remarkable because so little has been done to produce such complex effects. Its power comes from its elegance and simplicity.

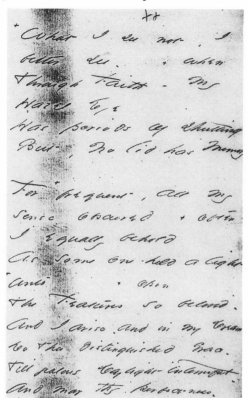

Fig. 18. Emily Dickinson,
"What I see not—I better see"

One moral of this story is that Dickinson's entire corpus needs to be closely reexamined at its primary material level. I close with two brief examples of some of the key issues involved.

The first example is J319, a poem Dickinson sent in her famous letter of April 15, 1862 to Higginson (fig. 19). He published the poem in his essay on Dickinson in the October 1891 *Atlantic Monthly* and again in the 1891 "Second Series" of Dickinson's *Poems*. None of these texts print the poem Dickinson wrote out for Higginson in her letter. Besides, Dickinson constructed another text of this work—the opening poem of fascicle 14 ("The maddest dream," J319) (fig. 20). When Johnson came to edit the poems in 1955 this entire scene of transcription and publication was normalized. The fact is that Dickinson, like William Blake, regularly reimagined and reconstructed her texts, not least when she would make variant and particular copies of her poems for different correspondents and occasions.

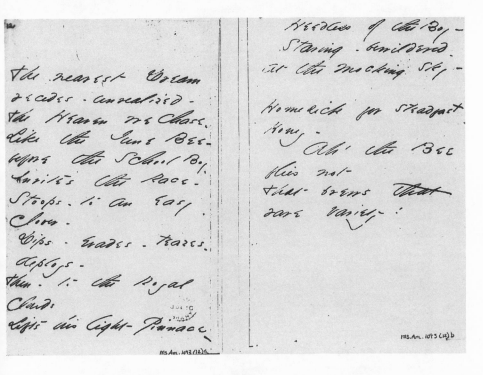

Fig. 19. Emily Dickinson, letter to T. W. Higginson. (By courtesy of the Trustees of the Boston Public Library.)

These variations underscore my earlier point—that we must trace the structure of Dickinson's writing forms to her epistolary habits and conventions. The letter form is absolutely central to Dickinson's poetry, since it is the letter form that encouraged her to seek an imaginative communion between the forms of prose and poetry. Poetical texts flow directly into (and out of) the epistolary texts. Through the interplay of this new kind of textuality Dickinson brought a new birth of freedom to writing.

We find these generically anomalous texts throughout Dickinson's letters—for example, in the letter to Samuel Bowles that contains the poem J691 ("Would you like Summer"; the letter is no. 229 in Johnson's edition) (fig. 21). In this case the poem slips into the prose without any marginal signals that the textual rhythms are about to undergo a drastic shift. This is not a poem sent with a letter or even *in* a letter; it is a poem that has grown up in a field of prose, like tares among the wheat.

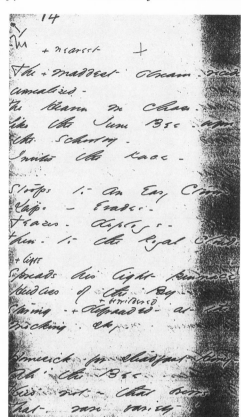

Fig. 20. Emily Dickinson, "The Maddest Dream"

Johnson's editions of both letters and poems go astray—misrepresent Dickinson's writing—because they approach her work as if it aspired to a typographical existence. On the contrary, Dickinson's scripts cannot be read as if they were "printer's copy" manuscripts or as if they were composed with an eye toward some state beyond their handcrafted textual condition. Her surviving manuscript texts take themselves at face value and urge us to treat all her scriptural forms as potentially significant *at the aesthetic or expressive level*. Calligraphic variations have to be carefully scrutinized, the same way we scrutinize all poetry for lexical nuances at the linguistic level. Some of her scripts are highly ornamental, some are not, and we must attend to these variant features of the texts. In the same way we have to read closely the lineation patterns and the spacing of the scripts at every level as well as the choice of papers and other writing materials. In a poetry that has imagined and executed itself

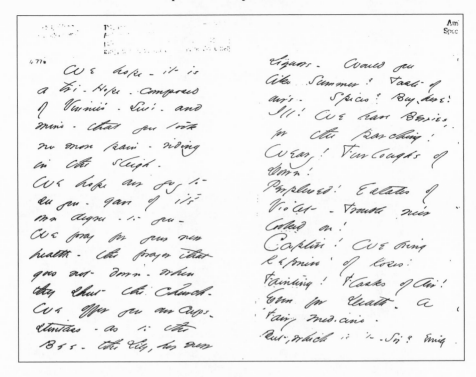

Fig. 21. Emily Dickinson, letter to Samuel Bowles

as a scriptural rather than a typographical event, all these matters fall under the work's initial horizon of finality. Emily Dickinson's poetry was not written *for* a print medium, even though it was written *in* an age of print. When we come to edit her work for bookish presentation, therefore, we must accommodate our typographical conventions to her work, not the other way round.

I conclude this brief survey of the bibliographical features of Modernist texts with a comment or two on the reception of this tradition among certain contemporary experimentalist writers.

As with the reception history of Blake, the printing history of Dickinson's writing testifies to the historically advanced character of her work. Only now are we beginning to develop adequate scholarly tools for representing what she wrote. Like the work of William Morris, her technical innovations constitute an antithetical response to her world's commercial traffic in poetry.

There is more at stake here than a mere technical inheritance. Much of our best recent poetry gains its strength by having disconnected itself from highly capitalized modes of production (by which I mean large university presses and trade publishers). Poets who work in those venues are far more alienated from their work—for instance, from its material features and its audience distribution—than are writers (for instance) who appear through contemporary small presses such as Roof, Burning Deck, The Figures, or Jargon. These are organizations founded, like Kelmscott Press, by writers themselves, so that the work is necessarily imagined as part of a social event of people intimately involved in day-to-day production. Along with such small presses contemporary writers have also founded and operated distributing mechanisms such as the Segue Foundation in New York or Small Press Distribution, Inc., in Berkeley. Writing carried out in these contexts comes into a fairly immediate confrontation with its material, its economic and social relations. In such immediacies they acquire a freedom that more conventional writers—"Fireside" writers—can never have.

"When composition begins, inspiration is already on the decline." Shelley is a great poet, and that is a great and important idea. It is not the whole truth about poetry, however, and it should always be read, like all great ideas, both for and against itself. It may indeed be the case that "inspiration" wanes before the material opportunities of writing, but the imagination need not grieve at "what remains behind" the departure of Shelleyan inspiration. On the other side is the opening of other fields, including the more physicalized inspiration—the poetry of human breath—that Whitman created from the ashes of transcendentalism. On the other side is William Morris, who understood that "you can't have art without resistance in the material." It is this artisanal thought of Morris, not Shelley's Neoplatonic thought, that would preside over imaginative writing in the twentieth century.

NOTES

This chapter is revised from "Composition as Explanation (of Modern and Postmodern Poetries)," in Jerome J. McGann, *Black Riders* (Princeton: Princeton University Press, 1993), copyright © by Princeton University Press. By permission of Princeton University Press.

1. First printed in 1906 in the *Contemporary Review;* here quoted from *Plays and Controversies* (London, 1923), 170.

2. See Basil Bunting, *Collected Poems,* 2d ed. (Oxford: Oxford University Press, 1978), 110.

3. See Humphrey Carpenter, *A Serious Character: The Life of Ezra Pound* (London: Faber and Faber, 1988), 52 (hereafter cited in the text).

4. See H. D.'s *End to Torment,* ed. Norman Holmes Pearson and Michael King (New York: New Directions, 1979), in which the text of the book is reprinted. It is interesting to note in passing that Yeats too was led by his Pre-Raphaelite inheritance to the production of a similar handmade book early in his career, one he made for Maude Gonne.

5. For an excellent discussion of Morris and his projects in decorative printing, see Norman Kelvin, "Patterns in Time: The Decorative and the Narrative in the Work of William Morris," in *Nineteenth-Century Lives: Essays Presented to Jerome Hamilton Buckley,* ed. Laurence Lockridge, John Maynard, and Donald Stone (Cambridge: Cambridge University Press, 1989), 140–68. See also Henry Halliday Sparling's classic work *The Kelmscott Press and William Morris Master-Craftsman* (London: Macmillan, 1924). Pound's initial serious involvement with Morris and his ideas continued during the time he worked with A. R. Orage and *The New Age,* for whom Morris was a central intellectual resource. See Tim Redman, *Ezra Pound and Fascism* (Cambridge and New York: Cambridge University Press, 1990), chap. 1, esp. pp. 21–22.

6. *An "Objectivists" Anthology* (Le Beaussett, Var, France, and New York: TO Publishers, 1932), 20.

7. Cunard bought this font when she purchased William Bird's printing equipment, in order to set up her new press.

8. The famous slogan The Revolution of the Word was applied to the program set forth in Eugene Jolas's important magazine *transition.* Brown's treatise *The Readies* made its first appearance—in an abbreviated version—in the June 1930 issue (hereafter cited in the text).

9. Dick Higgins might call Brown's texts "pattern poems"; see his two excellent studies, *George Herbert's Pattern Poems: In Their Tradition* (West Glover, VT, and New York: Unpublished Editions, 1977) and *Pattern Poetry: Guide to an Unknown Literature* (Albany: SUNY Press, 1987). But Higgins's pattern poems carry a strong element of Pythagoreanism and at least an abstract "musicality," which is entirely absent from Brown's texts.

10. *Readies for Bob Brown's Machine* (1931), 162.

11. *Readies,* 164.

12. For useful information about the publishing firm see Joe W. Kraus, *Messrs. Copeland and Day* (Philadelphia: George S. MacManus Co., 1979) and Stephen Maxfield Parrish, *Currents of the Nineties in Boston and London* (New York: Garland Publishing Inc., 1987), chap. 3. A curious but startling fact is that Crane was inspired to write his innovative free verse poems after hearing William Dean Howells give a reading from Emily Dickinson's recently published poetry. See Parrish, *Currents,* 268.

13. A few of the poems run beyond a single page. In no case, however, does a page print any part of another poem.

14. Throughout this discussion I shall be using R. W. Franklin's epochal *The Manuscript Books of Emily Dickinson* (Cambridge, Mass.: Harvard University Press, Belknap Press, 1981), which reconstructs the original fascicles (in facsimile); and Thomas H. Johnson's standard work *The Poems of Emily Dickinson*

(Cambridge, Mass.: Harvard University Press, Belknap Press, 1955). The poems will be referenced by their numbers in Johnson (hereafter cited in the text).

15. In my commentaries here I follow the lead of Susan Howe, who has done more to advance our understanding of Dickinson's texts than anyone else. See her essay "These Flames and Generosities of the Heart: Emily Dickinson and the Illogic of Sumptuary Values," *Sulfur* 28 (Spring 1991): 134–55. The important work of two of Howe's students, Marta Werner and Jeanne Holland (see her essay "Scraps, Stamps, and Cutouts," in this volume), should also be noted.

• 16. See especially Howe's "These Flames and Generosities," 134–55.

17. Susan Howe says that "around fascicles #6–12 . . . [Dickinson] begins to break her lines a new way" ("These Flames and Generosities," 152n.). It is possible to be more precise. In fact, the first experimental moment comes in fascicle 1, poem 31 ("Summer for thee, grant I may be"). Normatively a poem of two quatrains, Dickinson makes the second quatrain five lines and sets the crucial word *Anemone* on a line by itself, in the penultimate position. Fascicle 3 has one irregular text (in the second stanza of poem 11 ["I never told the buried gold"]). The next irregular text comes in fascicle 4, poem 136 ("Have you got a Brook in your / little heart"): this poem is the first to make its scriptural irregularities a regular feature of the entire work, rather than an isolated scriptural moment. Fascicle 5 has two irregular texts, poems 111 ("The Bee is not afraid of me") and 70 ("'Arcturus' is his other name"). Fascicle 6 has one, poem 132 ("I bring an unaccustomed wine"). In fascicle 7 there are two irregular texts, poems 148 ("All overgrown by cunning moss") and 61 ("Papa above"). In fascicle 8 we find three irregular texts, poems 174 ("At last to be identified"), 177 ("Ah! Necromancy Sweet!"), and 179 ("If I could bribe them by a rose"). In fascicle 9 these testing moves toward a practice of regular irregularity overwhelm the entirety of the writing.

18. The first text is taken from Franklin, *Manuscript Book*, 10. The second is letter 265 in Johnson's edition of *The Letters of Emily Dickinson* (Cambridge, Mass.: Harvard University Press, 1958) (hereafter cited in the text). The manuscript of the letter is reproduced from the original in the Boston Public Library.

19. Quoted from *The Recognition of Emily Dickinson,* ed. Caesar R. Blake and Carlton F. Wells (Ann Arbor: University of Michigan Press, 1968), 10 (hereafter cited in the text).

20. See Millicent Todd Bingham, *Ancestors' Brocades: The Literary Debut of Emily Dickinson* (New York: Harper and Brothers, 1945), 34.

21. This example was first brought to my attention by Susan Howe, in a lecture she delivered at the University of Virginia in 1991 on the texts of Dickinson.

Scraps, Stamps, and Cutouts: Emily Dickinson's Domestic Technologies of Publication

for Susan Howe

Jeanne Holland

Connections between unconnected things are the unreal reality of Poetry.
—Susan Howe, *My Emily Dickinson* (1985)

The tie between us is very fine, but a Hair never dissolves.
—Emily Dickinson, letter to Susan Gilbert Dickinson (1885)

Emily Dickinson had ample opportunity to market her poetry yet chose not to do so. In a detailed survey, Joanne Dobson examines the pleas of several Dickinson contemporaries and literary figures who repeatedly urged the poet to print.[1] To one of her most insistent admirers, the poet Helen Hunt Jackson, Dickinson is purported to have replied, "How can you . . . [p]rint a piece of your soul!"[2] Dobson concludes, "Contrary to prevalent opinion that Dickinson was discouraged by her friends from publishing, this continued solicitation . . . reveals that her non–publication was due to her own persistent refusal to publish."[3] Yet Dickinson *did* publish, after her fashion, by making fair copies into packets and distributing her poems to a select readership.

 Print is often the specific word that Dickinson mentions in describing her refusals. Martha Nell Smith elucidates that Dickinson, as well as her sister-in-law Susan Gilbert Dickinson, made careful distinctions between *publish* and *print* when the discussion concerned Emily Dickinson's poetry.[4] "Surrounded by lawyers (Dickinson's father and brother)," Smith notes, "these women are somewhat legalistic in their differentiations, using *publish* in the special sense 'to tell or noise abroad' (*OED*)."[5] Yet, as Dickinson readers, what should we make of the fact that Emily Dickinson chose never to print? Quite simply, if Dickinson did not intend to print, then the printing of her poetry misrepresents it. We should return to the manuscripts, or the nearest facsimiles thereof, to begin to appreciate the poetry that Emily Dickinson actually produced.[6]

This re-vision in Dickinson studies has been impelled by the landmark publication in 1981 of *The Manuscript Books of Emily Dickinson,* photographic reproductions of the poet's forty fascicles and fifteen sets as she organized them; the collection is edited by Ralph Franklin. Since then Dickinson scholarship has profited by a sharper focus on the poet's fascicles, the individually bound packets of her poems she sewed together beginning 1858–59 and ceasing about 1863–64.[7] After she stopped the book sewing process, Dickinson, until the late 1870s, continued writing on batches of similar sheets, a practice that suggests to later editors that these be grouped into separate sets.

But concurrently around 1870 and increasingly thereafter, Dickinson began to make fewer fair copies of her poetry in sets. Instead she wrote on odds and ends of paper and left poems in that form. Mabel Loomis Todd, who initially edited Dickinson's poems and letters for publication, called these bits "scraps." As her daughter, Millicent Todd Bingham, explains in her "Introduction" to *Bolts of Melody: New Poems of Emily Dickinson* (1945):

> Many [of Dickinson's late poems] are written on the backs of brown-paper bags or of discarded bills, programs, and invitations; on tiny scraps of stationery pinned together; on leaves torn from old notebooks (one such sheet dated "1824"); on soiled and mildewed subscription blanks, or on department- or drug-store bargain flyers from Amherst and surrounding towns. There are pink scraps, blue and yellow scraps, one of them a wrapper of *Chocolat Meunier;* poems on the reverse of recipes in her own writing, on household shopping lists, on the cut-off margins of newspapers, and on the inside of brown-paper wrappings.[8]

Interpreting this practice, Franklin remarks that Dickinson "finally gave herself up to the proliferation of shapes and sizes of her worksheets and miscellaneous manuscripts."[9] But I do not perceive resignation or carelessness in this activity. Rather I will argue that from the beginning, with her choosing to sew together her own fascicles (rather than purchasing ready-made blank notebooks); her including more and more variant readings in the fascicles; her circumscribing her readership to family, friends, and chosen outsiders; her refusal to print; and her ultimate writing on household detritus, Dickinson progressively refined her own domestic technologies of publication.[10]

Dickinson's movement from making fair copies in fascicles and then in unbound sets to inscribing her poetry on household scraps (food wrappers, torn envelopes, the backs of old letters) is a logical progression for a poet whose resistance to "going public" intensified as she grew older. Her technologies shift away from making The Book in fascicles toward materially locating her poems in the private home. It is significant that her writing on household refuse coincides with her agoraphobic withdrawal from public life.[11] Building upon Gillian Brown's brilliant *Domestic Individualism* (1989), which links domesticity and American nineteenth-century concepts of selfhood, I will begin to delineate how Dickinson's domesticity (her extreme withdrawal into the home, her refusal to print, her writing on household materials) reflects and shapes her explorations in the domain of selfhood and writing. Read in its domestic materiality, much of Dickinson's late work interrogates the relation of sexuality and textuality.

To illustrate my argument I will first analyze Dickinson's domestic practices of authorship, then examine the 1870 manuscript for Dickinson's poem 1167, "Alone and in a Circumstance—" (see figs. 1 and 2). This is a poem Dickinson chose to leave in worksheet form, even though at about this time, she had resumed her activity of fair-copying.[12] Her not making a fair copy implies that this specific manuscript was meaningful to her. I will argue that this scrap—and the dialogue it establishes between image and text—visually and textually dramatizes Dickinson's joyful play with writing's construction of the body. This scrap stages that interrogation by having child's play subvert the Law.[13] Yet we should not mistake Dickinson's play-activity and domestic creation as a complete escape from the public, commercial sphere. Rather the exchange between image and text exposes the inextricability of "private" epistolarity from the "public" literary culture of print, rehearsing Dickinson's class interests and her response to marketplace ideology.[14]

Visual/Visceral Poetry

To see the Summer Sky
Is Poetry, though never in a Book it lie—
True Poems flee—
                    —Emily Dickinson, poem 1472 (c. 1879)

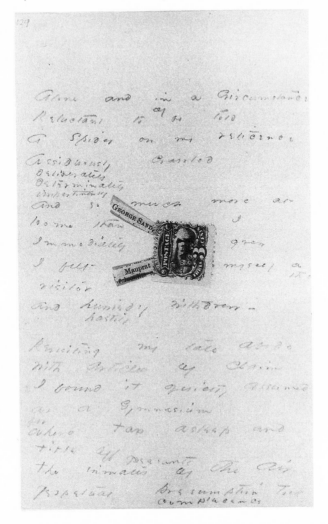

Fig. 1. Dickinson MS 129
(Amherst College Library)

In printed form, which is how the vast majority of modern readers see the text, Thomas Johnson in *The Poems of Emily Dickinson* reproduces the poem as follows:

> Alone and in a Circumstance
> Reluctant to be told
> A spider on my reticence
> Assiduously crawled

Fig. 2. Dickinson MS 129a.
(Amherst College Library.)

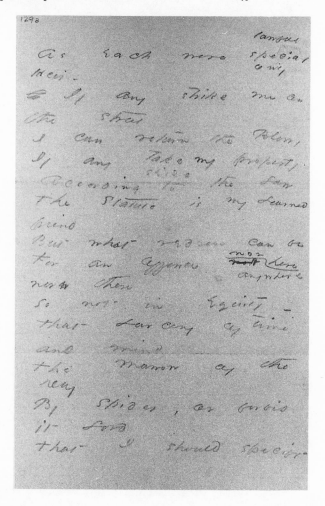

And so much more at Home than I
Immediately grew
I felt myself a visitor
And hurriedly withdrew

Revisiting my late abode
With articles of claim
I found it quietly assumed
As a Gymnasium
Where Tax asleep and Title off

The inmates of the Air
Perpetual presumption took
As each were special Heir—
If any strike me on the street
I can return the Blow—
If any take my property
According to the Law
The Statute is my Learned friend
But what redress can be
For an offense nor here nor there
So not in Equity—
That Larceny of time and mind
The marrow of the Day
By spider, or forbid it Lord
That I should specify.[15]

1. in] of	12. As] for
4. Assiduously] deliberately/	14. inmates] Peasants
determinately/ impertinently	15. presumption]complacence
7. a] the	16. special] lawful/ only
8. hurriedly] hastily	19. take] seize

Dickinson wrote the poem on the front and back of a half-sheet of standard notepaper. As Johnson notes, she affixed sideways on the face an unused three-cent stamp and two strips cut from a review of George Sand in *Harper's Magazine,* May 1870.[16] The stamp, which pictures a Baldwin locomotive, was issued in 1869 to commemorate the completion of the transcontinental railroad.[17] The review notes Roberts Brothers's new publication of Sand's novel *Mauprat* (1837) in "tasteful typography," although it later states that to those who " 'evil think' . . . it will prove a dangerous book"[18] (see fig. 3). Typical of most Victorian American reviews of Sand, this one recognizes her genius but laments her facility for rendering illicit passion.[19]

From the review, Dickinson cut out three strips: "GEORGE SAND," "it will prove a dangerous book. Mauprat" and "As to *Mauprat.*"[20] Interestingly Dickinson chose a strip where Sand's name appears in capitals—in sensationalized, not "tasteful typography"—suggesting a wry sensitivity to print's vagaries. Also although the review prints the novel's title in italics and Dickinson scissored that reference, the glued strip

Editor's Literary Record.

NOVELS.

WE are so weary of depending on England, and Scotland, and Ireland for our fiction, so hungry for some genuine American romance, that we are not inclined to read very critically the three characteristic American novels which lie on our table, and which, owing perhaps to our national prejudice rather than to their own superior excellence, we take up first. The most prominent author of "My Daughter Elinor," which last year we commended so cordially, follows his first work with a second—*Miss Van Kortland* (Harper and Brothers). On the whole, we see no signs of deterioration, and some of improvement. Comparing this new novel with its predecessor, we find it shorter, more compact, in some more original and effective, in composition more vigorous in incident and group-ing, and the excursion to the wild side, the mill, the strike and riot, and the falling Tamarack Lake and its results, and the des-ively told. "My Daughter Elinor" dragged a little; but with its splendid discomfort, the same pure spirit and the same Christian but unconventional tone pervades it. There is no female character to equal Elinor; but, on the other hand, Frescott is a much finer conception than Clive. The book is in its structure, its incident, genuinely, and freshly American. It is drawn from our life, not copied from for-eign sources. The most serious fault lies in the introduction of three or four absurdly unnatural characters, which are unnecessary to set off the story, and which only act as blemishes upon it—a fault which was venial in the first book, but has grown in its proportions to a serious offense in the second.—*Hedged In* (Fields, Osgood, and Co.), possesses by Miss Phelps's first novel—"Gates Ajar" was more a romance than a phi-losophy—is peculiar power, yet fails, on the whole, for short of it. It is not, like that, evolved out of the authoress's own experience, and lacks this intense vividness in the autobiography always invests the seeming novel. In "Hedged In" Miss Phelps has been compelled to depict experiences which by sympathetic imagination she must first make her own. It is the poet's privilege to so idealize his human expe-rience, which constitutes the secret of all true ro-mantic writing, Miss Phelps but partially pos-sesses. There is no indication that she has ever seen Thicket Street—or more than heard passin-g—or much that she has had any personal ex-perience with it. Still her style does not quite uncomfortably fragmentary, sententious, almost jerky; in treatment there is more effort to be new and fresh than to be true to life and nature. And when finally the curtain falls, in the midst of scenes, the rolling thunder, the climax that transformed by Eunice Trent, kneeling in her white dress at the foot of the great wooden cross, thus the authoress has quite crossed the verge which she has more than once approached, and has done herself and her theme a positive injustice by borrowing from the stage so thea-

---

trical a device.—*Askaros Kassis* (J. B. Lippin-cott and Co.) is an American novel only in that sense that Mr. Heilprin is an American, for it was written, we believe, United States Consul in Egypt. The scene is laid in the land of romance, and his book is scarcely less a study of Egyptian life than a novel; when a picture of that life in its guise of a novel. The field is new, in it Mr. De Leon is absolutely without a rival. He could hardly fail, with the material it affords him, to write a thoroughly fresh book; and certainly the coldest novel reader, to whom all the ordinary incidents of the conventional romance are more than "twice told tales," can not complain of "Askaros Kassis" that there is nothing new in it. The hero is an English-educated Egyptian; the heroine an American girl traveling in the Oriental Orient. The serpent is introduced, the Viceroy at home, the Khamseen wind of the des-ert, the harem with its splendid discomfort, the dogs of Cairo, the hippopotamus, the wild dance with its sensual passions, the abductions and assassinations, such as but in Egyptian life are only too true to nature, all are called in to aid in the portraiture of Egyptian life and the creation of dramatic inci-dents. Even written from fancy, such a book might vouch for the truthfulness of Mr. De Leon's pic-ture; but we judge that the reader, with very small allowance for the privilege of the romancer, will get a better conception of Egyptian life from these pages than from the innumerable books of travels for which a six weeks' sojourn is generally considered adequate preparation.

Madame George Sand, whose works Roberts Brothers are about introducing to the American public in tasteful typography, and, if we may judge from the first volume, in admirable trans-lation, has lived a romance as well as written it. By crooked paths, such as great families rarely travel outside of France, she traces her lineage back through misalliances of nobles and shop-girls to Marshal Saxe and the famous Au-rora de Königsmark. A wife at eighteen, a mo-ther at nineteen, separated from her husband at twenty-one, and begun her literary life in the back studio of the individual author of the nov-el and the melodrama, she is, in the sick-room scene between Esther and St. John, lack strength in male attire, partly for economy's sake, partly for freedom, and partly for safety, living on five francs a week, and finding it hard work to earn them. Now the critics did not accept this life, and for a year or two she had a hard fight, not for fame only, but for life. Her mother-in-law had, or fancied she had, some shadowy connection with noble families—her husband was a colonel in the army—and fearing this publicity would pollute the family name. So Madame Dudevant gave up even her husband's name—about all he had ever given her—and to the public became George Sand, the title by which the world now recognizes her ever since. About the same time that she wrote a novel in distinct; the marginal notes render it materially the court of the critics, she won a judgment in the

---

Mr. Froude has chosen for his theme what is perhaps the most critical period in the history of England. He begins with describing England in its condition in the early part of the sixteenth cen-tury. He closes it with the destruction of the Spanish Armada in 1588. The half century which intervenes is, perhaps, the most important in English history. It is that era which dates from Roman Catholic to Protestant England. It embraces the destruction of the monasteries and the emancipation of the Church of State from Papal rule under Henry VIII., the prog-ress of the Reformation under Edward VI., the brief restoration of Papal authority with its lit-ter rites under bloody Mary, and the long and exciting contest between Catholic and Protest-ant, between the cold, cautious, but unscrupu-lous Queen Bess and the "grand, but hateful, malignant and untamable" Queen of Scots, end-ing in the well-deserved and yet ever-regret-ted death of the charming adulteress and assas-sin, and the final, complete, and irretrievable overthrow of Papal power, not in England only, but in Europe as well, by the utter destruction with which God overwhelmed the Spanish fleet which ventured to avenge her. It is an era of history which, in these days, when in new forms had under new forms the old battle is like to be waged again, every Protestant has need to read, and study with care. For the Jesuitical spirit which canonized the assassin of William of Orange, and Elisabeth of England, is not far as sharp, though concealed beneath velvet. We do not hesitate to award Mr. Froude a first rank among the writers of history. He is cer-tainly surpassed by none; we doubt whether, in the rare combination of his qualities as a writ-er, he is equaled by any. As a painter, "I have worked, in it," says he, in a communication to the *Pall Mall Gazette*, "through nine hundred volumes of letters, notes, and other papers, vate and official, in five languages and in differ-from ancient archives some new material, and thrown light on much more than is now wholly new. It is a rare mind which would not be lost amidst such a mass of matter, in which careless gossip, maintaining report, unblushingly detailed falsehoods, literary frauds and forgeries, con-tradicted by other forgeries as fraudulent, are intermingled in apparently inextricable chaos. But Mr. Froude possesses in a peculiar meas-ure the legal mind. He intuitively seems to weigh evidence, to balance contradictory possi-bilities, to cross-examine the testimony of the dead past. We do not always agree with his conclusions. We think he awards too much credit to the court which condemned and slew Bobert, and too little to the verdict of later history, which has all but unanimously set the judgment of condemnation aside. We think he gives Elizabeth credit for greater sincerity than she possessed, and makes scarcely sufficient al-lowance for Scottish Mary's early education in the adulterous court and Jesuitical councils of France. But we can always commend his pa-tient research and his no less patient and impar-tial analysis of conflicting evidence.

HISTORY.

Mr. Froude brings his *History of England* (Charles Scribner and Co.) to a close with the twelfth volume, "Library Edition." Between this and the cheaper "Popular Edition" there is really but little to choose. In truth the more costly has the heavier and thicker and more convenient in size; the type is equally clear and more convenient for reference, and if it is not quite so handsome, it is quite handsome enough.

Fig. 3. "Editor's Literary Record," review of George Sand, *Mauprat*. *Harper's New Monthly Magazine* 40 (May 1870): [925]–26.

"Mauprat" indicates that Dickinson used a reference to the Heathcliffian protagonist's name, not the title.

Visually the manuscript of poem 1167 bears some resemblance to an addressed envelope and letter. The stamp and its two "legs" are an integral part of the text. Johnson remarks that these items must have been affixed first and the poem written later since the text accommodates its lines to their presence.[21] What are the connections between image and poem? To interpret the visual aspects of the holograph, we should examine how this particular stamp's iconography, the cutouts from the review, and Dickinson's practice of scissoring texts all figure in her poetics so that we may understand not merely what this poem says, but also how this specific production means.

That the stamp pictures a locomotive suggests that it is a synechdoche for the poet's father; a locomotive was named in his honor in 1862.[22] Bringing the railroad to Amherst was one of the consuming passions of Edward Dickinson's life.[23] In 1848, his efforts resulted in his being chosen to head the board of directors of the Amherst and Belchertown Railroad Corporation. As construction proceeded, he wrote to his son Austin in 1852, crowing: "The two great eras in the history of Amherst, are 1. The founding of the College [which Samuel Fowler Dickinson, Edward's father, had bankrupted his family to do]. and 2. The building of the rail road. We here 'set up our Ebenezer.' HaHa!!!" In 1853, the train arrived from Palmer to a nineteen-gun salute. Throughout the years, Dickinson continued to labor enthusiastically to expand Amherst's railroad facilities. Indeed, when he died in Boston on June 16, 1874, he had just addressed the legislature on the issue of a railroad tunnel.

Emily Dickinson's choice of a locomotive stamp thus resonates with patriarchal significance. To view the locomotive correctly, we have to turn the paper sideways. Yet that perspective makes the poem look skewed. Seen sideways, "Mauprat," the male protagonist's name is easily legible, as is the carefully crossed-out word "bandits" underneath. But from this angle, "GEORGE SAND" is more difficult to read. When we rotate the paper, privileging the father's perspective, the daughter's texts—poetry and "GEORGE SAND"—are thrown out of kilter, and vice versa. This visual pun recalls Dickinson's letter to her brother that "we do not have much poetry, father having made up his mind that its pretty much all *real life*. Fathers real life and *mine* sometimes come into collision, but as yet, escape unhurt!" (Letter 65). Locomotive and poetry collide, but neither is damaged here.

But the oppositions between locomotive/poetry, father/daughter, male/female are put into question by the cutout figure. Dickinson makes the locomotive the center of the image she constructs with cutouts. This suggests that she intuits the presence of the Father, a patriarchal power, at the heart of her work. Such an observation is further borne out by the poem's play with legal language (Circumstance, Articles, Claim, Tax, Title, Heir, Law, Statute, Equity, Larceny). The poem, as we will see, suggests that the constructed figure represents Dickinson's body. Consequently she embodies the locomotive's drive, possessing a phallus (quite literally, between the "legs" of the cutouts). Yet, since the cutouts lead/ read into the locomotive, its power appears to derive from a female literary genius (GEORGE SAND) and a male character (Mauprat) whom the genius created. The legs give the body locomotion, another visual pun that undermines the primacy of the locomotive/phallus.

What does GEORGE SAND signify to Dickinson? Sand is mentioned in an 1861 letter that the poet sent to her cousins Louise and Francis Norcross. Respecting Dickinson's privacy after she died, the Norcross cousins transcribed selections from several letters; they never allowed editors to see the originals that were destroyed after Louise's death.[24] As Johnson explains, this excerpt must have been written after June 29, 1861, the death of Elizabeth Barrett Browning.[25] Dickinson confides to Loo and Fanny:

> Your letters are all real, just the tangled road children walked before you, some of them to the end, and others but a little way, even as far as the fork in the road. That Mrs. Browning fainted, we need not read *Aurora Leigh* to know, when she lived with her English aunt; and George Sand 'must make no noise in her grandmother's bedroom.' Poor children! Women, now, queens, now! And one in the Eden of God. (Letter 234)

From Sand's *Story of My Life* (1854–55), Dickinson remembers how the tomboyish Aurore Dupin was restricted as a girl. Echoes of this scene reverberate in Dickinson's poem written about 1862:

> They shut me up in Prose—
> As when a little Girl
> They put me in the Closet—
> Because they liked me "still"—
>
> (*MB* 1:464)

Although it tells the story of an imprisoned child, the poem celebrates the Girl's freewheeling "Brain," which, like a bird, can look down upon "Captivity—/ And laugh—no more have I." In one sense, George Sand recalls for Dickinson a determined girl who overcame the restrictions on her child's play, or creativity, to become a literary genius, one whom the poet calls "woman" and "queen."

The dark, unconventional George Sand is the subject of a detailed November 1861 *Atlantic Monthly* essay by Julia Ward Howe, which Dickinson would have read.[26] One person in Dickinson's circle combines notable features of the mature George Sand—dark handsomeness, women's writing, queenly status. That person is her sister-in-law Susan Huntingdon Gilbert Dickinson, whom, as both Martha Nell Smith and Ellen Louise Hart convincingly demonstrate, Dickinson loved and desired her entire life.[27] Susan received more poems and letters from Dickinson than any other correspondent, more than 450 texts.[28] Although Dickinson nearly always made fair copies, when she sent her poetry to Susan, she often gave her penciled versions, poems obviously still in process. "The contrasts between the correspondences to others and the correspondence to Sue begins with this fact," Smith notes.[29] The 1861 exchange of letters over various versions of "Safe in their Alabaster Chambers" reveals that Dickinson involved Susan in her composition processes, revising to please her (Letter 238, 2:379–80). The dialogue also demonstrates the lengths to which Susan went to read Dickinson's work: she critiqued the first draft in "summer 1861," quite near the time she delivered her first child, Ned, on June 19, 1861.

In "George Sand," Julia Ward Howe frames her essay by associating Sand with Cleopatra, the dark, seductive queen who loomed large in the iconography of Dickinson's erotic life.[30] Reading repeated allusions in the letters, Judith Farr maintains that Dickinson self-consciously played Antony to Sue's Cleopatra.[31] "Egypt, thou knew'st" one cryptic note from Dickinson states (Letter 553), casting Susan as alluring Cleopatra and Emily as Antony, helplessly in love with her.

When Julia Ward Howe describes the pleasures of reading George Sand, other Susan Dickinson–George Sand physicality/textuality convergences are suggested:

We knew our parents wouldn't have us read her, *if they knew*. We knew they were right. Yet we read her at stolen hours, with waning and still entreated light; and as we read, in a dreary wintry room, with the flickering candle warning us of late hours and confiding expectations, the atmosphere grew warm and glorious about us,—a true human company with her, a living sympathy crept near us,—and the very world seemed not the same world after as before.[32]

This visceral description—being warmed by reading—parallels Susan's response to a second version she was sent of Dickinson's "Safe in their Alabaster Chambers." Susan's response, which begins, "I am not suited dear Emily with the second verse," indicates how closely she critiqued Dickinson's poetry. Remembering the first draft, Susan observes of its power, "I always go to the fire and get warm after thinking of it but I never *can* again."[33] Answering sometime after summer 1861, Susan may be unconsciously repeating what she had recently read about George Sand. Her "icy" response to reading Dickinson, inverting Howe's "warm" response to reading Sand, surfaces again when Dickinson explains to Higginson what she experiences when reading poetry: "If I read a book [and] it makes my whole body so cold no fire ever can warm me I know *that* is poetry. If I feel physically as if the top of my head were taken off, I know *that* is poetry. These are the only way I know it. Is there any other way."[34]

Hart, Smith, and Farr all importantly resituate Susan where she belongs—at the center of Dickinson's literary and emotional life. "GEORGE SAND," then, would seem to be an overdetermined sign that recalls the Frenchwoman literary genius, alludes to Susan Dickinson who was herself a writer and Cleopatra-figure, and refers to Dickinson, who knew herself as a misunderstood woman artist, as Sand is portrayed in the *Atlantic* essay.

Closer to the poet's heart and mind than any other person, Susan understood Dickinson's resistance to printing. As Farr recounts, after Austin's mistress, Mabel Loomis Todd, edited the first volume of Dickinson's poems with T. W. Higginson, Susan in 1890 wrote to Higginson, "'The Poems' will ever be to me marvellous whether in manuscript or type." Farr astutely notes, "To have written them, she meant, was enough. Dickinson's poems themselves make such a point repeatedly."[35] Susan's comment illuminates why she did not hurry Dickinson's poems into print. Keeping the poems "alive"—dynamic through intimate reading and oral performance—Susan read them repeatedly to herself and aloud to friends.[36] Only after Todd and the other Dickinsons began to publish the poems did Susan, in competition, try to stake her own legitimate claim to an intimacy with Dickinson's poetic genius.[37] Thus Susan was truer to Dickinson's wishes than were other well-intentioned family members—an understanding that further troubles our relation to the printed poetry and to the very question of reading Emily Dickinson.

A strategy Dickinson uses to keep her verse "alive," a concern voiced in her first letter to Higginson (Letter 260), is her scissoring of other texts, which she practices increasingly after 1870. In 1876, she cuts out an engraving in the August *Scribner's* from Helen Hunt Jackson's article "Hide-and-Seek Town" to enclose in a poem to her friend, Elizabeth Holland.[38] In late 1878, she scissors from the December *Scribner's* a reference to Henry James's *The Europeans,* presumably to remind herself to order it.[39] The Dickinson Collection at Harvard reveals that she cut up her own Bible, her *New England Primer,* and her father's Dickens.[40] Contrasting Dickinson's cutouts with the mutilations posthumously made of her writings, Martha Nell Smith makes an important point:

> That she did not regard works as untouchably sacred is obvious from her own role as reader, for Dickinson sometimes went so far as to cut up others' works to take an illustration or group of words to append to her own. Unlike the mutilations to her poems and letters, this is not an angry or hostile act to excise offensive expressions, but a sign of a reader at play or engaged in dialogic drama, combining hers with others' literary productions, remaking both in the process.[41]

As reader and writer at play/work, Dickinson drew upon a pool of such textual clippings. Johnson explains, when he notes that an 1856 clipping accompanied an 1871 poem, "The disparity in the date of the clipping and the poem leads one to conjecture that she kept a scrapbook or a file of items which to her were meaningful."[42] Thus not only did Dickinson work from a pool of manuscripts, making fair copies of poems over the years,[43] she also valued her collection of cutouts as a part of her poetic production. We should examine the significance of the scrap—visual and textual—as well as the art of scrap-writing in Dickinson's late works.

Pierre Glendenning and Emily Dickinson: Private Publishers

> For even at that early time in his authorial life, Pierre, however vain of his fame, was not at all proud of his paper.
> —Herman Melville, *Pierre* (1852)

To understand the dialogue between Dickinson's domestically produced text and image, we must consider her idiosyncratic habits of authorship. Her domestic technologies of publication result from her "agoraphobia," in the sense that Gillian Brown contextualizes that condition. Brown points out that in the wildly fluctuating economy of nineteenth-century America and the corresponding ideological construction of a stable, private domestic sphere, agoraphobia's symptoms figure "fear of the marketplace":

> The recourse of the agoraphobic, when outside the house, to the protection of interiors or companions or shielding edifices represents an effort to retain the stability and security of the private sphere. . . . By maintaining the integrity of the private sphere, this opposition sustains the notion of a personal life impervious to market influences, the model of selfhood in a commercial society.[44]

Although Brown does not make this comparison, her compelling discussion of a fictional author-figure who behaves as if "his personal life" were "impervious to market influences," whose actions uncannily predict Emily Dickinson's, illuminates Dickinson's practice. In *Pierre* (1852), Melville's Pierre Glendenning, the young beardless poet, refuses to have his daguerreotype made, believing that "when every body has his portrait published, true distinction lies in not having yours published at all."[45] Furthermore, we are told that Pierre

> was very careless about his discarded manuscripts; they were to be found lying all round the house; gave a great deal of trouble to the housemaids in sweeping; went for kindlings to the fires; and were forever flitting out of the windows, and under the door-sills. In this reckless, indifferent way of his, Pierre himself was a sort of a publisher.[46]

Pierre's scattered scraps reveal his disdain for the apparatus of publication as well as his wish to be intimately related to his writing. Brown observes, "So committed is Pierre to an organic relation between himself and his literary work that he needs no copyrights, no public record of himself or his authorship other than the work itself. Indeed he and his productions constitute an ecological system: he smokes cigars bought from his magazine publication earnings, lit by pages of his work. . . ."[47]

When asked by young women to autograph their keepsake books, Pierre kisses the paper and sends candy instead. As Brown explains,

> Just as he would transform autographs into kisses and confections, literary signs into bodily gestures and pleasures, Pierre would translate literary production, both the work's materiality and its monetary value, into another oral pleasure, realizing the sentimental model of literary production as affective and nurturing.[48]

Pierre's tightly controlled cycle of literary and personal production, in its resistance to the wage-driven, public literary market, replicates domestic values:

> So Pierre wants what the sentimental family and sentimental literature strive to achieve: a perfect domestic circle . . . in which industry and individuality are independent from the marketplace; an intimacy between self and labor, writer and book, which assures the integrity of the individual. The representative form of this alternative formation of individuality is autobiography or, more precisely, a reconception of literature as fundamentally autobiographical—primarily self-expressive and self-determined.[49]

As we will see, Dickinson reproduces some of Pierre's attitudes, but as a woman, she bears a much different relation to the sentimental model of literary production. In her scrap-writing, she resembles Pierre, "a sort of a publisher"; pressured by household responsibilities, she recalls the maid who sweeps up the scraps. The ideological split between "male" literary creativity and "female" domestic labor collapses in Dickinson's experience. Because she combines ideological positions that her culture struggles to separate—indeed her late works meld literary creativity and domesticity—Dickinson's multiply gendered perspective enables her to resist the possessive individualism that drives Pierre's autobiographical impulse. At the heart of her enterprise, she swerves from Pierre's pursuit of an unproblematic "I." The scrap for "Alone and in a Circumstance—" and its thematics of violated body and failure of the Law recognize the mobility of sexuality and the impossibility of a monolithic identity.[50]

Dickinson and Domesticity: Agoraphobia and Technophobia

Preserve the backs of old letters to write upon.
—Lydia Maria Child, *The Frugal Housewife* (1832)

Like the American aristocrat Pierre, Dickinson's determination not to publish certainly reflects class privilege, her sense of being a well-to-do, insulated self defined against the mob (see *MB* 2:915, "Publication—is the Auction / Of the Mind of Man—"). Upper classes such as Dickinson's were disturbed by the impact print technology had upon nineteenth-century America. As John Kasson states:

> Furthering the development of shared class values and eroding the authority of older conceptions of fixed rank and gentility was the extraordinary transformation in the culture of print and reading in the second quarter of the nineteenth century. Economic and technological developments converged to produce what was arguably "the greatest single advance in . . . [printing] since the fifteenth century."[51]

Calling herself the "Queen of Calvary" (*MB* 1:356) and "Empress of Calvary!" (poem 1072), exulting "Mine—by the Royal Seal!" (*MB* 1:452), Dickinson occasionally alludes to herself and, as we have seen, to other women writers such as George Sand, Elizabeth Barrett Browning, and Susan Gilbert Dickinson as queenlike. Not only recognition of female literary talent, but also perhaps a sense of her elevated class status further impels her to adopt the vocabulary of "older conceptions of fixed rank and gentility."

Doubtless, the Dickinson family's wealth and class position allow the poet to withdraw into the home and write. But it should be noted that once Dickinson is within that home, she does not become the leisured household member whom Betsy Erkkila portrays.[52] Dickinson's writing is filled with references which suggest that she wrote late at night or early in the morning, when she was free from domestic responsibilities; her letters refer repeatedly to her household duties.[53] Erkkila wants to argue that "by enclosing herself in the traditionally female space of home, [Dickinson] ends by enforcing the sexual division of labor and the division of public and private spheres she seeks to resist and protest in her life and work."[54] Yet the economic aspects of Dickinson's domesticity are not that simple. As a nineteenth-century woman writer, one whose class frees her from the necessity of writing for money, Dickinson retires to the domestic to confront, and thwart as best she can, its ideological stranglehold.[55]

On some level, Erkkila seems to recognize this strategy. Near the end of her essay, she stops lambasting Dickinson long enough to observe that "[a]t a time when the traditionally productive space of the home and traditional female housework were being devalued, Dickinson also appears to have been engaged in reclaiming the home and women as producers of valuable and enduring work."[56] Dickinson's domestic technologies of publication do reflect a reaction against local industrialization. From 1800 to 1860, as factory villages developed within Amherst, local self-sufficiency in food and produce shifted to reliance on outside markets; more pertinently for Dickinson's poetry, Amherst witnessed the change from household production to workshop manufacture and entrepreneurship.[57] The old ways of home production and exchange with neighbors, which, according to Christopher Clark, represented values of self-sufficiency, household integrity, and family advancement, may have become even more acute once they were colored with nostalgia.[58] At any rate, even after mercantilism's ascension, many Connecticut Valley farmers "continued [into the 1860s] to use the household system to protect themselves from the vagaries of the marketplace."[59] Erkkila locates Dickinson's resistance to the marketplace in "the more specifically Federalist, anticommercial, and ruling class heritage of John Adams and later John Quincy Adams."[60] While these political interests may inform her withdrawal, it is equally likely that, similar to the resistance of some local farmers, Dickinson chose a "publication" method that reflected the folk economies of her hometown.

Not only did the poet draw her market-resisting economics from the town, but also from the household. Dickinson probably first learned the art of using scraps from *The Frugal Housewife* by Lydia Maria Child. Edward Dickinson presented the second edition to his wife, Emily Norcross, in 1832. *Emily Dickinson: Profile of the Poet as Cook* describes the well-thumbed copy: "From its worn pages, one gathers it was as much a household staple as the Bible."[61] *The Frugal Housewife* opens, "The true economy of housekeeping is simply the art of gathering up all the fragments, so that nothing be lost. I mean fragments of *time,* as well as *materials*."[62] Wasting neither time nor paper, Dickinson combined domestic duties with poetry-writing. As Ellen Dickinson, the wife of Dickinson's cousin Willie, reminisced in 1892:

> Emily Dickinson was a past mistress in the art of cookery and housekeeping. She made the des[s]erts for the household dinners; delicious confections and bread, and when engaged in these duties had her table and pastry board under a window that faced the lawn, whereon she ever had pencil and paper to jot down any pretty thought that came to her, and from which she evolved verses, later.[63]

Remembering Dickinson as domestic poet, Louise Norcross wrote a defense of housekeeping published in the Boston *Woman's Journal* in 1904:

> ... I know that Emily Dickinson wrote most emphatic things in the pantry, so cool and quiet, while she skimmed the milk; because I sat on the footstool behind the door, in delight, as she read them to me. The blinds were closed, but through the green slats she saw all those fascinating ups and downs going on outside she wrote about.[64]

Gary Scharnhorst, who discusses this letter, posits that Loo must have observed her cousin "during Dickinson's period of greatest productivity between 1858 and 1865."[65] While it is impossible to date which era Loo describes, the manuscript evidence leads me to place Dickinson's pantry-writing and domestic productions in the late 1860s and beyond. As she performed her household labors, she produced worksheets using scraps and later refined chosen verses when she could concentrate, alone in her room. But rather than themes of domesticity dominating her writing, Dickinson's poetry reflects her engagement with domesticity's ideology of intimacy, privacy, and self-protection.

These ideological concerns Dickinson shares with Pierre as seen not only in their private publications, but also in their mutual distrust of being photographed. Only one daguerreotype of Dickinson, taken when she was seventeen at Mt. Holyoke, survives.[66] When Higginson asked her to send a "portrait," she described herself in diminutive terms, then added: "It often alarms Father—He says Death might occur, and he has Molds of all the rest—but has no Mold of me, but I noticed the Quick wore off those things in a few days, and forestall the dishonor—" (Letter 268). As far as she was concerned, mechanical reproduction of her self was somehow "killing." Instead Dickinson prefers to "textualize" her body through poems and letters, substituting a more individualized portrait for the daguerreotype, which many believed made the sitters look "half-dead."[67]

Dickinson's refusal to be photographed, to be forced again to assume the rigid position at the daguerreotypist's orders, may be read as a parable of her resistance to print technology. Walter Ong specifies the inflexibility of print versus the more fluid nature of manuscript: "Print situates words in space more relentlessly than writing ever did. Writing moves words from the sound world to a world of visual space, but print locks words into position in this space. Control of position is everything in print."[68] As she associates reading true poetry with seeing a summer's day, feeling freezing cold, experiencing her head as removed, Dickinson's phrases illustrate her sensitivity to the reader's response—a response she wished to intensify with her visual bricolage, her selective manuscript distribution, and her personally produced texts.

This technophobia influenced her refusal to print her poetry. "I had told you I did not print—," an angry Dickinson reminded Higginson in 1866, explaining how her poem "The Snake" was pirated from her, then its third line "defeated" by the printed inserts of punctuation (Letter 316). As if to highlight the contrast between print and manuscript, Dickinson enclosed in the letter to Higginson a clipping of "The Snake" from the February 17 issue of the Springfield *Weekly Republican* and a manuscript of "A Death blow is a Life blow to Some" (*Letters,* 2:451).[69]

For Dickinson, printing, as opposed to her own writing, would destroy the "aura" of her work, to use Walter Benjamin's term. According to Benjamin,

> We know that the earliest art works originated in the service of a ritual—first the magical, then the religious kind. It is significant that the existence of the work of art with reference to its aura is never entirely separated from its ritual function. In other words, the unique value of the 'authentic' work of art has its basis in ritual, the location of its original use value.[70]

Dickinson's sacred ritual was the circuit of letter-writing, poetry-making, and reading, which, for her, constituted one activity. "A Letter is a joy of Earth—/ It is denied the Gods" (poem 1639), Dickinson wrote.

She resisted the inflexibility of print through the ritualized methods she used to exchange her poems with a select body of readers. Versions of the same poem would often be sent out to different readers on different occasions, inflecting each poem's immediate reception by each reader (e.g., poem 816, "A Death blow is a Life blow to Some" sent to Higginson was also previously sent to Susan about 1864). Her "letters to the World" blurred the distinctions between poem and intimate letter.[71]

Dickinson's "publishing" thus reinscribes a potentially impersonal and passive reader/consumer in the more domestic—personalized and confidential—terms of epistolarity.[72] Even in poems which were not sent to others, in poems that seem "autobiographical" (such as the manuscript for poem 1167), the emphasis remains on epistolarity. The whispered tone of "Alone and in a Circumstance" establishes an intimate relation to the addressee, the "I." But rather than recuperating the subject dispersed by the visual image, the poem's text only complicates the issue further.

Sexuality/Textuality: A Case of Female Fetishism

> The normal prototype of all fetishes is the penis of the man, just as the normal prototype of an organ felt to be inferior is the real little penis of the woman, the clitoris.
> —Sigmund Freud, "Fetishism" (1927)

In manuscript, when we see the poetry between the stamp-figure's splayed legs, it becomes clearer that these opening lines are perhaps the bawdiest/body-est Dickinson ever wrote:

> Alone and in a Circumstance
>   of
> Reluctant to be told
> A spider on my reticence
> Assiduously crawled
> Deliberately
> Determinately
> Impertinently

Beginning in secrecy, Dickinson's poem alludes to her going to the bathroom when she is interrupted by a spider's crawling across her bare bottom.[73] To be sure, other interpretations of the opening scene may be proposed. But the phrase "a Circumstance / Reluctant to be told," the immediate, redoubled assertion of resistance/chagrin ("on my reticence"), and the admission that the speaker flees a specific place and returns ("Revisiting my late abode") leads me to surmise that this indeed is an extremely private and embarrassing situation, rather than Dickinson's sitting at her writing desk or being involved in a more innocuous activity. Dickinson coyly substitutes "reticence" for "arse"; the genteel discourse requires the reader to fill in the omitted center, Dickinson's body.[74] Rhetorically, Dickinson's choice of "reticence" is suggestive. In her 1844 edition of Noah Webster's dictionary, one definition of "reticence" is "[i]n *rhetoric,* aposiopesis or suppression; a figure by which a person really speaks of a thing, while he makes a show as if he would say nothing on the subject."[75]

Interpretation becomes intimate revelation and violation at once and must be limited to select eyes/I's. Perhaps this is one reason why the poem was not made into a fair copy nor sent out; this "personal" scene is meant for Dickinson's eyes only. Strangely, however, the subject of the poem, the "I," is erased from its invocation; "Alone and in a Circumstance . . . A spider . . . Assiduously crawled" displaces the subject even as it is sought in autobiography. Unlike Pierre, Dickinson, in her domestic literary production, problematizes whether the writer may possess the "I" through literature-as-autobiography. The status of subject and body is at stake in her poem.

After the spider's intrusion, Dickinson bemusedly notes her response:

> And so much more at
> Home than I
> Immediately grew
> I felt myself a
>   the
> visitor
> And hurriedly withdrew—
>   hastily

So far, the poem sounds a lot like a "high-toned 'Little Miss Muffett.'"[76] As many critics have noticed, throughout her poetry Dickinson often uses the child's voice to articulate desires forbidden to nineteenth-century adult women. This poem, which begins playfully, repeating a famous scene from the nursery rhyme, adheres to that strategy.[77]

The stamp-figure sits within/among the lines that describe her fleeing. The stamp and its "legs" emblematize Dickinson's female body,
with its "omitted center." The poetry derives from and surrounds the
open space between the legs, a feminine, interior site. Visually the image
alludes to Dickinson's female body in a vulnerable situation, legs spread.
The opened legs represent the "ground zero" of the domestic sphere, the
space that lacks a phallus, suggesting the feminized (and, later in the
poem, lawless) site from which Dickinson's writing proceeds. Yet the
absence of the phallus is offset by the locomotive, situated between her
legs. The cutouts and text oscillate between portraying phallus/no phallus; the gendered status of this subject and body is ultimately undecid-
able. The locomotive is present, but the space between the legs gapes.
Yet that space is filled with poetry. Is the poetry a metaphorical phallus?
Or rather, does the complicated dialogue between image and text decon-
struct simplistic, fixed ideas such as "phallus" and "lack"?

Dickinson's polymorphously sexed body-image is constructed
through references to technology and intertextuality: by a locomotive
stamp, a printed name that refers to an admired but scandalous woman
author, and another printed name that identifies the sort of brooding
male figure that saturates so much of Dickinson's writing.[78] In terms of
technology, that the body-image is made from a locomotive and two
printed strips acknowledges Dickinson's ambivalence toward technology. Even as she resists it in other areas of her life, especially her poetry-
making, she recognizes that she cannot completely elude its power and
influence, its shaping of herself.

Intertextually speaking, the image recognizes the discursive construction of *any* body, the invasion of language, like the spider, into our
most private space. Specifically, Dickinson's cutout figure insinuates
that she understands *her* body, *her* desires through "GEORGE SAND" and
"Mauprat"—female and male signs of passion. The cutouts trace the
circulation of the letter, in print and writing, that necessarily (de)con-
structs Dickinson's subjectivity. Is this a love letter sent from Emily
Dickinson to George Sand? To Mauprat? From each or both to her? The
answer is all of the above, as the letter/signifier, powered by the locomotive (or is it the other way around?) circulates endlessly among the three,
transforming each from sender to addressee to receiver, from lover to
beloved. Rather than fixed identities, "female" and "male" are revealed
to be linguistic points on a continuum of desire.

At first reading, *Mauprat* does not provide immediate parallels between the novel and this specific Dickinson poem. Johnson suggests of

the carefully constructed collage and text: "Such deliberateness would suggest that the poem is autobiographical; that 'in a circumstance reluctant to be told' Emily Dickinson had been guided to *Mauprat* and had found the book a 'larceny of time and mind.'"[79] Certainly this may be one interpretation. Yet we should recall that this is a poet who once said of the Sea, "We correspond, though I have never met him" (Letter 1004). What is the subtle correspondence between *Mauprat* and a poem that portrays a playfully violated body? A Gothic romance, *Mauprat* consists of the recollections of eighty-four-year-old Bernard Mauprat, who narrates his escape from a barbaric family as a spoiled, rustic youth to be redeemed by the love of his virtuous and cultivated cousin Edmée. But Naomi Schor's focus on Edmée's initiation into sexuality helpfully highlights *Mauprat*'s leitmotif—the repeated eroticized wounding of the female body.[80] In the following scene, for example, Bernard has been crying at Edmée's rejection of him when she appears on the other side of a chapel window:[81]

> "Edmée, I order you to kiss me."
>
> "Let go, Bernard!" she cried; "you are breaking my arm. Look you have scraped it against the bars."
>
> "Why have you intrenched yourself against me?" I said, putting my lips to the little scratch I had made on her arm. "Ah, woe is me! Confound the bars!"[82]

> At that period it was the fashion for women to have their arms half bare at all times. On one of Edmée's I noticed a little strip of court-plaster that made my heart beat. It was the slight scratch I had caused against the bars of the chapel window. I gently lifted the lace which fell over her elbow, and, emboldened by her drowsiness, pressed my lips to the darling wound.[83]

In *Mauprat,* this wounding, or the threat of it, goes both ways. Later, after the chaste Edmée admits that she loves Bernard, he tries to kiss her. As their startled horses gallop into the woods, Bernard states, "She repulsed me, therefore, with scorn; and as I followed her distractedly, she raised her whip and threatened to leave a mark of ignominy on my face if I dared to touch even her stirrup."[84] Immediately thereafter, Edmée is shot twice in the breast and nearly dies.[85] Although innocent, Bernard is accused and tried for the assault, but he is eventually exonerated and marries Edmée.[86]

That Emily Dickinson is fascinated with this kind of eroticized wounding is especially clear from the Master letters.[87] Wounding as a prelude to sexuality is a dominant theme. Master hurts Daisy: "I cannot [talk] stay any [more] longer / tonight [now], for this pain / denies me— / How strong when weak / to recollect, and easy / quite to love" (*Master* Letter 1); "I've got a Tomahawk / in my side but that / dont hurt me [h] much, / [if you] Her Master / stabs her more—" (*Master* Letter 2); "One drop more from the gash / that stains your Daisy's / bosom—then would you *believe*?" (*Master* Letter 3). Daisy hurts (or fears she has insulted) Master: "Oh—did I offend it— / [Did'nt it want me /to tell it the truth] / Daisy—Daisy—offend it . . ." (*Master* Letter 2); "You say I do / not tell you all—Daisy 'confessed— / and denied not'" (*Master* Letter 3).

According to Freud, who studied only male patients in this instance, all fetishists are male and all are horrified by the absence of the phallus in the female.[88] "Probably no male human being is spared the terrifying shock of threatened castration at the sight of the female genitals," Freud sympathizes.[89] The fetishist's obsession is an attempt to resolve his anxiety at the "nothing" of female genitalia by eroticizing "some thing," a penis-substitute.[90] But what of female fetishism, Schor asks, especially as seen in Sand's novels?[91] Schor explains, "By appropriating the fetishist's oscillation between denial and recognition of castration, women can effectively counter any move to reduce their bisexuality to a single one of its poles . . . female fetishism is not so much, if at all, a perversion, rather a *strategy* designed to turn the so-called 'riddle of femininity' to women's account."[92] For Sand's predilection to wound/castrate her women as part of their sexual initiation, Schor coins the term *bisextuality:*

> The wounds inflicted on the female protagonist's body as a prelude to her sexual initiation are the stigmata neither of a turning away from femininity, nor even of a feminist protest against woman's condition under patriarchy, but rather of a refusal firmly to anchor woman—but also man—on either side of the axis of castration.[93]

In *Mauprat* and in Dickinson's text, who is castrated? Who isn't? Who has the phallus? Is there or isn't there a locomotive between Emily Dickinson's legs?

Dickinson did not need Freud to define "bisexuality" for her, nor poststructuralist theory to illuminate how the signifier deconstructs stationary poles of sexual identity. Her life and writing are suffused with "bisextuality." She calls herself "a Boy, and / Barefoot—" (*MB* 2:1137), associates poetry-writing with male creativity ("The Poet—it is He"[*MB* 1:465], "The Merchant of the Picturesque" [poem 1131]), identifies with Antony, maintains a thirty-five-year love for Susan,[94] flirts with Samuel Bowles,[95] has a passionate affair with Judge Otis Lord,[96] writes "he [Santa Claus] is your boundless Aunt" to her nephew Ned (Letter 526), and appears to act as domestic angel, dressed in white.

In the specific exchange between text and image for poem 1167, Dickinson's bisexuality is noted through a number of subject positions: she is the lover of George Sand, she is the lover of Mauprat (whose brute passions signify the carnality Dickinson both invokes and censors), she is the writer of a letter/poem to them, she is the subject of the letter/ poem she writes, and she is the reader of the letter/poem she never sent. What Dickinson finds, then, when she withdraws intensely to the private domestic realm is that there is no stable self at home.

How Spiders Defeat the Law

> The Spider as an Artist
> Has never been employed—
> Though his surpassing Merit
> Is freely certified
> > —Emily Dickinson, poem 1275 (c. 1873)

The spider is Dickinson's conventional shorthand for "poet" (as in poem 1138, "A Spider sewed at Night—" written near the same time as "Alone and in a Circumstance—"). In the poem under consideration, Dickinson is concerned with how much agency to invest in the spider, as evident in the many variants that modify its crawling: Assiduously, Deliberately, Determinately, Impertinently. Since it is the spider which causes her to run away, the spider/poet as culprit suggests that writing is implicated in the transgression, causing the body to flee.

After detailing the scene of the crime, the poem shifts, in the second half, to note the failure of the Law:

> Revisiting my late abode
> With Articles of Claim
> I found it quietly assumed
> As a Gymnasium
> for

Where Tax asleep and
Title off
        peasants
The inmates of the Air
Perpetual presumption took
            complacence
                lawful
As each were special
                only
Heir—
If any strike me on
the street
I can return the Blow—
If any take my property
        seize
According to the Law
The Statute is my Learned
friend
But what redress can be
For an offense nor here
                anywhere
nor there
So not in Equity—
That Larceny of time
and mind
The marrow of the
Day
By spider, or forbid
it Lord
That I should specify.

At first in this witty inquisition, Dickinson appeals to the Law for recourse.[97] A glance at Dickinson's 1844 Webster's dictionary, which she
referred to as her "Lexicon" and "companion" (Letter 342a), illuminates
the legalistic definitions. She returns to the scene armed with "Articles
of Claim"; in her Webster, an "article" is defined as "A single clause in
a contract, account, system of regulations, treaty, or other writing. . . ."
But legal contracts are useless; the usurpers, the many insects, have
turned the site into a "Gymnasium," a "place where athletic exercises are
performed; *originally, in Greece,* by persons naked," according to Webster.

Consequently, a carnivalesque scene unfolds, with "Tax asleep and / Title off." Webster quotes Blackstone's definition of "title":

> Right; or that which constitutes a just cause of exclusive possession; that which is the foundation of ownership; as, a good *title* to an estate; or an imperfect *title*. The lowest degree of *title* is naked possession, then comes the right of possession, and lastly the right of property, all which united complete the *title*. *Blackstone.*
>
> But *possession* is not essential to a complete title. A title to personal property may be acquired by occupancy. A *claim* is not a title.

These lower orders, be they peasants or inmates, exercise their naked bodies and take "presumption," or "naked possession." The Law cannot arrest this nakedness.

The remainder of the poem distinguishes between public and private, "on the street" versus "Alone and in a Circumstance." In public, the "I" is protected by Statute and Law. In privacy, however, the "I" is assaulted—just the opposite of what Victorian domestic ideology maintained. Through its line drawings, the manuscript asks what recompense can there be for an offense "nor here"—drawn with a curved line on top of "anywhere" and "not" crossed out—"nor there" on the next line. Where has the crime occurred? Where has the "I" been wounded? What loss can be shown? The poet knows that this particular crime is "not in Equity." Using Blackstone again, Webster defines "equity" as:

> In *jurisprudence,* the correction or qualification of a law, when too severe or defective; or the extension of the words of the law to cases not expressed, yet coming within the reason of the law. Hence a court of equity or chancery, is a court which corrects the operation of the literal text of the law, and supplies its defects by reasonable construction, and by rules of proceeding and deciding which are not admissible in a court of law. Equity, then, is the law of reason, exercised by the chancellor or judge, giving remedy in cases to which the courts of law are not competent.

If the offense is not in "Equity," then it is nowhere in relation to the Law as it stands, not even in any possible interpretation. The poet's grievance is outside the jurisdiction of any existing Law, any language of exactitude and compensation, any patriarchal order.

The crime is "That Larceny of time / and mind / the marrow of the

/ Day." According to Webster, "Larceny" is a specific legal term with varying degrees of seriousness:

> Larceny is of two kinds; *simple larceny,* or theft, not accompanied with any atrocious circumstance; and *mixed* or *compound larceny,* which includes in it the aggravation of taking from one's house or person, as in burglary or robbery. In *England,* when the value of the thing stolen is less than $25, the crime is *petty larceny*.

But when "Time" and "mind" are taken, the "marrow of the day" lost, what dollar amount can be put on the damages?

Considered in relation to the cutout figure and in the context of Dickinson's domestic explorations, "Larceny" suggests writing's theft of any subjectivity supposed to inhere in the private sphere. What the poem illustrates is a transgression, an intimate wounding without re-dress. The loss occurring in the most personal space, "an offense nor here nor there," is at once tangible and indeterminate. Dickinson feels language's wounding of the subject as it forces an adult to abandon childhood's polymorphous sexuality and name oneself as either a "fe-male" or "male"[98] and its continual loss and slippage, whereby the "I" speaking and the "I" spoken of never coincide.[99]

In the end, the poem recedes into the silence from which it pro-testingly emerged. Who perpetrated the offense? The poet refuses to testify. "By spider, or forbid / it Lord / That I should specify." From a nursery-rhyme beginning, Dickinson has taken the Law to a place where it breaks down—confronted with the body and desire in poetry. Emily Dickinson does not make another Law to substitute for the insufficient one. Instead she flaunts the uselessness of the Law, enjoying the dis-order created by peasants, inmates, and spiders.[100]

Child's Play, Dickinson's Poetry

> The playfulness of the artist is felt to fulfil the same function in the laboring life process of society as the playing of tennis or the pursuit of a hobby fulfils in the life of the individual.
>   —Hannah Arendt, *The Human Condition* (1958)

Playfulness organizes much of Dickinson's late writing, an aspect easy to miss when we do not see the manuscripts. Dickinson's delight in play, I believe, earns her the class-based criticisms of Dobson and Erkkila.

America's Calvinist legacy has dictated that "[p]layfulness is associated with the apolitical, the acultural, with escape from the most productive of social constraints."[101] But in her development of a feminist theory of play, Yaeger affirms the outlandish imagination of the child, her propensity for a lawless creativity using the shards of culture. Yaeger notes, "In play the child experiences a continual slippage, a to-and-fro motion between the world that restricts desire and desire itself."[102] In *Playing and Reality* (1971), D. W. Winnicott analyzes the back-and-forth bricolage construction of child's play, a description that mimics the there/not-there oscillation of fetishism:

> Into this play area the child gathers objects and phenomena from external reality and uses these in the service of some sample derived from inner or personal reality. Without hallucinating the child puts out a sample of dream potential and lives with this sample in a chosen setting of fragments from external reality.[103]

In the holograph for "Alone and in a Circumstance," with its oscillation between the sign for a female writer (who dressed as a man), the sign for a violent, rustic male lover [in a Master letter, Dickinson wondered whether "her odd—Backwoodsman /[life] ways [troubled] teased his finer sense nature" (Letter 2), the image of a technologized patriarchal power in a text that resists print technology, and the poem of a hilarious private wounding/castration and the Law's failure to provide redress, fixed positions of female and male sexuality are put into play. They slip and slide, with none being given primacy or a rigid definition.

Textually, in its play of secrecy and disclosure, the poem at once celebrates and mourns the "Larceny of time and mind," the loss of a determinate self sought in domesticity. Materially, Dickinson's abandoning the process of book-sewing and set-making arises from an awareness of this loss, from her ongoing interrogation of issues of totality and ontology. In her famous (non)revelation, "My Business is Circumference" (Letter 268), Dickinson is, I would suggest, alluding to her concern with linguistic boundaries and boundary-breaking. Thus the endgame of Dickinson's refusal to publish—her scrap-writing—shows her extending the play of the signifier into the materiality of its production. As Jacques Derrida explains in *Of Grammatology* (1976):

> The idea of the book is the idea of a totality, finite or infinite, of the signifier; this totality of the signifier cannot be a totality, unless a

totality constituted by the signified preexists it, supervises its in-scriptions and its signs, and is independent of it in its ideality. The idea of the book, which always refers to a natural totality, is pro-foundly alien to the sense of writing. It is the encyclopedic protec-tion of theology and of logocentrism against the disruption of writ-ing, against its aphoristic energy; and . . . against difference in gen-eral.[104]

The death of The Book, for Emily Dickinson, liberates the life of her writing. The artifacts produced by her domestic technologies of publica-tion celebrate the disruption of totality and writing's play of difference.

What uncanny prescience Emily Dickinson had. Roberts Brothers, who tastefully printed George Sand, also printed Dickinson's "Success is counted sweetest," in its collection of anonymous writings, *A Masque of Poets* (1878). The poem was sent to them by Helen Hunt Jackson. Leyda provides a facsimile of the published version[105] that may be com-pared to Dickinson's manuscript (*MB* 1:76). Although we cannot be certain that Dickinson sent an exact copy of the manuscript to Jackson, its existence suggests that editorial changes were made, most notably in the manuscript's final line: "Burst agonized and clear!" has been altered to "Break, agonizing clear." Dickinson, who seldom used exclamation points, had this one taken away from her. The cadence of the conclusion, mimicking the military trumpet's call, is lost.

But Roberts Brothers wasn't finished with Dickinson yet. As Willis J. Buckingham remarks, "Late in 1890, in time for the Christmas trade, Roberts Brothers of Boston issued a delicately pretty book of poems by a deceased and unknown writer named Emily Dickinson."[106] The pub-lishers understood the tastes of their customers. Their marketing of Dickinson, along with the editors' alterations, normalized her for public consumption:

The poems chosen for publication in the nineties are among her least difficult. . . . The editors [Mabel Loomis Todd and T. W. Higgin-son] also did what they could to reduce the oddity of the poems they did choose, making changes in fifty of the one hundred fifteen poems published in the first volume. They further conventionalized the manuscripts by adding generalizing titles of a type used in the decade, such as "Reticence" and "Disenchantment." The editors' topical divisions, sectioning all three volumes into categories headed "Life," "Love," "Nature," and "Time and Eternity," brought the architecture of Dickinson's books into conformity with others of the period.[107]

Like being forced again to sit stiffly for a daguerreotype, Emily Dickinson was posthumously framed. As she was transformed into "Emily Dickinson," her poetry was organized into marketable, printed commodities. Roberts Brothers knew their clientele: *Poems* (1890) went through eleven editions by the end of 1892 and *Poems* (2d series, 1891) went through five editions by 1893.[108]

After surveying the reviews of Dickinson's popular first volumes of printed poetry, Buckingham states: "She was published at the moment when the nineteenth century could feel, and take pleasure in, the alien force of her voice. These documents reveal how quickly and fundamentally Dickinson's first audience delighted in her 'strangeness.'"[109] I must qualify this observation. Clearly 1890s readers/consumers did respond positively to Dickinson's printed verse. But it is one hundred years later, as we study her manuscripts, that we are finally beginning to appreciate the true "alien force" of Emily Dickinson's "strangeness."

NOTES

Special thanks are due to John Lancaster, Curator, Special Collections, Amherst College, and to Beth Kinder-Kiley, Permissions Editor at Harvard University Press, for granting permission to reproduce this Dickinson manuscript. I am indebted to Martha Nell Smith who sent me the galleys for *Rowing in Eden,* which was in press when I first wrote this essay. Smith's insights and encouragement have helped me enormously. Jim Lewis, Curator of Houghton Library, kindly assisted me with details from the Lydia Maria Child book. Carol Birtwistle, Curator of the Homestead, helpfully discussed bathroom facilities that existed there during and after Dickinson's residence. While all the assistance I have received has been crucial, responsibility for errors remains fully my own.

1. Joanne Dobson, *Dickinson and the Strategies of Reticence: The Woman Writer in Nineteenth-Century America* (Bloomington: Indiana University Press, 1989), 128–30 (hereafter cited as Dobson, *Strategies*).

2. As quoted in Millicent Todd Bingham, *Ancestors' Brocades: The Literary Debut of Emily Dickinson* (New York: Harper and Brothers, 1945), 166.

3. Dobson, *Strategies,* 130.

4. Her most sympathetic editor, Susan occasionally submitted Dickinson's poems for publication while Emily was alive but mostly respected her wish not to print. Over their thirty-five year relationship, Susan received more letters from Emily Dickinson, more copies of her poetry, than did any other correspondent [see *The Letters of Emily Dickinson,* eds. Thomas H. Johnson and Theodora

Ward, 3 vols. (Cambridge, Mass.: Harvard University Press, Belknap Press, 1958), 3:964–65] (hereafter cited as *Letters*). As Smith explains, when Susan submitted a few Dickinson poems for publication in 1891 (as other family members were publishing Dickinson's works), she defended the poet's "lack of rhyme and rhythm" to the editor, asserting "but I have learned to accept it for the bold thought, and everything else so unusual about it." Even five years after Dickinson's death, Susan, her closest literary correspondent, displays ambivalence about having the poems *printed:*

> I think if you do not feel that your own literary taste is compromised by it, I would rather the three verses of the "Martyrs" ("Through the Straight Pass / of Suffering" [Fasc. 36; poem 792]) should be published if any. I shall not be annoyed if you decide not to publish at all. I should have said *printed.* . . . (as quoted in Martha Nell Smith, "Gender Issues in Textual Editing of Emily Dickinson," *Women's Studies Quarterly,* nos. 3 and 4 [1991], 80; hereafter cited as Smith, "Gender Issues").

The "everything else so unusual about it" may have included how the poem looked on the page and other manuscript details, aspects which would be erased by print technology.

Martha Nell Smith's *Rowing in Eden: Rereading Emily Dickinson* (Austin: University of Texas Press, 1992) (hereafter cited as Smith, *Rowing*) corrects earlier negative caricatures of Susan and assesses the complex and vital influence Susan Dickinson had upon the poet, as beloved, friend, and literary critic.

5. Smith, "Gender Issues," 80.

6. I recognize that problems and questions abound in my suggestion that readers focus on the Dickinson manuscripts. At present, other than *The Manuscript Books,* ed. Ralph W. Franklin, 2 vols. (Cambridge, Mass.: Harvard University Press, Belknap Press, 1981; hereafter cited as *MB*) and *The Master Letters,* ed. R.W. Franklin (Amherst, Mass.: Amherst College Press, 1986; hereafter cited as *Master*) access to the hundreds of other Dickinson manuscripts is severely limited. Even when one is lucky enough to work with holograph photocopies, Dickinson's handwriting is often difficult to decipher. Furthermore, the various sizes, shapes, and details of the late works (such as the manuscript I am interpreting) can be daunting, since even the best photographic reproduction cannot provide all pertinent details of the material artifact and, in fact, many of those details have altered (such as the fading of a page's color) over time. I would still argue that a reader's edition of Dickinson's manuscripts, especially of the "scraps," is essential. I realize that in such a reproduction, the collection's editorial apparatus will inevitably reflect the ideology of those who organize the publication. Many problems with interpretation will arise: readers will be confused when exposed to her variants written down a page and sometimes up the sides of margins. One wonders how poems would be included in anthologies and taught in the classroom. Yet I believe these struggles are both necessary and worthwhile in appreciating Dickinson's work.

To answer fully these editorial concerns is outside the purview of this essay. Rather I would hope that we may recall Jerome McGann's observation that "an author's intentions toward his [*sic*] manuscript may be quite different—have special aims and reflect special circumstances—from his [*sic*] intentions toward his [*sic*] published text" (*A Critique of Modern Textual Criticism* [Chicago: University of Chicago Press, 1983], 42). Every time a Dickinson poem has been printed, other editorial intentions have shaped it. To read *Emily Dickinson,* we must begin to discern, as best we can, her intentions. This task necessitates reading the manuscripts.

7. See Ruth Miller, *The Poetry of Emily Dickinson* (Middletown, Conn.: Wesleyan University Press, 1968), a study that antedates the *Manuscript Books*'s publication; Ralph W. Franklin, "The Emily Dickinson Fascicles," *Studies in Bibliography* 36 (1983): 1–20 (hereafter cited as Franklin, "Fascicles"); and Franklin, *Manuscript Books.*

8. Millicent Todd Bingham, "Introduction" to *Bolts of Melody: New Poems of Emily Dickinson,* ed. Mabel Loomis Todd and Millicent Todd Bingham (New York: Harper and Brothers, 1945), xii, xv.

9. Ralph W. Franklin, "Introduction" to *The Manuscript Books of Emily Dickinson,* 2 vols. (Cambridge, Mass.: Harvard University Press, Belknap Press, 1981), xiii.

10. Franklin, *Manuscript Books,* ix, and Smith in *Rowing* also point out that Dickinson is engaged in her own personal forms of publication.

11. In a June, 1869, letter to Higginson, Dickinson noted her retirement from public society. She declined Higginson's request that she visit Boston: "Could it please your convenience to come so far as Amherst I should be very glad," she demurred, "but I do not cross my Father's ground to any House or town" (Letter 330). The holograph I am reading was produced about May 1870; Higginson visited Dickinson at the Homestead in August 1870. As her withdrawal intensified, Dickinson wrote more and more of her poetry on scraps.

Unless otherwise noted, all correspondence quoted in the text is from Johnson and Ward, *Letters.* For Dickinson's poetry, the notation "P" plus a number indicates the poem's location in the Johnson edition; *MB* identifies Franklin's edition of *The Manuscript Books.* When both Johnson and Franklin reproduce the poem, I choose Franklin's manuscript version, imitating its details, as best I can, in print. I refer readers to *The Manuscript Books* and *The Master Letters.*

12. According to Franklin, in *The Manuscript Books,* Set 7 consists of 129 poems copied and organized about 1864–66 (2:1157). There is roughly a four-year break until Dickinson returns to copy and organize 12 poems in Set 8a, about 1870–74 and 10 poems in Set 8b, 1871–73 (2:1264). Sets 8a and 8b inaugurate Dickinson's brief practice of copying only one poem per recto and verso. All previous sets and fascicles either put another poem on back of an unused sheet or use any leftover space to begin a new poem. She retains this practice through Set 9, 1871–74 (2:1310). Yet Set 10, 12 poems copied between 1871–72, for the most part, returns to the old habit of copying as many poems on fronts and backs of sheets as is possible in her "performance" script; see Smith, *Rowing* chapter 2 for the distinction between Dickinson's "performance" versus her "casual" script. In addition see Susan Howe, "Visual Intentionality in Emily Dickinson," *HOW(ever)* 3, no. 4 (1986): 11–13, for persuasive interpretations of

the interplay between Dickinson's careful, elaborate orthography and the poems' thematics.

13. Gillian Brown's *Domestic Individualism: Imaging Self in Nineteenth-Century America* (Berkeley: University of California Press, 1990) (hereafter cited in the text as Brown, *Domestic Individualism*) examines how "nineteenth-century American individualism takes on its peculiarly 'individualistic' properties as domesticity inflects it with values of interiority, privacy, and psychology" (Brown, *Domestic Individualism*, 1). Nineteenth-century rhetoric and material culture locate the "true self" in the peaceful home, secure from the risks of an unstable public market. As Brown reveals of this feminized, domestic discourse, "Far from an account of the female subject, domesticity signifies a feminization of selfhood in service to an individualism most available to (white) men" (ibid., 7).

Dickinson's withdrawal into the home, I will argue, should be interpreted for its complex influence on how the poet tests the "Circumference" of female selfhood and sexuality. This movement into the home ironically frees her in her writing from the domestic constraints that bound so many nineteenth-century women who were forced to write for money. Yet her decision to withdraw into the home has been disparaged by class-based arguments from Joanne Dobson and Betsy Erkkila. Dobson, comparing Dickinson to other nineteenth-century women writers such as Harriet Beecher Stowe, Catharine Maria Sedgwick, and Elizabeth Stuart Phelps, does begin by providing a helpful corrective:

> Let us not romanticize Dickinson's withdrawal. While isolation may well have been her peculiar necessary condition for creation, we must not forget that her fear and seclusion cost her dearly in personal pain and limited the range of her experience. Whereas other women writers forged satisfactory social and professional lives for themselves, often courageously flouting convention to do so, Dickinson retreated into the home and eschewed—as a refined woman was taught to do—the jostling and strife of the world. In marked contrast with the groundbreaking activities of her contemporaries, this behavior appears conservative, indeed, strongly acquiescent to cultural demands. (*Strategies* 48)

The emotional price Dickinson paid for her agoraphobia should not be ignored. But in associating "public" women writers with courage and initiative, Dobson implicitly portrays Dickinson as one who selfishly adopted an easy path. While it is undeniable that Dickinson was enabled by her class position—and while I am in sympathy with some criticisms of Dobson and Erkkila—I am unsatisfied with merely pointing out that Dickinson was lucky enough to have an affluent family and that she used their resources to enable her writing. Rather, I would propose that if domesticity "limited the range of [Dickinson's] experience," we notice what she does within that limited range. She does not, as would the woman portrayed by Dobson and Erkkila, lie upon her divan suffering from fits of the vapors. Instead, she is a working poet.

14. As will become apparent, I take issue with Betsy Erkkila's "Emily Dickinson and Class," *American Literary History* 4 (1992): 1–27 (hereafter cited in the text as Erkkila, "Class") in which Erkkila concludes that Dickinson's "poetic

revolution was grounded in the privilege of her class position in a conservative Whig household whose elitist, antidemocratic values were at the very center of her work" ("Class," 23). Dickinson's occasional class snobbery and apathy regarding social justice are offensive, as Erkkila demonstrates (her most convincing examples are in Dickinson's own words on ibid. 10, 12–13). And I agree that "Dickinson's refusal to publish was marked by a similar aristocratic resistance to the twin forces of democratization and commercialization" (ibid., 17).

Yet Erkkila's tunnel-vision focus on class, which marginalizes gender, distorts Dickinson's achievement. Erkkila's criticism depicts Dickinson as a "rich bitch" who should have worked publicly to make America more egalitarian: "But while Dickinson's poetic assault on the patriarchal orders of language parallels the more public agitation for a change in women's social, economic, and legal status in the US, it is unclear how her poetic revolution might become an agent of political change" (ibid., 22). In other words, Dickinson was not "political" in the right way—which is defined only as laboring to better the less fortunate. If the line of argumentation sounds familiar, it's not surprising. This patriarchal guilt-trip has effectively made women artists feel selfish because it labels their dedication to their work as "turning their backs on needy others." Such narrow rhetoric discounts any positive political significance in Dickinson's choice to become a private poet. Evidently Erkkila sees no political inspiration in the example Dickinson set for the women around her and for later generations of women readers who have learned to articulate their own desires through Dickinson's work.

15. Poem 1167 and Johnson's notations regarding Dickinson's substitutions appear in *The Poems of Emily Dickinson,* ed. Thomas H. Johnson, 3 vols. (Cambridge, Mass.: Harvard University Press, Belknap Press, 1955), 2:815–16 (hereafter cited as Johnson, *Poems*).

16. Jay Leyda, *The Years and Hours of Emily Dickinson,* 2 vols. (New Haven: Yale University Press, 1960) 2:148 (hereafter cited in the text as Leyda, *Years and Hours*) imagines that Dickinson makes the cutouts to remind herself to order the novel, but changes her mind before doing so. The anonymous review appears as "Editor's Literary Record," review of George Sand, *Mauprat, Harper's New Monthly Magazine* 40 (May 1870): [925]–26 (hereafter cited in the text as "Editor's Literary Record").

17. According to Wayne Fuller, *The American Mail: Enlarger of the Common Life* (Chicago: University of Chicago Press, 1972), 345, the stamp was common after 1851 when postage was reduced to three cents for a letter going less than three thousand miles. For a color photograph of the medium blue stamp, see Charles Davidson and Lincoln Diamant, *Stamping Our History: The Story of the United States Portrayed on Its Postage Stamps* (New York: Lyle Stuart Book by Carol Publishing, 1990), 112 (hereafter cited in the text as Davidson and Diamant, *Stamping*). Artistically this stamp was part of a group that represented something of a breakthrough in the era of American stamp-production. As Davidson and Diamant explain,

Postal graphics during our first two decades of stamp design continued with enscrolled busts of Franklin and Washington—and occasionally Jefferson,

Jackson, and Lincoln. Finally, in 1869, the government's printing contractor, the National Bank Note Company, took a creative plunge. To the heads of those presidents (and Franklin, our first Postmaster General), the company designers added some delicately engraved early American iconography: *Columbus Landing on San Salvador,* the *Declaration of Independence,* a pair of bald eagles, a Pony Express rider, the *S.S. Adriatic,* and a Baldwin locomotive. (*Stamping* xiii)

Dickinson, then, had a choice of stamps she could affix to her manuscript. Her selection of the locomotive stamp, as I will explain, resonates with recognition of her father's achievements.

18. "Editor's Literary Record," 926.

19. "In the antebellum era only three women authors were discussed in American magazines as though they were eligible to be thought of as examples of genius," Nina Baym explains in *Novels, Readers, and Reviewers: Responses to Fiction in Antebellum America* (Ithaca: Cornell University Press, 1984), "George Sand, Harriet Beecher Stowe, and Charlotte Brontë" (259). Sand posed the most troublesome case for moralistic reviewers because

she was the only one of the three whose genius could not be debated; because the morality of her private life was problematic, to say the least; because it was the intention of her writing to attack the one moral position to which women were supposed to be committed, the sanctity of secular marriage; and because her intellectual powers were clearly equal to or greater than those of most men. (Ibid., 259)

As another woman literary genius who was critical of marriage (in Letter 204 to Elizabeth Holland who had just announced her engagement, Dickinson describes herself as "by birth a Bachelor"), Dickinson clearly felt an affinity for the audacious Sand. See Baym, esp. 259–63, for an analysis of antebellum reviews which confronted Sand's unconventional lifestyle (her "dressing as a man," her failed marriage, her affairs) as well as her disturbing talent for dramatizing revolutionary politics through well-crafted fiction. I appreciate the assistance of Cedric Reverand concerning *Mauprat.*

20. The Dickinson Collection at the Houghton Library, Harvard University, owns the May 1870 copy of *Harper's New Monthly Magazine* that the poet scissored. I thank Reference Librarian Emily Walhout who pointed out to me the three cuttings. Only two are glued onto the holograph.

21. Johnson, *Poems,* 2:816.

22. Details in this paragraph about Edward Dickinson's involvement in railroad ventures are from Leyda's invaluable *Years and Hours,* 2:71, 1:204, 2:233, 1:273, 2:223–24.

23. In this sense, Edward Dickinson was following in the footsteps of his quite successful father-in-law. Emily Dickinson's maternal grandfather, Joel Norcross, was a shrewd entrepreneur who was involved in railroad ventures. "He [Joel Norcross] had large stock holdings and served as a director of the Western Railroad, as the Worcester to Albany section of the Boston and Albany

Railroad was known. In addition, he promoted and helped build the Petersham and Monson Turnpike which extended the Connecticut line to New Hampshire." (Mary Elizabeth Kromer Bernhard, "Portrait of a Family: Emily Dickinson's Norcross Connection," *New England Quarterly* 40 [1987]: 373.) Within Emily Dickinson's family, railroads figured largely as the means for men to gain community accolades and profit.

24. Gary Scharnhorst, "A Glimpse of Dickinson at Work," *American Literature* 57 (1985): 483 (hereafter cited in the text as Scharnhorst, "Glimpse").

25. Johnson, *Letters*, 2:376.

26. "The Dickinson family subscribed to *The Atlantic Monthly, Harper's New Monthly Magazine,* and *Scribner's Monthly* along with the *Springfield Republican* and two other newspapers . . ." notes Cristanne Miller, *Emily Dickinson: A Poet's Grammar* (Cambridge, Mass.: Harvard University Press, 1987), 155; hereafter cited as Miller, *A Poet's Grammar.* Julia Ward Howe's essay, "George Sand," appears in *Atlantic Monthly* 8 (November 1861): [513]–34; hereafter cited in the text as Howe, "George Sand."

27. On the issue of Dickinson's sexual attraction to Susan, see Ellen Louise Hart:

> For many it has been impossible to conceive of erotic love between two adult women, between Dickinson, a poet who wrote passionately of men, and Susan, a wife and mother. They have difficulty accepting that Dickinson had intense romantic relationships with men at different times in her life, which coexisted with her lifelong attachment to Susan. It may also be difficult for critics to see language between two women as marked by desire when the biography suggests that the relationship did not necessarily involve physical intimacy. Such is the power of the taboo against homoeroticism and so narrow the range of definitions of love in our culture. ("The Encoding of Homoerotic Desire: Emily Dickinson's Letters and Poems to Susan Dickinson, 1850–1886," *Tulsa Studies in Women's Literature* 9 (1990): 253; hereafter cited as Hart, "Encoding.")

28. Smith, *Rowing,* 3.

29. Ibid., 152.

30. Howe, "George Sand," 513, 534.

31. Judith Farr, *The Passion of Emily Dickinson* (Cambridge, Mass.: Harvard University Press, 1992), 171–77 (hereafter cited in the text as Farr, *Passion*).

32. Howe, "George Sand," 514.

33. *Letters,* 2:380.

34. *Letters,* 2:342a.

35. Farr, *Passion,* 322.

36. Smith, *Rowing,* 213.

37. Farr, *Passion,* 322.

38. Leyda, *Years and Hours,* 2:254–55.

39. Ibid., 2:302.

40. Smith, *Rowing,* 6.

41. Ibid., 52.

42. Johnson, *Poems*, 3:966.

43. Franklin, "Fascicles," 12.

44. Brown, *Domestic Individualism*, 174.

45. Herman Melville, *Pierre, or The Ambiguities* (Evanston and Chicago: Northwestern University Press and Newberry Library, 1971), 254; hereafter cited in the text as Melville, *Pierre*.

46. Ibid., 263.

47. Brown, *Domestic Individualism*, 150.

48. Ibid., 150.

49. Ibid., 150–51.

50. Although it is not in the Dickinson Collection, from the increase in her scrap-writing and other allusions, it would seem that around 1870 Dickinson read *Pierre*. One of the first statements Higginson recorded after his August 1870 visit with Dickinson was her admission, "I never had a mother" (*Letters*, 2:475), a phrase that echoes Isabel's words to Pierre, "I never knew a mortal mother" (Melville, *Pierre*, 114). Certainly before 1870 Dickinson had produced some poetry on household refuse (for two examples, see poem 1102, written about 1866, on the back of a tradesman's bill, and poem 1147, written about 1869, on the back of a kitchen memorandum). Yet after 1870, this activity increases, suggesting that she may have adopted the scrap-authorship style of Pierre. Yet unlike Pierre, her gendered relation to domesticity causes her not simply to view scraps as trash. Rather, using the domestic as a productive site for creativity, she attends to the types of scraps she chooses, their sizes, and the witty interplay resulting between domestic materials and her poetry.

51. John Kasson, *Rudeness and Civility: Manners in Nineteenth-Century Urban America* (New York: Hill & Wang, 1990), 36–37.

52. Erkkila accepts uncritically Dickinson's sister Lavinia's statement that Lavinia "managed the house, Dickinson *thought*" ("Class" 2).

53. See Letter 36 in 1850 to Abiah Root, "Twin loaves have just been born into the world under my auspices. . . . *My* kitchen I think I called it, God forbid that it was, or shall be my own—God keep me from what they call *households* . . ."; Letter 89 in 1852 to Austin, "I have made the fires, and got breakfast, and the folks wont get up, and I dont care for it because I can write to you"; Letter 145 to Austin in 1853, "I add a word to say that I've got the fires made and waked the individuals . . ."; in 1856, "Emily's bread wins second prize at Agricultural Fair" (Richard Sewell, *The Life of Emily Dickinson* [New York: Farrar, Straus and Giroux, 1980], xxii; hereafter cited as Sewell, *Life of Emily Dickinson*); Letter 286 to the Norcross cousins in 1863(?), "I finish mama's sacque, all but the overcasting. . ."; in 1870, Higginson about Dickinson in Letter 342a, "She makes all the bread for her father only likes hers & says '& people must have puddings' this *very* dreamily, as if they were comets—so she makes them"; Letter 722 in late summer 1881 to Susan, "The Loaf for Ned, I will send Wednesday evening, unless he prefer before. . . ." *Emily Dickinson: Profile of the Poet as Cook*, ed. Guides at the Dickinson Homestead (Amherst, Mass.: Hamilton I. Newell, 1976) reprints several recipes that were copied in Dickinson's hand.

Kathryn Whitford, "Why Emily Dickinson Wore White," *Dickinson Studies*

55 (1985 First Half): 12–17, persuasively argues that, although the Dickinsons had household help (including Margaret O'Brien and Margaret Maher), Emily executed many household duties. In a sensible analysis, Whitford surveys Dickinson's and other's references to her cooking, cleaning, and laundry duties. She concludes that Dickinson's withdrawal and wearing of white gowns "were both efforts to gain time for herself. Emily's choice of white was clear-headed and practical. Her dresses were the farthest removed from bridal finery. They were in fact, more nearly a uniform. The uniform was white for the same reason that the uniforms of doctors, nurses, cooks and butchers were white and towels, pillowcases and table linen were uncompromisingly white. White linen and cotton were the easiest fabrics to wash" (16). While we should not ignore the symbolic significance of Dickinson's "white election," the domestic aspect should also be stressed so we understand Dickinson's omnipresent domestic responsibilities.

54. Erkkila, "Class," 13.

55. Dickinson's extreme withdrawal to the private sphere of the home ironically enabled her to escape some of the domestic fetters that bound public American women writers in the nineteenth century. As Mary Kelley, *Private Woman, Public Sphere: Literary Domesticity in Nineteenth-Century America* (New York: Oxford, 1984) observes of women writers such as E.D.E.N. Southworth, Catharine Maria Sedgwick, and Susan Warner:

> The circle of domestic concerns was a closed, absorbing, and consuming one for these women, and although literary careers obviously extended the boundaries of their lives, the focus of their beings revolved around and fastened them to a common and conventional ground. They became popular writers, but the inner compass of their lives held them to a familiar course. By a process peculiar to themselves they could only involuntarily and in ironic fashion impose themselves upon the alien male role of published writer. Unable to separate themselves from domestic callings governed by the interests and behavior of others, the domestic and literary became one, or rather the domestic absorbed the literary and the private woman of the home intruded upon the pages of a public literature. (221)

In Dickinson's late works, the domestic absorbed the literary materially. But her literary "career" became a thing apart from domesticity, by the poet's tunnelling within it.

56. Erkkila, "Class," 20.

57. Christopher Clark, "Household Economy, Market Exchange, and the Rise of Capitalism in the Connecticut Valley, 1800–1860," *Journal of Social History* 13 (1979): 169, 171.

58. Ibid., 175.

59. Ibid., 183.

60. Erkkila, "Class," 13.

61. *Emily Dickinson: Profile of the Poet as Cook,* eds. Guides at the Dickinson Homestead (Amherst, Mass.: Hamilton I. Newell, 1976), 5.

62. Lydia Maria Child, *The Frugal Housewife*, 2d edition (Boston: Carter and Hendee, 1830), 3.

63. As quoted in Leyda, *Years and Hours*, 2:482.

64. As quoted in Scharnhorst, "Glimpse," 485.

65. Ibid., 485.

66. See Judith Farr's comparison of the circa 1847–48 daguerreotypes taken of Emily Dickinson and another young woman Margaret Aurelia Dewing (*Passion*, 18–19). The figures are rigid mirror images of each other, down to the right elbow's resting on a table with a book near it. Juxtaposed, the two daguerreotypes dramatize the technology's erasure of the sitter's individuality. "Very different in appearance and (no doubt) personality from Margaret Aurelia Dewing," Farr notes, "[Dickinson] had been made to assume the typical pose convenient to the daguerreotypist" (ibid., 20). In a brilliant chapter, Farr argues that the poet chooses flamboyantly to hide her face in order to pursue the relation between "honor, art, and immortality. Daguerreotypes pretended to confer the latter. But Emily Dickinson knew that it was art—for her, the art of poetry— that led both to honor and immortality and that poetry was written alone, in seclusion" (ibid., 23).

67. Farr, *Passion*, 21.

68. Walter Ong, *Orality and Literacy: The Technologizing of the Word* (London: Routledge, 1982), 121; hereafter cited in the text as Ong, *Orality and Literacy*.

69. In note 2 to chapter 1 of *Rowing*, Martha Nell Smith elucidates: "'The Snake' was printed in both the weekly and daily *Republican*. To the weekly version, which Dickinson sent to Higginson, they added a question mark after the third line; to the daily version, they added a comma. No mark of punctuation appears in either manuscript copy. . . . Both the question mark and comma determine interpretations for the reader that Dickinson did not wish to impose" (222). For a facsimile of the daily *Republican's* version, see Leyda, *Years and Hours*, 2:110.

70. Walter Benjamin, "The Work of Art in the Age of Mechanical Reproduction," *Illuminations*, ed. Hannah Arendt, trans. Harry Zohn (New York: Schocken Books, 1969), 223–24.

71. Analyzing how print and manuscript establish different relations between text and reader, Ong explains:

> The readers of manuscripts are less closed off from the author, less absent, than are the readers of those writing for print. The sense of closure or completeness enforced by print is at times grossly physical. A newspaper's pages are normally all filled—certain kinds of printed material are called "fillers"— just as its lines of type are normally all justified (i.e., all exactly the same width). Print is curiously intolerant of physical incompleteness. (*Orality and Literacy*, 132–33)

72. The distinction between poetry and epistolarity in Dickinson's work is shifting and dynamic. Dickinson sent hundreds of her poems either enclosed in

personal letters or actually incorporated in the body of the letter. Many lines
written as prose in personal letters scan poetically; see Hart, *Encoding* for poems
that were written in bodies of letters to Susan but which later editors have not
reproduced as poems.

Often Dickinson sent a variant of one poem to a certain friend and another
variant to a different person, keeping the poem "alive" and flexible to suit different contexts. Epistolarity afforded Dickinson the opportunity to exploit lack of
closure in her poetry, to push back the "Circumference" of poetic representation
and reception. That Dickinson enjoyed the play of intimacy and distance, the joy
of private consumption, that epistolarity necessitates is suggested in her gleeful
poem: "The Way I read a Letter's—this—/ 'Tis first—I lock the Door—. . ."
(*MB*, 2:787).

For further manuscript study analyzing the dialogue between epistolarity and
poetry, see my "'Knock with / tremor': When Daughters Revise 'Dear Father,'"
in *Emily Dickinson: Woman of Letters,* ed. Lewis Turco (Albany: SUNY Press,
1993), 84–97.

73. The layout of the Homestead as it was arranged during Dickinson's
lifetime shows no bathroom facilities (for blueprint, see Leyda, *Years and Hours,*
2:2–3). The first floor "wash room" was for laundry. According to Carol
Birtwistle, Curator of the Homestead, by the time Reverend Hervey Parke
purchased it in 1915, one bathroom had been added at the very back of the
second story. Parke sold the Homestead to Amherst College in 1965. No documentation indicates that the Homestead had an outhouse, but photographs show
that Austin's house, the Evergreens, built next door in 1856, did. Birtwistle
conjectures that the Homestead also had an outhouse and/or that the Dickinsons
may have used "commode chairs," wooden chairs with openings for chamber-
pots which were kept underneath. These "chairs" were common in New England homes of the mid- to late-nineteenth century.

When I made this interpretation at a departmental Works-in-Progress series,
two faculty members were outraged and tried to shout me down in their vigorous denials. Although this essay is not the occasion, a consideration of why
patriarchal ideology finds the knowledge of a woman's using the bathroom so
threatening would be fascinating to explore. For an account of the furor erupting
over Jane Tompkins's "personal" admission in "Me and My Shadow," *Gender
and Theory: Dialogues on Feminist Criticism,* ed. Linda Kauffmann (New York:
Basil Blackwell, 1989), 121–39, see Nancy K. Miller, *Getting Personal: Feminist
Occasions and Other Autobiographical Acts* (NewYork: Routledge, 1991), 1–30.

74. See David S. Reynolds, *Beneath the American Renaissance: The Subversive
Imagination in the Age of Emerson and Melville* (New York: Knopf, 1988), 443, for
a helpful discussion of the kinds of "subversive" and "reputable" humor in
cultural circulation that may have influenced Dickinson's bawdy/genteel poem.

75. All definitions are taken from Noah Webster, *An American Dictionary of
the English Language,* 2 vols. (Amherst, Mass.: J., S., and C. Adams, 1844);
hereafter cited in the text as Webster, *Dictionary.*

76. The observation is Jerrald Ranta's; I thank him for pointing this out to
me. "Little Miss Muffett" was certainly well-known during Dickinson's life.
As William and Ceil Baring-Gould explain in their edition of *The Annotated*

Mother Goose (New York: Clarkson N. Potter, 1962), the doggerel is thought either to allude to Mary, Queen of Scots, or to the daughter of Dr. Thomas Muffett (d. 1604), he who wrote *The Silkwormes and their flies* (114).

77. Cristanne Miller's reading of this poem omits the first sixteen lines, causing her to read it as a humorless indictment of God's caprice. Focusing on the second half, Miller states that "the poet indirectly accuses God of an injustice far worse than any human kind. . . . here human 'Statute' is greater protection than His inexplicable, or perhaps, nonexistent, law. Dickinson always trusts herself first and all things human second before heavenly salvation or under-standing or reward" (*A Poet's Grammar*, 170–71). While Miller's conclusion is apt, she misses the poem's playfulness, especially because she does not see Dick-inson's cutouts and manuscript.

78. All of us make sense of our bodies through language, or specific dis-courses (medical, religious, fashionable) about the body. Discourse thus medi-ates and organizes our most intimate relation with our own corporeality. Dickin-son's manuscript foregrounds this discursive construction of the body. Or, as Francis Barker in *The Tremulous Private Body* (London: Methuen, 1984) explains the body/text issue:

> [T]he body in question is not a hypostazied object, still less a simple biological mechanism of given desires and needs acted on externally by controls and enticements, but a relation in a system of liaisons which are material, discur-sive, psychic, sexual, but without stop or centre. It would be better to speak of a certain "bodiliness" than of "the body." (12)

79. Johnson, *Poems*, 2:816.

80. See Naomi Schor, "Female Fetishism: The Case of George Sand," in *The Female Body in Western Culture*, ed. Susan Rubin Suleiman (Cambridge, Mass.: Harvard University Press, 1985), 366–67; hereafter cited in the text as Schor, "Female Fetishism."

81. George Sand, *Mauprat*, trans. Stanley Young (New York: P.F. Collier, 1902), 136; hereafter cited as Sand, *Mauprat*.

82. Ibid., 141.

83. Ibid., 154.

84. Ibid., 319.

85. Ibid., 324.

86. Ibid., 349–415.

87. All following quotes are from R. W. Franklin's manuscript reproduction edition of *The Master Letters*. Readers should be advised that I have not reprinted exactly from Franklin's transcription the arrows that indicate whether a certain phrase occurs above or below the line or the angled brackets that indicate what has been crossed out. I have omitted the arrows, and I have substituted square brackets for angled ones.

88. Sigmund Freud, "Fetishism," in *Sexuality and the Psychology of Love*, trans. Joan Riviere, ed. Philip Rieff (New York: Collier Books for Macmillan, 1963), 215.

89. Ibid., 216.

90. Ibid., 216.

91. Schor, "Female Fetishism," 365.

92. Ibid., 368–69.

93. Ibid., 369.

94. See Hart, *Encoding,* Smith, *Rowing,* and Farr, *Passion,* 100–177.

95. Farr, *Passion,* 178–244.

96. Sewell, *Life of Emily Dickinson,* 642–67.

97. In "ED: 'Vicinity to Laws,'" *Dickinson Studies* 56 (1985 Second Half), B. J. Smith notes that while legal language can be found in roughly three hundred of Dickinson's poems (38), her usage of it changes. In the early poems, Dickinson, the daughter and sister of lawyers, tends to laugh at the law. "In later poems she looks at the law nostalgically in a recognition of both its usefulness and uselessness" (ibid., 40). While Dickinson's use of visual images decreases from 1858–69—and legal images also decrease—legal language, Smith reveals, "continues to find its way into the meaning and sense of the later 'cooler' poems until the end of Dickinson's life" (ibid., 50).

98. In *The Daughter's Seduction: Feminism and Psychoanalysis* (Ithaca: Cornell University Press, 1982), Jane Gallop explicates Lacan's notion of how language polices desire by forcing the subject to take up her/his position as either "female" or "male" (or, in Lacan's parable, to enter a restroom marked either "Ladies" or "Gentlemen"). She clarifies that "in some mythical prehistory prior to the signifier's arrival, the doors are identical. Similarly, it is not the biological given of male and female that is in question in psychoanalysis . . . but the subject as constituted by the pre-existing signifying chain, that is, by culture, in which the subject must place himself" (11).

99. Discussing Lacan and Benveniste, Anthony Easthope in *Poetry as Discourse* (London: Methuen, 1983) notes:

> Identity is ever only possible as misrecognition. For vision, I can only see myself in a mirror by seeing this reflection from somewhere else. For discourse, I can only identify myself in discourse by speaking about this character ('myself') from somewhere else; the 'I' as represented in discourse (subject of the enounced) is always sliding away from the 'I' doing the speaking (subject of enunciation). (44)

In February 1885, Dickinson wrote to Higginson, "Biography first convinces us of the fleeing of the Biographied—" (Letter 972). In principle, Dickinson recognizes the inadequacy of language to capture immediately a subject's complex, full identity.

100. Dickinson's resistance to the Law, to the symbolic order's attempt to "shut her up in Prose," is remarked not only through the poem's text, but through a visual pun. Her glee, associated with "GEORGE SAND," recalls her lawyer father's stern edicts. Higginson, in notes he made after meeting Dickinson, summarizes her tale of how Edward Dickinson legislated her reading: "One day her brother brought home Kavanagh hid it under the piano cover & made signs to her & they read it: her father at last found it & was displeased" (Letter

342b). If Edward Dickinson "did not wish them to read anything but the Bible" (Letter 342b) and disapproved of Longfellow's *Kavanagh,* what would he have thought of George Sand? Clearly Dickinson violates her father's law in connecting his sign—the locomotive—with her desired author—"GEORGE SAND." But then these contradictions textually, joyfully construct "Emily Dickinson," the absent/present "I" of the poem.

101. Patricia Yaeger, *Honey-Mad Women: Emancipatory Strategies in Women's Writing* (New York: Columbia, 1988), 211; hereafter cited in the text as Yaeger, *Honey-Mad Women.*

102. Ibid., 231.

103. As quoted in Yaeger, *Honey-Mad Women,* 231.

104. Jacques Derrida, *Of Grammatology,* trans. Gayatri Spivack (Baltimore: Johns Hopkins University Press, 1976), 18.

105. Leyda, *Years and Hours,* 2:302.

106. Willis J. Buckingham, ed. *Emily Dickinson's Reception in the 1890's: A Documentary History* (Pittsburgh: University of Pittsburgh Press, 1989), xi; hereafter cited in the text as Buckingham, *Reception.*

107. Ibid., xv.

108. Sewell, *Life of Emily Dickinson,* xxviii.

109. Buckingham, *Reception,* xii.

Beyond Artifacts: Cultural Studies and the New Hybridity of Rap

Houston A. Baker, Jr.

Artifact presupposes a plan of work, a moment of visual arrest, and an instant of social evaluation. On the seventh day one sees the artifact, pronounces it "good," and relaxes for the weekend. *Purposive making* defines the artifactual process. Its results are overdetermined by a social imaginary. It is the social imaginary that assigns primary use value to artifacts and maps their integration into rounds of daily life.

An African ritual mask, for example, is an artifact because it has a socially determined range of formal variation and ceremonial use. No matter how creative the mind and soul of its maker, the mask must remain within the limits of the social imaginary if it is to function precisely as an artifactual African ritual mask. New materials and technologies may alter the formal properties of a particular representative mask, but these alterations must follow accepted social lines. Robert Farris Thompson, the celebrated art historian, has elaborated these artifactual dynamics of African tradition and individual talent in striking ways, which need no further elaboration at the moment.

It would be a mistake, however, to assume that what I have called "artifactual dynamics" are confined to technologically primitive societies and their social imaginaries. For the "creation-in-seven-days" paradigm, with its assumptions of omniscient design and utilitarian social purposiveness, has retained a stubbornly metaphysical hold on the human imagination. How many times have we heard an awe-struck observer faced with an assortment of rocks and stones and trees say: "How can anyone see this and not believe in a supreme maker?"

Perhaps it is because we are programmed for order that we read order "all the way down" in the universe. (Gestalt psychology claims that at the slightest hint of order we go the whole nine yards: we spontaneously connect even imaginary dots into familiarly human forms, perceiving, for example, not craters on the lunar surface but, instead, "the man in the moon.") We assign responsibility for rocks and stones and trees to an inferred but always-already-unseen creator because we want rocks and stones and trees to stand in and for order. And having posted our claims for supreme artifaction, we consider even our own narratives of such artifice formal, finite repetitions of what Coleridge called the "infinite I am."

The social artifact is, thus, held to be the product of a transcendentally reflective process of human making. Rather than a transitory percept, it is considered a material emblem of God's making power on earth. In its materiality it is deemed socially significant—a synecdoche for culture as a whole, complete with a comprehensible place in a fixed order of use and meaning.

We may be able to shift the artifact around a bit, but we can never—or so familiar wisdom dictates—dislodge it from its proper place in a transcendental narrative of supreme making. The transcendentally reflective, or mimetic, character of the artifact is surely what commentators have in mind when they speak of the "sacredness" of the *book* or the "timelessness" of the *classics*. As "made" products that have relentlessly held their place in the social imaginary, some *books*—like all *classics*—are instanced as proof positive that they have been invested by human makers with some mimetic aura of the transcendental. Surely this state of affairs is what Walter Benjamin has in mind when he speaks of the "aura" as the distinguishing aspect of the work of art prior to an age of mechanical reproduction.

The translation of such stock phrases as the "sacredness of the book" would seem to be: God, the Supreme Artificer and protagonist of our grand narrative of making, is in heaven, and all is right with the valued artifacts of the world.

Artifactual thinking requires that the eye never be averted from some "thing" called, say, "actual writings," "real poems," "genuine books," or "original paintings." Such thinking reads the world as though it is an enormous jigsaw puzzle of rigorously distinctive artifactual units.

Artifactual order is intolerant of comingling, co-implication, and, I think, cultural studies. The God of artifactual thinking and order is one who makes the human body in his own image—the Supreme Design, as it were. In turn, the human body crafts—in finite repetition of this Supreme Design—discrete, ordered, and comprehensible material units that constitute books, pages, and images.

Artifactual criticism locates discrete meanings in discrete formal units received as pages, books, and images. Such criticism scrupulously details the manner in which such finite meanings repeat, or reflect, a transcendental design.

Now, cultural studies, while it does read the world in material terms, stands in energetic contrast to artifactual thinking on almost every count. Cultural studies views the world not in fixed and discrete units but, instead, as a complex array of momentary relationships. It defines *culture* in a very political and ideological sense as a signifying domain of asymmetrical relations of power and permeable boundaries. A fluid and always "in motion" culture replaces the agency of a Supreme Artificer in the making and unmaking of the world. The universe of cultural studies is far more Heraclitean than Aristotelian. Rather than concentrating on a point of arrest and evaluation, cultural studies focuses our attention on fluid situations in which boundaries and the discrete units they are supposed to hold in place are virtually impossible to discern.

To return to the example of the African mask, one might say that cultural studies would never ignore the material planes of the mask. The mask is granted tangible material existence. But cultural studies would be far more interested in the mask *in motion* than in its existence as a cultural artifact.

The relations of interest to cultural studies are not artifactual; there is little concern for how, say, a mask exists in relationship to other discrete things such as a Yoruba measuring weight. Rather, cultural studies is concerned to discover how precisely any mask gains significance by virtue of its ritual and ceremonial motions among a huge array of motions and relationships of order and disorder, silence and speaking, stasis and dynamism.

The origin of artifactual thinking seems to be a rage for order and transcendental significance. The motivating insight for cultural studies, by contrast, seems to be the recognition that any stated, perceived, or proclaimed symmetry is always and inevitably a "fearful symmetry." Under the merest interrogation even the most stable material symmetry explodes like the blow-out diagram for a difficult Christmas toy purchased under the illusion that only "limited assembly" was required.

The artifactual thinker inquires of the native informant: "What is the ritual significance of this mask?" The informant replies: "It keeps evil away." The answer is recorded by the artifactualist. The mask is cataloged among "things" that keep evil away.

The cultural studies investigator observes the ritual and ceremonial motions of the mask at work and asks a further question: "Does the mask keep evil away?" The informant replies: "No, unfortunately, it does not." Symmetry is always fearfully and momentarily attained.

Rather than the signifiers *maker* and *made,* the words *in the making* and *unmaking* describe the cultural studies universe of work. Seeing and visual arrest are complemented in a cultural studies universe by every sensible means. The aural, tactile, olfactory, and gustatory immediacy of social imbrication reveals unseen connections and "unmakes" familiarly accepted, artifactual designs of mere *things.* There are no arrested *things,* only myriad relations "in the making."

Of course, from one perspective we can dismiss artifactual thinking with the wave of a deconstructionist hand: God, History, Self, and the Book disappear in the foamy wake of a metaphysics of presence. But what I have in mind is far more akin to the symbolic anthropology of Clifford Geertz or the new ethnography of James Clifford. Cultural studies is like the type of revisionist, intellectual stock taking that marked the career of W. E. B. Du Bois in his seventies. At seventy the sage of Great Barrington remarked that all of his earlier analyses had suffered from the absence of Freudian insight.

Perhaps our situation is very akin to that of Du Bois. For surely we have all found it necessary to pay far more attention to chaos than to order. We have been compelled to add new sensible dimensions to our analytical reading projects. And we have been forced to recognize in the dizzying, asymmetrical motions of actually existing reality meanings and forms in the making that have changed our ways of thinking forever.

"Hybridity" replaces the discreteness of artifactual distinctions. Boundaries between the "popular" and the "scholarly" disappear. And notions of what precisely *can* and *must* be taught are reformulated in a new pedagogy for a coming century.

I consider "rap" music and its analytical and pedagogical entailments for the American academy a case par excellence for cultural studies. Rap is, I believe, the new poetical story of "the work of art" in a postmodern age of electronically mediated production. And the story of rap's nonartifactual embodiment begins in "the hood." It begins, as well, with turntables decisively out of place—in dramatically unaccustomed locations . . .

Turntables in the park displace the machine in the garden. Postindustrial, hyperurban, black American sound puts asunder that which machines have joined together . . . and dances . . . to hip-hop acoustics of Kool DJ Herc. "Excuse me, Sir, but we're about to do a thang . . . over in the park and, like how much would you charge us to plug into your electricity?" A B-Boy, camp, site, is thus established. And Herc goes to work . . . with two turntables and a truckload of pizzazz. He takes fetishized, commodified discs of sound and creates—through a trained ear and deft hands—a sound that virtually commands (like Queen Latifah) assembled listeners to dance.

> It was the "monstrous" sound system of Kool DJ Herc which dominated hip hop in its formative days. Herc came from Kingston, Jamaica, in 1967, when the toasting or DJ style of his own country was still fairly new. Giant speaker boxes were essential in the competitive world of Jamaican sound systems . . . and Herc murdered the Bronx opposition with his volume and shattering frequency range.[1]

It was Herc who saw possibilities of mixing his own formulas through remixing prerecorded sound. His enemy was a dully constructed, other-side-of-town discomania that made South and West Bronx hip hoppers ill. Disco was not *dope* in the eyes, ears, and agile bodies of black Bronx teenagers, . . . and Queens and Brooklyn felt the same.

There are gender-coded reasons for the refusal of disco. Disco's club DJs were often gay, and the culture of Eurodisco was populously gay. Hence, a rejection of disco carried more than judgments of exclusively musical taste. A certain homophobia can be inferred—even a macho redaction. But it is also important to note the high-marketplace maneuvering that brought disco onto the pop scene with full force.

The LeBaron Taylor move was to create a crossover movement in which black R&B stations would be used as testing grounds for single recordings headed for largely white audiences.[2] Johnnie Taylor's 1975 "Disco Lady" was one of the first hits to be so marketed; 2.5 million singles sold. And the rest is history.

What was *displaced* by disco, ultimately, was R&B, a funky black music as general "popular" entertainment. Also displaced (just *dissed*) were a number of black, male, classical R&B artists. Hey, some resentment of disco culture and a reassertion of black manhood rights (rites)—no matter who populated discotheques—was a natural thing. And what the early hip-hoppers saw was that the break between "general popular" and being "black by popular demand" had to be occupied. And as Albert Murray—that longtime stomper of the blues, who knows all about omni-Americans—put it: in the *break* you have to be nimble or not at all![3]

Queens, Brooklyn, and the Bronx decided to "B," to breakdance, to hip hop to rhythms of a dismembered, sampled, and remixed sound meant for energetic audiences—in parks, in school auditoriums, at high school dances, on the corner (if you had the power from a light post . . . and a crowd). And Herc was there before Grandmaster Flash and Afrika Bambaataa. And hip hop was doing it as in-group, urban style, as music disseminated on cassette tapes . . . until Sylvia Robinson realized its general popular possibilities and sugared it up at Sugarhill Productions. Sylvia released "Rapper's Delight" (1979) with her own son on the cut making noises like "To the hip hop, hippedy hop / You don't stop. . . ." The release of "Rapper's Delight" began the recommercialization of B-ing. The stylistic credo and cryptography of hip hop were pared away to a reproducible sound called "rap." And rap was definitely a mass market product after "Rapper's Delight" achieved a stunning commercial success. B-style came in from the cold. No longer was it—as crossover/commercial—"too black, too strong," for the popular charts. (But, of course, things have gotten stranger and 2 live since then!)

So, rap is like a rich stock garnered from the sudden simmering of titanic B-boy/B-girl energies. Such energies were diffused over black cityscapes. They were open-ended in moves, shoes, hats, and sounds brought to any breaking competition. Jazzy Jay reports:

> We'd find these beats, these heavy percussive beats, that would drive the hip hop people on the dance floor to breakdance. A lot of times it would be a two-second spot, a drum beat, a drum break, and we'd mix that back and forth, extend it, make it 20 minutes long. If you weren't in the hip hop industry or around it, you wouldn't ever have heard a lot of these records.[4]

Twenty minutes of competitive sound meant holding the mike not only to B, but also to set the beat—to beat out the competition with the "defness" of your style. So . . . it was always a *throwdown:* a self-tailored, self-tutored, and newly cued game stolen from the multinational marketplace. B-style competed always for (what else?) consumers. The more paying listeners or dancers you had for circulating cassettes or ear-shattering parties in the park, the more the quality of your sneakers improved. The idea was for youth to buy your sound.

Herc's black, Promethean appropriation of the two-turntable tech tnology of disco and his conversion of "discotech" into a newly constructed blackurban form turned the tables on analysts and market surveyors alike. For competing disco DJs merely *blended* one disc into a successor in order to keep the energized robots of a commercial style (not unlike Lambada) in perpetual motion on the dance floor. *To disco* became a verb . . . but one without verve to blackurban youth. What Herc, Flash, and their cohort did was to actualize the immanent possibilities of discotechnology. They turned two turntables into a sound system through the technical addition of a beat box, heavy amplification, headphones, and very, very fast hands.

Why listen—the early hip-hop DJs asked—to an entire commercial disc if the disc contained only twenty (or two) seconds of worthwhile sound? Why not *work* that sound by having two copies of the same disc on separate turntables, moving the sound on the two tables in DJ-orchestrated patterns, creating thereby a worthwhile sound? The result was an indefinitely extendable, varied, reflexively signifying hip-hop sonics . . . indeed, a deft sounding of postmodernism.

The techniques of rap were not simply ones of selective extension and modification. They also included massive archiving. Black sound (African drums, bebop melodies, James Brown shouts, jazz improvs, Ellington riffs, blues innuendos, doo-wop croons, reggae words, calypso rhythms) were gathered into a reservoir of threads that DJs wove into intriguing tapestries of anxiety and influence. The word that comes to mind is *hybrid*.

Discotechnology was hybridized through the human hand and ear—the DJ turned wildman at the turntable. The conversion produced a rap DJ who became a postmodern, ritual priest of sound rather than a passive spectator in an isolated DJ booth making robots turn. A reverse cyborgism was clearly at work in the rap conversion. The high technology of advanced sound production was reclaimed by and for human ears and the human body's innovative abilities. A hybrid sound then erupted in seemingly dead, urban acoustical spaces. (By *postmodern* I intend the nonauthoritative collaging or archiving of sound and styles that bespeaks a deconstructive hybridity. Linearity and progress yield to a dizzying synchronicity.)

The Bronx, Brooklyn, Queens—called by the Reagan/Bush era

black "holes" of urban blight—became concentrated masses of a new style, a hybrid sonics hip-hoppingly full of that piss, sass, and technological vinegar that tropes Langston Hughes, saying: *"I'm still here!"*[5] This is a *blackhole* shooting hip-hop quasars and bum-rushing sucker, political DJs.

What time was it? Time to get busy from the mid-1970s into the wild-style popularizations of the 1980s. From Parks to Priority Records—from random sampling to Run DMC. Fiercely competitive and hugely braggadocious in their energies, the quest of the emergent rap technologists was for the baddest toasts, boasts, and signifying possible. The form was male dominant... though KRS One and the earliest male posses will tell you the "ladies" were *always* there—answering back, dissing the ways of menfolk and kinfolk alike who tried to ease them into the postmodern dozens. Hey, Millie Jackson had done the voice-over with musical backdrop—had talked to wrongdoing menfolk (at length), before Run or Daryl had ever even figured out that someday they might segue into each other's voices talking 'bout some "dumb girl." Indeed!

Rap technology includes "scratching": rapidly moving the "wheels of steel" (i.e., turntables) back and forth with the disc cued, creating a deconstructed sound. There is "sampling": taking a portion (phrase, riff, percussive vamp, etc.) of a known or unknown record (or a video game squawk, a touch-tone telephone medley, verbal tag from Malcolm X or Martin Luther King) and combining it in the overall mix. (The sample was called a "cut" in the earliest days.) "Punch phrasing": erupting into the sound of turntable #1 with a percussive sample from turntable #2 by def cuing.

But the most acrobatic of the techniques is the verb and reverb of the human voice pushed straight out or emulated by synthesizers or emulating drums and falsettoes—rhyming, chiming sound that is a mnemonic for blackurbanity.

The voice is individual talent holding the mike for as long as it can invoke and evoke a black tradition that is both prefabricated and in formation. "Yo, man, I hear Ellington, but you done put a new (W)rap on it!" For the rap to be defly *yours* and properly original, it has got to be *ours*—to sound like *us*.

The voice, some commentators have suggested, echoes African griots, black preachers, Apollo DJ's, Birdland MC's, Muhammed Ali, black streetcorner males' signifying, oratory of the Nation of Islam, and get-down ghetto slang. The voice becomes the thing in which, finally, raptechnology catches the consciousness of the young.

What time is it? The beginning of the decade to end a century. It is postindustrial, drum machine, synthesizer, sampling, remix, multitrack studio time. But it is also a time in which *the voice,* and *the bodies* of rap and dance beat the rap of technologically induced (reproduced) indolence, impotence, or (in)difference.

Why?

Because sales figures are a mighty index. But also . . . the motion of the ocean of dancers who fill vast, olympian spaces of auditoriums and stadiums transnationally when you are (à la Roxanne) "live on stage" is still a principal measure of rap-success. Technology can create a rap disc, but only the voice dancing to wheels of steel and producing a hip hopping, responsive audience gives testimony to a full-filled *break.* You ain't busted a move, in other words, until the audience lets you know you're in the groove.

What time is it? It's "hardcore" and "message" and "stop the violence" and "2 live" and "ladies first"—1990s—time. Microcomputers, drum machines, electric keyboards, synthesizers, are all involved in the audio. And MTV and the grammarians of the proper Grammy Awards have had their hands forced.

Rap is a too-live category for the Grammies to ignore, and Fab Five Freddy and "Yo! MTV Raps" have twice-a-week billing these days. Jesse Jackson and Quincy Jones proclaim that "rap is here to stay." Quincy has even composed and orchestrated a cross-generational album (*Back on the Block*) on which he announces his postmodernity in the sonics of rap. Ice-T and Big Daddy Kane prop him up "on every leaning side."

But it is also time to "fight the power," as Public Enemy (PE) knows—the power of media control. In their classic rap "Don't Believe the Hype," PE indicates that prime-time media is afraid of rap's message, considering it both offensive and dangerous. In Philadelphia one of the principal popular music stations confirms PE's assessment. For WUSL ("Power 99") proudly advertises its "no-rap workday." Secretaries fill a sixty-second ad spot with kudos for the station's erasure of rap. Hence, Federal Communications Commission (FCC) "public" space is contoured in Philly in ways that erase the energy of rap's postmodern soundings. "Work" (defined as tedious office labor) is, thus, publicly constructed as incompatible with rap. Ethics and outputs of wage labor are held to be incommensurate with postmodern, black expressive culture. Implicit in a no-rap workday, of course, is an agon between industrial ("Fordist") strategies of typing pool (word processing pool?) standardization and a radical hybridity of sound and morals. For rap's sonics are disruptive in themselves. They become even more cacophonous when they are augmented by the black voice's antiestablishment injunctions, libido urgings, and condemnations of coercive standardization. To "get the job done" or "be paid in full" in the economies of rap is scarcely to sit for eight hours cultivating carpal tunnel syndrome. Nope. To get the job done with rap style is to "get busy," innovative, and outrageous with *fresh* sounds and defly nonstandard moves. One must be undisciplined, that is to say, to be "in effect."

Eric B and Rakim, Twin Hype, Silk Tymes Leather, Kingpin Redhead, De La Soul, Q-Tip, the DOC—the names in themselves read like a Toni Morrison catalog of nonstandard cultural denomination. And such named rap ensembles and the forms they produce are scarcely local or parochial. For rap has become an international, metropolitan hybrid. From New Delhi to Ibadan it is busy interrupting the average workday.

3rd Bass is a prime example of rap's hybrid crossovers. The duo is prismatically white, but defly blackurban in its stylings and "gas face" dismissals of too-melodic "black" artists such as MC Hammer.[6] ("Holy Moly!" as a notorious media character used to say: white boys, and one of them a graduate of Columbia, dissing a melanin-identified black boy for being not black or strong enough.) Which is to say that "we" are no longer in a Bronx or Brooklyn or Queens era but at the forefront of transnational postmodernism. The audience begins at eleven or twelve years of age and extends, at least, through post-B.A. accreditation. Rap is everywhere among adolescents, young adults, and entry-level professionals. It is a site of racial controversy, as in the antisemitism fiascos of Public Enemy.[7] It is a zone of gender problematics, ranging from charges against the form's rampant sexism (2 Live Crew is too flagrant here) through the throwdown energies of Queen Latifah and her *ladies first,* to the irony of squeaky-clean "Good Girls." It is a domain of the improper, in which copyright and "professional courtesy" are held in contempt. Rappers will take what is "yours" and turn it into a "parody" of you—and not even begin to pay you in full: for example, N.W.A's "It's not about a salary" line signifying on Boogie Down Productions (BDP) whom, so I am told, they can't abide. Rap is a place of direct, vocal, actional challenge to regnant authority: N.W.A., again, with

" . . . Tha Police." Class is also a major determinant in the rap field. Its postmodernity is a lower-class, blackurban, sonic emergent speaking to (as PE has it) "a nation of millions."

Microcomputation, multitrack recording, video imaging, and the highly innovative vocalizations and choreography of blackurban youth have produced a postmodern form that is fiercely intertextual, open-ended, hybrid. It has not only rendered melody virtually anomalous for any theory of "new music" but also revised a current generation's expectations where "poetry" is concerned. Technology's effect on student expectations and pedagogical requirements in, say, "English Literature Classrooms," is tellingly captured by recent experiences that I have had and would like to share. To prepare myself for a talk I was to give at New York's Poetry Project symposium entitled "Poetry for the Next Society" (1989) I decided to query my students in a course devoted to Afro-American female Writers. "What," I asked, "will be the poetry for the next society?" To a man or woman, my students responded, "Rap" and "MTV."

We didn't stop to dissect their claims, nor did we attempt a poetics of the popular. Instead, we tried to extrapolate from what seemed two significant forms of the present era a description of their being-in-the-world. Terms that emerged included: *public, performative, audible, theatrical, communal, intrasensory, postmodern, oral, memorable,* and *intertextual*. What this list suggests is that my students believe that the function of poetry belongs in our era to a telecommunal, popular space in which a global audience interacts with performative artists. A link between music and performance—specifically, popular music and performance—seems determinative in their definition of the current and future function of poetry.

They are heirs to a history in which art, audience, entertainment, and instruction have assumed profoundly new meanings. The embodied catharsis of Dick Clark's bandstand or Don Cornelius's soultrain would be virtually unrecognizable—or so one thinks—to Aristotle. Thus, Elvis, Chuck Berry, and the Cherelles foreshadow and historically overdetermine the Boss, Bobby Brown, and Kool Moe Dee as, let us say, People's Poets.

My students' responses, however, are not nearly as natural or original as they may seem on first view. In fact, they have a familiar cast within a history of contestation and contradistinction governing the relationship between poetry and the State.

The exclusion of poets from the republic by Plato is the primary Western site of this contest. (One envisions a no-poetry workday, as it were.) In Egypt it is Thoth and the King; in Afro-America it is the Preacher and the Bluesman. It would be overly sacramental to speak of this contest as one between the letter and the spirit, and it would be too Freudian by half to speak of it as a struggle between the law and taboo. The simplest way to describe it is in terms of a tensional resonance between homogeneity and heterogeneity.

Plato argues the necessity of a homogeneous State designed to withstand the bluesiness of poets who are always intent on worrying such a line by signifying and troping irreverently on it and continually setting up conditionals. "What if this?" and "What if that?" To have a homogeneous line Plato advocates that philosophers effectively eliminate poets.

If the State is the site of what linguists call the *constative,* then poetry is an alternative space of the *conditional.* If the State keeps itself in line, as Benedict Anderson suggests,[8] through the linear, empty space of homogeneity, then poetry worries this space or line with heterogeneous performance. If the State is a place of reading the lines correctly, then poetry is the site of audition, of embodied sounding on State wrongs such as N.W.A's ". . . Tha Police" or PE's "Black Steel in the Hour of Chaos." What, for example, happens to the State line about the death of the Black Family and the voiceless derogation of Black Youth when Run DMC explodes the State line with the rap:

> Kings from Queens
> From Queens Come Kings
> We're Raising Hell like a Class When the Lunch Bell Rings!
> Kings Will be Praised
> And Hell Will Be Raised
> Suckers Try to Phase Us
> But We Won't be Phased!

In considering the contestation between homogeneity and heterogeneity, I am drawing on the work of the scholars Homi Bhabha and Peter Stallybrass,[9] who suggest that nationalist or postrevolutionary discourse is always a discourse of the split subject. In order to construct the Nation it is necessary to preserve a homogeneity of remembrance (such as anthems, waving flags, and unifying slogans) in conjunction with an amnesia of heterogeneity. If poetry, like rap, is disruptive performance, or, in Homi Bhabha's formulation, an articulation of the melancholia of the people's wounding by and before the emergence of the State line, then poetry can be defined, again like rap, as an audible, or sounding, space of opposition.

Rap is the form of audition in our present era that utterly refuses to sing anthems of, say, whitemale hegemony.

A final autobiographical instance of rap-shifted student expectations on the pedagogical front will conclude my sounding of postmodernism. I recently (February 1990) had the experience of crossing the Atlantic by night, followed by a metropolitan ride from Heathrow Airport to North Westminster Community School in order to teach Shakespeare's *Henry V* to a class of General Certificate of Secondary Education (GCSE) students. Never mind the circumstances occasioning the trip . . . no, on second thought, the circumstances are popularly important. A reporter for London's *Mail on Sunday* had gotten onto the fact that I advocated rap as an absolute prerequisite for any teacher attempting to communicate with students between the ages of twelve and twenty-five.[10] So, there I was in London, in a school with students representing sixty-seven nationalities and speaking twenty-two languages, in the Paddington/ Marylebone area.

> Once more into the breach dear friends
> Once more into the breach
> or let us close the wall up with our English dead

was the passage the students were supposed to have concentrated on, paying special attention to notions of "patriotism."

Introduced by the head of the English Department to a class doing everything but the postmodern boogie on desktops, I pulled up a chair, sat down, and calmly said: "I've come from the United States. I've been awake for thirty-six hours, and I have to listen to you so that I can answer questions from my teenage son about what you are listening to, what you are *into*. So, please, start by telling me your names." Even as they began to give me their names (with varying degrees of cooperative audibility), a black British young woman was lining up twelve rap cassette boxes on her desk immediately in front of me. (Hey, she knew I had *nothing* to teach her!)

To make an exciting pedagogical story brief we took off, as a group. I showed them how "Henry V" was a rapper—a cold dissing, def con man, tougher-than-leather and smoother-than-ice, an artisan of words.

His response to the French dauphin's gift of tennis balls was my first presentational text. And then . . . "the breach." We did that in terms of a fence in the yard of a house that you have just purchased. A neighbor breaches it . . . "How, George? How could your neighbor breach it?" George jerked up from that final nod that would have put him totally asleep and said, "What?" "Could your neighbor do anything to breach your fence, George?" "No, Sir, I don't think so." "Come on George!" "Sir . . . Oh, yeah, he could break it."

And then the anterior question about breaches and fences was arrived at by another student, and I leaped out of my chair in congratulation. "Sir, the first question is 'Why was the fence there in the first place?'" Right! What time was it?

It was time for Public Enemy's "Don't Believe the Hype." Because all of that Agincourt admonition and breach rhetoric (the whole hybrid, international class of London GCSE students knew) was a function of the English church being required to pay the king "in full," and the State treasury can only get the duckets if ancient (and spurious) boundary claims are made to send "Henry V" and the boys into somebody else's yard. "Patriotism," a show of hands by the class revealed, is a "hype" if it means dying for England. Bless his soul, though, there was *one* stout lad who held up his hand and said he would be ready to die for England. My black British young lady, who had put her tapes away, shouted across the room: "That's because you're English!"

Hybridity: a variety of sounds coming together to arouse interest in a classic work of Shakespearean creation.

The *Mail On Sunday* reporter told me as we left North Westminster that the English Department head had asked her to apologize to me in advance for the GSCE group because they would never listen to what I had to say and would split the room *as soon as the bell rang*. What the head had not factored into her apologetics was the technology I came bearing. I carried along my very own Panasonic cassette blaster as the postmodern analogue of both "the message" and the "rapper's delight" that Shakespeare himself would include in his plays were he writing today. At a site of postmodern, immigrant, sonic (twenty-two languages) hybridity produced by an internationally accessible technology, I gained pedagogical entrée by playing in the new and very, very sound game of rap. Like Jesse, I believe rap is here to stay. Other forms such as "house" and "hip-house" and "rap reggae" may spin off, but rap is now classical black sound. It is the in-effect archive where postmodern-ism has been *dopely* sampled for the international 1990s.

NOTES

This chapter was revised from "Hybridity, the Rap Race, and Pedagogy for the 1990's," in *Technoculture,* ed. Andrew Ross and Constance Penley (Minneapolis: University of Minnesota Press, 1991), copyright © by the University of Minnesota. By permission of the University of Minnesota Press.

1. David Toop, *The Rap Attack* (Boston: South End Press, 1984), 78.

2. Nelson George, *The Death of Rhythm and Blues* (New York: Dutton, 1989), 149–58.

3. *The Hero and the Blues* (Columbia: University of Missouri Press, 1973).

4. John Leland and Steve Stein, "What It Is," *Village Voice* 33, January 19, 1988, 26. Leland and Stein's article is one moment in this special issue of the *Voice* devoted to hip hop.

5. "Still Here," *Selected Poems of Langston Huges* (New York: Alfred Knopf, 1969), 123.

> I've been scarred and battered.
> My hopes the wind done scattered.
> Snow has friz me, sun has baked me.
> Looks like between 'em
> They done tried to make me
> Stop laughin', stop lovin', stop livin'—
> But I don't care!
> I'm *Still here*!

6. Playthell Benjamin, "Two Funky White Boys," *Village Voice* 35, January 9, 1990, 33–37.

7. Robert Christgau, "Jesus, Jews, and the Jackass Theory," *Village Voice* 35, January 16, 1990, 83–84, 86, 89.

8. *Imagined Communities* (London: Verso, 1983).

9. Bhabha presented his brilliant insights on hybridity and heterogeneity in two lectures at the University of Pennsylvania on April 20–21, 1989. Stallybrass's essay on heterogeneity I read in manuscript, but it is destined for *Representations*. For the insight of Bhabha one can read "The Other Question." In *Literature, Politics, and Theory,* ed. Francis Barker et al. (London: Methuen, 1986), 148–72. For Stallybrass one might turn to his coedited monograph entitled *The Politics and Poetics of Transgression* (Ithaca: Cornell University Press, 1986).

10. Clarence Waldron, "Could Students Learn More If Taught with Rap Music," *Jet* 77, January 29, 1990, 16–18. I had the honor of featuring prominently in this article. My picture even appeared in the gallery of Kurtis Blow, Kool Moe Dee, DJ Jazzy Jeff and the Fresh Prince, and Run DMC.

Narrative, Memory, and Slavery

for Hortense Spillers

W. J. T. Mitchell

[Author's note: This essay was first read at the conference on "Textual Technologies" at Texas A&M University in March of 1992. It turned out that my role at this conference was to serve as the voice of anxiety about technology, the voice of suspicion about our pleasure in the powers afforded by new technologies of information storage and retrieval. "All this stuff," as Hamlin Hill put it so eloquently, "is the devil's work!" My essay, therefore, was an attempt to take us back to a time and place "before" technology, a sort of "state of nature," as Rousseau puts it, that never existed and never will. My aim was to take us back—way back—to an archaic period when communities were based in oral tradition, when communication was mainly spoken, gestural, and bodily, when writing (if any) was by pictures. I wanted us to remember memory, the faculty we had before computers and before writing; a time when narrative—especially first-person autobiographical narrative—had a different social and epistemological function, when having an account of one's life, feeling impelled to produce a story of oneself was an obligatory, even ordinary practice in the construction of private and public identity.

When and where was this time and place? Was it England and America in the eighteenth and nineteenth centuries, when "spiritual autobiography" and the rise of secular "confessions" articulated the self-consciousness of a new class of bourgeois subjects? Does it emerge in postrevolutionary moments (as in post–cultural revolution China), when the lifting of censorship and the freeing of previously silenced voices releases a massive wave of self-reflection? Or is it best located in archaic societies, in which the passage from childhood to adulthood requires a ritual of self-identification deeply involved with narratives of an emergent, transformed, newly created self?

As these questions suggest, the historical location of this essay is hopelessly and necessarily indeterminate, except perhaps for its location in the late twentieth century, when the emergence from the global order of the cold war requires a recasting of all the cultural histories organized by narratives of modernity and postmodernity. (A few weeks after the Texas A&M conference a special issue of *Newsweek International* appeared, documenting the widespread survival of slavery as an international social and economic institution.) The conceptual location of the essay, on the other hand, is precise: it seeks to explore the nexus of narrative, memory, and slavery, to connect the visual/textual technologies of storytelling (whether historical or fictional) with the psychotechnologies of human memory (whether constitutive of personal or social identity) with the fact of radical social inequality, the possibility of absolute domination, abjection, and the reduction of the human individual to a commodity form.]

I was cautioned not so long ago that "we already know about slavery," which amounts to saying that we can only look forward to repeating what everybody "knows."

—Hortense Spillers

I have a survivalist intention to forget certain things.

—Toni Morrison

I do not remember to have ever met a slave who could tell of his birthday.

—Frederick Douglass

Description is *ancilla narrationis,* the ever-necessary, never-emancipated slave of narrative.

—Gerard Genette

The natural place to start an investigation of narrative, memory, and slavery, I suppose, would be with that genre of literature known as "the slave narrative." Hundreds of American slave narratives survive from the nineteenth century.[1] Some of them, most notably Frederick Douglass's *Narrative,* are acknowledged literary masterpieces. Taken together with the enormous outpouring of historical documents on the economics and sociology of slavery, the archive of American slave narratives provides unprecedented access into one of the great atrocities of modern history, an access to horror paralleled, perhaps, only by the body of Holocaust survivor narratives. Slavery occupies a position in the American national memory similar to that of the Holocaust in German memory: it is what we think we know, what we can never forget, and what seems continually to elude our understanding.

I want to attempt a different starting place, one that comes at the problem from the standpoint of some formal problems in the construction of narratives, memories, and their interrelations and that circles back only very indirectly to the "main story" of slavery itself. I take this indirect route partly as a matter of professional competence: that is, I feel much better prepared to say something of substance about the construction of narrative and memory than I do about "slavery itself." But I also want to contribute, in a very minor way, to Hortense Spillers's gestures of resistance to the historical "knowledge industry" that has turned slavery into an object of "massive demographic and economic display," a phenomenon so well-known that nothing more is to be known about it.[2] My subject, then, is not "slavery itself" but, rather, the representation of slavery in narrative and memory. More specifically, I want to examine the ways in which the descriptive aspects of narrative and the visual-spatial features of memory figure in accounts of servitude.

Ideally, this essay should be read in tandem with a companion piece, "Ekphrasis and the Other," an exploration of the tradition of verbal description of works of visual art.[3] The typical ekphrastic text might be said to speak to or for a semiotic "other"—an image, visual object, or spectacle—usually *in the presence* of that object. The point of view of the text is the position of a seeing and speaking subject in relation to a seen and usually mute object. But suppose the "visual other" was not merely represented by or "made to speak" by the speaking subject? Suppose that the other spoke for herself, told her own story, attempting an "ekphrasis of the self"? Suppose further that this "self" is a *former* self, not present to the speaker but mediated and distanced by memory and autobiographical transformation? What would it mean for the ekphrastic "object" to speak of and for itself in a former time, from the standpoint of a present in which it is no longer an object but now has become a subject? The answer, I will argue, is to be found in the nexus of narrative, memory, and slavery.

It is a commonplace in the criticism of slave narratives that description is the dominant rhetorical feature. Early reviewers of slave narratives regularly compare them to "windows" and "mirrors" that provide "transparent access" to slavery and are to be praised in proportion to the sense of "ocular conviction" they provide.[4] Although the title of George Bourne's *Picture of Slavery* is somewhat unusual, it typifies the dominance of visual, graphic metalanguages to describe slave narrative as assemblages of "scenes" and "sketches" linked in an episodic structure that confines temporality to particular "incidents."[5] This feature seems answerable both to the desire for "eyewitness authenticity," the "unvarnished truth," and to what James Olney has characterized as a severe limitation on slave narrative—the poverty of the whole genre with respect to complex plot devices or what Paul Ricouer calls "configurational time," the large, complicated reflections on temporality and memory he finds in canonical Western narratives, particularly autobiography.[6]

The opening of Frederick Douglass's *Narrative* illustrates the dominance of visual and spatial codes and their relation to a sense of lack. Douglass begins by insisting that, while he has exact knowledge of the place of his birth, he was systematically deprived of the knowledge of time ("I have no accurate knowledge of my age"). Temporal consciousness is a privilege of white children, of the master. Spatial consciousness, focused on place, on scene, on the sketching of incidents linked in an episodic structure, is what is left as material for the slave's literary labor.

The descriptive textual strategies associated with vision and space play a double role, then, as symptoms of both lack and plenitude, erasure of time, memory, and history, and direct access to its sensory actuality.

The role of memory in slave narrative admits, similarly, of absolutely contradictory descriptions. On the one hand, it is a transparent window into past experience. James Olney suggests that there is "nothing doubtful or mysterious about memory" in slave narrative: "On the contrary, it is assumed to be a clear, unfailing record of events sharp and distinct that need only be transformed into descriptive language." Olney argues that memory is simply an instrumental feature of slave narrative, not a topic of reflection: "Of course ex-slaves do exercise memory in their narratives, but they never talk about it as Augustine does, as Henry James does. . . ."[7] On the other hand, the transparent window seems to reveal strange gaps and blind spots.[8] There are indications of a blankness in memory so radical that it can't be described as forgetting, amnesia, or repression but, instead, as the absolute *prevention* of experience, the excision not just of "memories" as a content but also the destruction of memory itself, either as an artificial technique or a natural faculty.[9] When Frederick Douglass opens his autobiography by saying "I do not remember to have ever met a slave who could tell of his birthday," we cannot read his words literally without noticing what Olney claims is unheard of in slave narrative, a complex reflection on memory and the very possibility of remembered experience.

Douglass seems at first to cast the radical blankness of slave consciousness in the moderated form of "forgetting," as if he might have met a slave who remembered his birthday but has simply forgotten about it. The fact is that if Douglass had ever met a slave with such memories, he would certainly have remembered it. What he is really saying (we suppose) is that slavery is a *prevention* of memory: no slave was allowed to "remember" his or her birthday, either in the sense of knowing when it was or celebrating its annual return. But there is an even more literal sense in which, of course, no one, free or slave, can remember his or her birthday. Some experiences—birth, the origins of existence—certainly "happened" but are simply prior to the formation of memory. This literal reading erases the slave's difference from other human beings; none of us can "tell of" our birthdays in the sense of narrating a remembered experience. How could we remember a time before memory? What sense could "forgetting" have for a creature that lacks the faculty of memory?

Yet Douglass's words pretend as if we could remember the immemorial. They conjure with the possibility of a memory of the blankness prior to the formation of memory. He doesn't say that no slave could tell of his birthday; only that he can't remember having met one. It could be that he has simply forgotten. Douglass plays here with two meanings of memory, the recollection of past experience by an individual and the "passing on" ("telling") of memory from one person to another, as when we ask to be remembered to someone. There is a simple reason that Douglass and other slaves had no (collective) memory of their birthdays. They were separated from the one person who might pass on this memory, who might connect the personal and social, the directly experiential and the mediated forms of memory, namely, the mother who would likely be the only one with exact knowledge of the birthday based on personal experience. By eliding in a single sentence the personal and intersubjective senses of memory, Douglass opens up the possibility of remembering a time before memory, in both senses. This impossible feat is exactly what it means, of course, to remember slavery—that is, to remember the time, not just of "forgetfulness" or amnesia, but to remember the time when there was nothing to remember with.

I hope this laborious reading of Douglass's sentence will have planted two suspicions: first, the notion that "there is nothing doubtful or mysterious about memory" in slave narrative is, like the related notion of descriptive transparency, an aspect of the ideological packaging of these writings and not an adequate account of the way they actually work. Perhaps this is only to remind ourselves of what is simply a truism in the contemporary analysis of cultural forms, that representation (in memory, in verbal descriptions, in images) not only "mediates" our knowledge (of slavery and of many other things) but also obstructs, fragments, and negates that knowledge.[10] This isn't to say that we learn nothing from memory and narrative but, rather, that their construction does not provide us with straightforward access to slavery or anything else. They provide something more like a site of cultural labor, a body of textual formations that has to be worked through interminably.

The blankness of personal memory that Douglass evokes is matched by the collective, national amnesia about his subject after the Civil War. Slave narrative virtually disappeared from American cultural memory for over a century, surfacing only as grist for the mill of "history," or as an object lesson in the poverty of subliterary genres (with Douglass always granted a grudging exceptional status).[11] In the last generation it has reappeared as the object of serious reading, and the present effort is an attempt to contribute to that reappearance, not so much by rereading the slave narratives themselves, but by using it to redescribe our picture of narrative and memory and the access or knowledge they mediate.

The second suspicion has to do with the relation of slave narrative to something called "Western autobiography," the canonical tradition that runs from Augustine to Rousseau to Henry Adams. Perhaps there are, after all, self-conscious reflections on memory in slave narrative if we only knew where to look. Or, more precisely, perhaps slave narrative teaches something fundamental about the nature of memory, something that might actually reflect on the strange turns of memory in the "master" narratives of Western autobiography, especially those forms of bourgeois and spiritual autobiography that were so important to the formation of slave narrative. If "the truth of the master is in the slave,"[12] the truth of Western autobiography may be in slave narrative.

These suspicions about the transparency of description and memory are not doubts about the veracity of narrators but, rather, about the perspicuity of readers and their illusion of access. The dilemma of our access to slave narrative is not new; it isn't a consequence of our historical distance from slavery but is fundamental to the genre from its beginnings. Slave narrative is not just difficult to read; in a literal sense it is impossible to write. Impossible because the slave narrative is never literally that of a slave but only of an ex-slave, already removed from the experience by time, forgetfulness, and often by editings, rewritings, and interpolations by sentimental abolitionist transcribers. The slave narrative is always written by a former slave; there are no slave narratives, only narratives about slavery written from the standpoint of freedom. It is not even quite accurate to say that the slave narratives are "about" slavery; they are really about the *movement* from slavery to freedom. A narrative that was simply about slavery (like a narrative that was simply about freedom) is conceivable, but unlikely, and neither could find an author to "own" it as autobiography, as a record of an actual life. Actual narratives, like actual lives, always play off slavery against freedom, which is perhaps why *pure* slave narrative is both impossible and fundamental to the understanding of narrative as such.

Rather than talk of what we "know" about slavery, then, we must talk of what we are prevented from knowing, what we can never know, and how it is figured for us in the partial access we do have. This raises a question that goes beyond the genre of slave narrative to narrative modes of representation generally. Narrative seems to be a mode of knowing and showing that constructs a region of the unknown, a shadow text or image that accompanies our reading, moves in time with it, like Douglass's blankness, both prior to and adjacent to memory. It is a terrain crisscrossed by numerous internal borders, fringes, seams, and frontiers. This is not only a question of the "content" of the slave narrative, which invariably recites a moment (or several moments) of "crossing" or "passing" the frontiers that divide slavery from freedom or from one kind of slavery to another. Slave narrative is notable for its formal frontiers as well, its textual heterogeneity, its multiple voices, boundaries, and frames—prefaces, frontispieces, and authenticating documents.[13] But narrative in general is, as structuralism taught us long ago, a hybrid form, patching together different kinds of writing, different levels of discourse. It is the form of this heterogeneity, this difference, that solicits our attention when we look at the resistances and blockages, the boundaries that we, as readers, must pass to get at something we call slavery.

The specific formal boundary we are concerned with here is canonical to narrative in general and crucial to slave narrative in particular: Gerard Genette calls it the "frontier" between narration "proper," the unfolding of actions in time, and its improper twin, the mode of description, the rendering of a spatialized scene or state of affairs, often marked by a densely visual or multisensory rhetoric.[14] This is not the only frontier in narrative, nor necessarily the most important. The distinctions between diegesis and mimesis (telling the story and "miming," or performing, it, as in dialogue), or discourse and narration, are at least as important, and more ancient, than the description-narration distinction. It is, as Genette notes, a relatively recent and fragile distinction; from a strict structuralist standpoint, focusing on the semiotic fabric of the text, it is really a phantom distinction, with no clear boundary between narrative and description.[15] Nevertheless, it seems to be part of the pragmatic metalanguage of stories (and especially of slave narrative), one of the ways the seamless web of textuality is crossed by the difference between temporal and spatial modes, visual and aural codes.

It will be obvious by now that the narration-description distinction has a strong connection with the medium of memory. It may seem odd to speak of memory as a medium, but the term seems appropriate in a number of senses. Since antiquity memory has been figured not just as a disembodied, invisible power but also as a specific technology, a mechanism, a material and semiotic process subject to artifice and alteration.[16] More specifically, memory takes the form in classical rhetoric of a dialectic between the same modalities (space and time), the same sensory channels (the visual and aural), and the same codes (image and word) that underly the narrative-descriptive boundary.[17] That is, the classical memory technique is a way of reconstructing temporal orders by mapping them onto spatial configurations (most notably architectural structures, with various "loci" and "topoi," or "memory places," inhabited by striking images and sometimes even words); it is also a way of mapping an oral performance, an oration from memory, onto a visual structure. Memory, in short, is an imagetext, a double-coded system of mental storage and retrieval that may be used to remember any sequence of items, from stories to set speeches to lists of quadripeds.

Now it might be objected here that it is inappropriate to connect the ancient memory systems of classical rhetoric with the problematics of memory in slave narrative. The problem isn't only one of anachronism (shouldn't one have a "history of memory" that would reconstruct the appropriate models for memory in the nineteenth century?) but also of "fit." The ancient memory systems are artificial, cultivated techniques designed as aids to public verbal performance; the modern sense of memory treats it as something more like a natural faculty, an aspect of private consciousness. The appropriate terms for this kind of memory would seem to be located in psychology rather than rhetoric. Insofar as this essay has an argument to make about memory, it would dispute every one of these objections. The difference between "artificial" and "natural" memory was regarded as quite permeable by the ancient rhetoricians. And the difference between public and private recollection (say, between the memorial oration and the psychoanalytical session) is exactly what is under most pressure in autobiographical narratives whose function is to bear witness to a collective, historical experience. Even more fundamentally, while the specific cultural articulations of memory may vary from one place and time to another, the composite imagetext structure of memory seems to be a deep feature that endures all the way from Cicero to Lacan to the organization of computer memory.

"Stories," in the sense of a temporal sequence of events, are not the only elements of memory that can be withdrawn from the storehouse of memory. Descriptions come out too, and they have an odd status in relation to the visual and spatial order from which they emerge. Description might be thought of as the moment in narration when the technology of memory threatens to collapse into the materiality of its means. Description typically "stops," or arrests, the temporal movement through the narrative; it "spreads out the narrative in space," according to Genette.[18] But the point of the spatial memory system is orderly, reliable movement through time. Description threatens the function of the system by stopping to look too closely and too long at its parts— those "places" with their "images" in the storehouse of memory. Memory, like description, is a technique that should be subordinate to free temporality: if memory becomes dominant, we find ourselves locked in the past; if description takes over, narrative temporality, progress toward an end, is endangered, and we become paralyzed in the endless proliferation of descriptive detail.

That is why both description and memory are generally characterized as instrumental, or "servant," functions in the realms of textuality and mental life. Memory is a technology for gaining freedom of movement in and mastery over the subjective temporality of consciousness and the objective temporality of discursive performance. To lack memory is to be a slave of time, confined to space; to have memory is to use space as an instrument in the control of time and language. Description is, in Gerard Genette's words, "the ever-necessary, ever submissive, never emancipated slave" of narrative temporality.[19] Genette is not talking about slave narrative here, of course, but about narrative in general and the internal hierarchies of typical narrative structures. The questions we need to answer, then, are deceptively straightforward: How do these formal or structural hierarchies in narrative and memory engage with various forms of social hierarchy and domination? How do the descriptive components of narrative and the visual-spatial technology of memory "serve" the articulation of the "servant voice"? What happens when the "servitude of description" is explicitly addressed to the *description of servitude,* when the memory of slavery is narrated?[20]

A full account of these questions would engage not just the power relations of master-slave in the structure of representation but would address as well the whole issue of economics and exchange—the value of narrative and memory, the conversion of the slave-as-commodity into the slave *narrative–as–commodity*. In place of such a full account, let me simply offer an inventory of the narrative-memory-slavery intersection in terms of what Derrida has called "economimesis."[21]

Narration as enumeration. We need to be mindful of the whole panoply of figures that link narration to counting, recounting, "giving an account" (in French, a *conte*), "telling" and "tallying" a numerical total, and the relation between "stories" and "storage." Description in particular is often figured as the textual site of greatest wealth, an unbounded cornucopia of rich detail, rendered in the rhetoric of "copiousness."

Memory as a countinghouse. We need to recall the figures of memory as a storehouse in which experience is "deposited" (sometimes to accrue "interest") and the memory technology characterized as a device for "withdrawing" these deposits on demand.[22] Cicero's account of the invention of artificial memory in *De Oratore*[23] tells the story of the invention of memory as a story of misguided thrift, the failure to give the poet-rhetorician, and by implication the gods, their due. Simonides dedicates half his poem to the twin gods Castor and Pollux, half to his noble patron, Scopas, who meanly refuses full payment and tells Simonides to collect the other half from the gods. Simonides is then called from the banquet hall by a servant, who tells him that two young men want to see him outside. While he is outside, the banquet hall collapses, crushing Scopas and all his guests, leaving their bodies disfigured and unrecognizable to all but Simonides, who is able to identify the bodies because he has been using the architectural places in the hall as a memory system for his own recitation. The memory palace of praise, lyric celebration, and free generosity is transformed into a charnel house; the memory of words gives way to the re-membering of dismembered bodies.

The slave as commodity. The central issue is clearly the reduction of human personhood and individuality to the status not just of mere instrumentality and servitude but to commodity, object of economic exchange. In his analysis of the fetish character of commodities Marx imagines what it would be like if the commodity could speak. The deepest answer, I suggest, is contained in the nexus of narrative, memory, and slavery. It is not just that the slave speaks of a time when she was a commodity but also that her speaking itself becomes a new form of commodity.[24] The slave's memory of suffering is traded in for cash and credit, and the "authenticating documents," the "letters of credit" that verify the truth of the narrative, are as important as the story proper. The slave's narrative becomes her principal stock in trade, the cultural capital that she invests by putting it into circulation. Her memories are money, her account earns "interest" in a market that is beyond her control. The collapse of slavery after the Civil War was a disaster for the literary market in slave narrative. "Essentially," say Davis and Gates, "the slave narrative proper could no longer exist after slavery was abolished."[25] The value of slave narrative seemed to depend on the real existence of chattel slavery, as if a gold reserve of "real wealth" in human suffering had to back up the paper currency of the writings on slavery.

Marcel Mauss's studies of exchange in archaic societies suggest that slavery is inseparable from the general problem of the human being as object of exchange, as an item to be "given freely" in rituals of gift giving or bought and sold in the marketplace.[26] (Sethe, the central character in Toni Morrison's *Beloved*, is a "timely present for Mrs. Garner"[10];[27] Frederick Douglass is given by his master to a relative in Baltimore.) The slave regularly appears as a commodity along with movable furniture, symbolic and ornamental artifacts, animals, and (most notably) women and children.[28]

This conjunction suggests that the special problem of slave discourse might be illuminated by the contexts of "object discourse," or ekphrasis (when mute objects seem to speak), prosopopoeia, or personification (when the nonhuman acquires a voice), and, most obviously, the narratives of women and children. "Ekphrasis and the Other" explored the problem of object discourse, especially the object-as-person.[29] In the remainder of this essay I want to work back toward the problem of slave narrative with a series of snapshots of specific conjunctions of description and memory in the imagetexts of women, children, and "survivors"—representatives of groups that have, in various ways, suffered forms of subjection and abject powerlessness that compel public acts of autobiography. At the outset, of course, we have to register some distinctions. Women's narrative often describes memories of subjection and victimization comparable to slave narrative, but it rarely does so from the standpoint of an "ex-woman," while the slave narrative, as we've noted, always seems to be that of an "ex-slave." Narratives of childhood memories are often, like slave and women's narratives, recollections of abjection and powerlessness, but they recall a domain of experience that, unlike slavery and womanhood, seems as close to being universal as we can imagine. The survivor's narrative comes close to the border of "blankness" in memory that Frederick Douglass describes, but that blankness is figured not as a durable, extended condition of servitude and commodification but, instead, as the threat of the total extinction of all witnessing memory, on the one hand, and the unendurable pain of experiential memory, on the other.

Wordsworth's *Prelude* will serve as my paradigm for the autobiographical narrative focused on memories of early childhood. Wordsworth's characterization of his childhood as a "fair seed time" of blessed freedom and sensual delight may seem an odd example to juxtapose with the horrors of slave narrative, but it is precisely the remoteness and freedom of *The Prelude* from these issues that makes it an interesting comparison. *The Prelude* is about narrative and memory as technologies of freedom and power. It is riddled with exactly those sorts of complex reflections on memory that are supposed to be absent from slave narrative and emerges from a social position of "bourgeois consciousness" very similar to the sentimental liberalism that enframes the early white abolitionist reception of slave narrative.

Like the slave narratives, Wordsworth's autobiography is punctuated by intensely visualized descriptive passages he calls "spots of time," a transference of the classical memory architecture onto scenes (usually) of natural landscape. The experiences stored in these memory places play a double role, as (1) repositories of poetic "wealth," storehouses of impressions that nourish the mature poet's imagination, and (2) reminders of power, reassurances that "the mind is lord and master," outward sense the "obedient servant" of the mind's "will." What Wordsworth calls the "eye" of his song roams freely over these memory scenes, "recollecting" the "interest" invested in them and employing their visionary power to undo the "despotism of the eye."

This, at any rate, is the Wordsworthian ideology of a stabilized master-slave dialectic between temporal narration and spatial description, adult maturity and childish sensuality. In fact, however, the positions of dominance and servitude are not as secure as Wordsworth might wish. The spots of time do not typically show us the "mastery" of the mind or will but, rather, the unruliness of imagination and sensation. They don't show a freely moving temporal subjectivity but, instead, a compulsive tendency to return to scenes of traumatic experience, often characterized by a "visionary dreariness" and impoverishment and invested with a nameless, exorbitant guilt. The mature poet may claim to have "mastered" the sensuous child he once was, but the Child still asserts itself as Father to the man, an image of lost power and freedom that recedes in the face of a future of declining power and imaginative poverty. Wordsworth's mastery, in short, is the ambivalence of the bourgeois "sovereign subject," a rather more modest role than his unqualified egotism might like to claim. Wordsworth's narrative progress through the time-space structure of his memory system is as much an account of a man flying from something he dreads as seeking something he loves.

If *The Prelude* exemplifies the ambivalent conjunction of narrative, memory, and subjection characteristic of male "poetic sensibility" in the early nineteenth century, Charlotte Brontë's *Jane Eyre* provides a corresponding type of the poetical female. For Jane, however, the sublime egotism of *The Prelude* (and its accompanying ambivalence about the self as master or slave) is not so readily available. *Jane Eyre* seems designed to affirm both the thematized social position of servitude (the governess's progress from orphaned social outcast to security as wife and mother) and the formal servitude of description of visual space, the renunciation of narrated actions in time. This feature is announced in the first sentence of the novel, a negative declaration that "there was no possibility of taking a walk that day," followed almost immediately by an affirmation of this negativity: "I was glad of it."[30]

I don't mean, of course, that *Jane Eyre* has no action or temporality, only that the narration of action is subordinated to and organized by the description of—indeed the fixation on—spatial settings. The narrator of *Jane Eyre* doesn't even have the illusion of Wordsworthian freedom to roam "at will" over space and time, picking places and actions in accordance with the requirements of a liberation narrative. Her telling is strictly confined to a sequence of places that are also to be understood as times. In each of these place-times (Gateshead Hall, Lowood School, Thornfield, Marsh End, Ferndean) the circumscribing of point of view mirrors the immuring of the heroine. These spots of time are more like prisons. When Jane surveys an infinite Wordsworthian prospect from her window ("there was the garden; there were the skirts of Lowood; there was the hilly horizon") and longs for the "liberty" it suggests, her immediate reaction is to abandon her petition in favor of a prayer for "a new servitude" (117). Within each of these memory places the narrative emphasizes Jane's role as a seeing subject, a sharp-eyed observer and visionary painter, and the passages between these places are regularly occluded by episodes of relatively unstable vision and uncertain narrative representation. The transition from Gateshead to Lowood occurs in a dreamy night journey; the move from Lowood to Thornfield is presented as the unrepresented gap between the acts of a play; the flight from Thornfield to Marsh End is told by a narrator lost in a storm.

In both *The Prelude* and *Jane Eyre,* then, the role of memory and the technology of memory as a composite image-text system, is ostensibly constructive and positive. Memory, like description, is the servant of the narrative, and of the narrator's identity. The spots of time and place-times allow the narrator's life to be retraced, re-membered, and re-experienced in a mutual interchange with the reader. Wordsworth's addressed "friend" becomes a "we" who goes back with him to the origins of his own consciousness, a collaborator in the process of turning Wordsworth's private memory places into public commonplaces that will be a shareable patrimony, the renewed national identity of an "English soul." Jane Eyre's reader is, like Rochester, in the paradoxical position of mastery and subservience, "led by the hand" (in Virginia Woolf's phrase) and forced to see what Jane sees. Jane "serves" as our eyes; like Hegel's master, the reader becomes a dependent overseer. Like Wordsworth, she publicizes her memory, not so much to establish a utopian public sphere of English "nature" but to stabilize a sphere of feminine privacy in which a certain limited and therapeutic freedom may be exercised.

But memory, as Borges loves to remind us, may be a mixed blessing, and not merely "mixed" in the manner of the stabilized ambivalence narrated by Wordsworth and Brontë. What if memory took us back to that blankness before memory conjured with by Frederick Douglass? What if the materials of memory are overwhelming, so traumatic that the remembering of them threatens identity rather than reconstitutes it? What if identity had to be constituted out of a strategic amnesia, a selective remembering, and thus a selective *dis*(re)membering of experience? What if the technology of memory, the composite visual–verbal architecture of the memory palace, becomes a haunted house? What if recollection led us back not to a stabilized public or private sphere but into what Hortense Spillers calls "the dizzying motions of a symbolic enterprise" that must be continually reinvented?[31]

The negativity of memory, the need to forget while remembering, is perhaps most vividly illustrated in Holocaust survivor narratives. Claude Lantzmann's *Shoah,* for instance, rigorously excludes a certain kind of visual memory and narration, refusing to show any documentary footage of the concentration camps or of the war.[32] All visual representation of the camps is situated in the present of the film's narration, from the standpoint of its *récit,* in the *now* of the 1980s. Auschwitz is presented as a springlike pastoral landscape in which all the signs of horror and suffering are muted and nearly forgotten. Memory is carried by the soundtrack, the voice of the interviewer and his interlocutors painstakingly reconstructing not only "what happened" (the *histoire* of the narrative), but also how it felt, how it looked, what the experience was. While Lantzmann's camera eye seems to wander blindly, almost aimlessly, over the unreadable surface of a landscape that effaces all but the most general contours of memory, the voice-over dialogue penetrates and probes like a surgeon searching out a hidden cancer. At times the patient cries out in protest, as when one survivor explodes in resentment against Lantzmann's insistent, seemingly impertinent questions about the color of the trucks that carried them to the camps.

> "What color were the trucks?"
> "What color? I don't remember! Perhaps green, I think. No. I can't say. I will tell you what happened, but don't ask me to go back in memory. I don't go back in memory."

The refusal to "go back" in memory, triggered by the request to recall a color, is a refusal to revive a visual memory, to remember the experience in a form that brings it too close, too near to a reexperiencing of the unspeakable. "Telling," or "passing on," a story—the public, verbal recounting of a temporal sequence of events—is possible, allows perhaps a mastery of the materials. But *describing* the experience, recounting the experiential density of visual details, especially those trivial details that do nothing to advance the narrative but, instead, "spread the narrative in space," as Genette puts it—this way of telling is too dangerous. It threatens to master the narrator, to produce all too vividly an *effet de réel* and to take the narrator "back in memory" to a place he or she cannot endure. The visual imagery in narrative description activates the mnemotechnique as an uncontrollable technology; the phantom figures in the landscape or memory palace threaten to come alive, to be remembered and resurrected from the dead as ghosts who act upon the material world and the body of the narrator. We should recall here that legendary origin of the rhetorical memory system involves Simonides's being asked to identify the disfigured bodies of those killed when the banqueting hall/memory palace collapses on them. Simonides has to convert the function of memory from its proper function as an artificial aid to public performance into a mode of private, experiential recollection that will make possible, in its turn, the public commemoration of the dead. Although cheated by Scopas, Simonides as the lone survivor owes his listeners that much. The Holocaust survivor narrative is also the payment of a debt owed to the dead; failure to bear witness may be even more unendurable than the act of recollection. As Mauss notes, "the punishment for failure to reciprocate" the gift in archaic systems of exchange "is slavery for debt" (49).

Toni Morrison's *Beloved* insists upon a similar obligation to remember, to carry memory back into materials both forgotten and immemorial, to explore both repressed experience and experience located in the blankness prior to memory.[33] Morrison describes her own method of "literary archeology" in her essay "Sites of Memory," as a "recollection that moves from the image . . . to the text." Starting with "a journey to a site to see what remains were left behind and to reconstruct the world that these remains imply," she goes on to a text, a narrative, an account of the temporal processes that produced the image. "By 'image,'" Morrison insists, "I don't mean 'symbol,'" a prefabricated literary sign. "I simply mean 'picture' and the feelings that accompany the picture."[34] Much of the novel is built accordingly upon intensely vivid visual descriptions of memorable scenes, what Sethe calls her "rememories":

> Some things you forget. Other things you never do. . . . Places, places are still there. If a house burns down, it's gone, but the place—the picture of it—stays, and not just in my rememory, but out there, in the world. What I remember is a picture floating out there outside my head.

These pictures, Sethe insists, are not private or subjective. They are not mere "memories," but "rememories," a term that suggests a memory that contains its own independent mechanism of retrieval, as if memory could remember itself. Even if Sethe dies, "the picture of what I did, or knew, or saw is still out there" (36). One thing that gives rememories endurance and objectivity is, of course, the very act of telling about them, which has the potential to produce a reexperiencing of the original event, a "passing on" of the rememory. When Beloved tells her memories to Denver, her sister "began to see what she was saying and not just to hear it" (77).

But the narrative voice of Morrison's novel repeatedly suggests that her purpose is not just the traditional fictional aim of "making us see" these events in vivid detail, nor is it the traditional historical aim (as articulated by Collingwood) of constructing "a picture, a coherent whole," and filling in the gaps, penetrating the "veil" that pain, propriety, and national amnesia have placed over the unspeakable experience of American slavery. Morrison's story aims to make the very process of passing on the story and its rememories a problem—the very subject of the story—in itself. The narrator concludes the final chapter by repeating three times, "It was not a story to pass on," an ambiguous refrain that suggests both the imperative to remember and to forget. Does *passing on* emphasize the "passing," implying that it is not a story that one can avoid, a story one cannot "take a pass on"? Is the story actually a blockage or impossible border that prevents the teller or hearer from passing from negritude and slavery to freedom?[35] Or is passing on a story compared to "telling" or "recounting" it something like the difference between handing over a story as something like a material object, a gift, legacy, or commodity and simply "reporting" a series of events as a way of getting rid of them? This difference is much like the division between descriptive *fixation* on visual re-membering and re-experiencing and the forms of narrative that aim at a temporal passing through a sequence of events, passing beyond them with an account that puts the story, as we say, "behind us" or even "before us," as a story to be read and reread. Genette admits that the narration-description "frontier" may be nothing but a late development in the history of narrative structures; perhaps it is a modern formation connected with secular autobiography, the narrative form in which subjective memory and privacy establish their "classic" relation to the public sphere.[36] The narrative-descriptive boundary may be nothing more than a phantom difference, an ideologeme imposed on the seamless web of language and narration. That does not keep it from impinging on actual practices of storytelling and reception. The difference between vision and voice, the narrator as seeing and speaking subject, between passing on and telling a story, haunts the practice of storytelling the way ghosts haunt the living memory.

The descriptive passages of *The Prelude* are haunted by "mighty forms" that veil a guilt about an abandoned child and childhood Wordsworth can never quite specify.[37] *Jane Eyre* is haunted by the marginally representable figure of Bertha Mason, the Creole madwoman in the attic. The construction of Jane's secure identity depends, as Gayatri Spivak has shown, on the erasure of her memory—literally, the burning of her along with the place she inhabits.[38] But Toni Morrison's task is to remember slavery, to reconstruct the experiential place-times of racial degradation, loss of identity, and abject servitude. The "haunting" of memory can, therefore, not be marginalized in representation; it must be allowed full sway. The ghost has to be re-membered so vividly and physically that it can lift chairs, eat, be seen by the neighbors, get sick, get pregnant, and finally disappear in full view of an entire community. *Beloved* is arguably the most physically literal and material ghost story ever written, and the reason is that its rememories are too powerful and dangerous to pass on without elaborate defenses and mediations, including the defense of laughter and the presentation of a ghost who walks in the noonday sun. Beloved, the slaughtered baby, must be simultaneously remembered and forgotten, resurrected and dismembered:

> Everybody knew what she was called, but nobody anywhere knew her name. Disremembered and unaccounted for, she cannot be lost because no one is looking for her, and even if they were, how can they call her if they don't know her name? Although she has claim, she is not claimed. In the place where the long grass opens the girl who waited to be loved and cry shame erupts into her separate parts, to make it easy for the chewing laughter to swallow her all away. (274)

> It was not a story to pass on.

> They forgot her like a bad dream. After they made up their tales, shaped and decorated them, those that saw her that day on the porch quickly and deliberately forgot her.

But Toni Morrison's narrator, the speaking/seeing voice of *Beloved,* has not forgotten. She tells the story of remembering, dismembering, and disremembering. Who is she? We cannot say, even about her gender. She is a classic, omniscient narrative voice—not an autobiographical "I"/"Eye" as in the slave narrative but, instead, a disembodied, anonymous voice/inscription that cannot be located except by a kind of proximity to Sethe, Denver, Paul D, Beloved, and, most generally, the places in which most of the story transpires and is recollected. *Beloved*'s narrator is the ghost of the "sites," the textual place-times or pictorial rememories that she haunts relentlessly. The central place-time of *Beloved,* the memory palace that structures its narrative, is a haunted house, 124 Bluestone Road in Cincinnati, Ohio, the place in which all the other place-times of the story (the landscape setting of "The Clearing," the slave pastoral of "Sweet Home," the hells of the Georgia prison camp and the Middle Passage) may be reassembled.

The centrality of this house is stressed from the opening sentence of the novel: "124 was spiteful. Full of a baby's venom. The women in the house knew it and so did the children." The first "character" to be introduced in the narrative is the house, but it is not even named as a house (though it is given an emotion of its own). Only a number designates the house, a number that (as we learn by the end of the first paragraph) "it didn't have . . . then, because Cincinnati didn't stretch that far." The narrative begins, in other words, with a simultaneous immersion in and distancing from the *histoire* it recounts: "spiteful" designates the condition of the house from 1855 to 1873, the period when it was haunted by an invisible baby ghost who shatters mirrors and leaves handprints on the cake. But "124" designates the house at a much later period, when Cincinnati has extended its suburbs, when the story has passed on into legend and, finally, into forgetfulness and laughter.[39] The opening sentence is thus anachronistic, temporally impossible. 124 never was spiteful; "the gray and white house on Bluestone Road" was spiteful. The contradiction is between an "account," or "recounting" from a historical distance (when 124 has a meaning), and describing, remembering, placing, and seeing the colors and location on a specific road itself named for local colors like "bluestone."

The insistence on producing this chronologically impossible sentence is the opening move in a narrative of "disrememberment." It shows us how to tell a story that is not a story to pass on. Morrison also shows us what it would mean *not* to be able to disremember, to be overwhelmed by the remembering and reexperiencing of slavery, in her account of Grandma Baby Suggs's withdrawal from her active life as a leader of the black community after their betrayal of Sethe and the death of Beloved. Grandma baby puts herself to bed: "Her past had been like her present—intolerable—and since she knew death was anything but forgetfulness, she used the little energy left her for pondering color." It is as if Baby Suggs were performing an exercise in amnesia, veiling the disfigured images of memory in shrouds of pink and blue. Perhaps she is also "pondering color" in a more abstract sense, as the "veil" or color line that doesn't merely cover the memory figures but disfigures them in the first place.

124 Bluestone Road, like all memory palaces, is both a private site and a public location, a "commonplace" in a social, even a national imaginary. "Not a house in the country ain't packed to its rafters with some dead Negro's grief," is Baby Suggs's practical response to being haunted. The house is thus "a person rather than a structure" (29), and yet it is also a structure (like a person) of intersubjective memory spaces.

Sethe's daughter Denver has "lived all her life in a house peopled by the living activity of the dead" and thus sees it simultaneously as a person, a building, and a narrative riddled with puns on "story" and the "storage" of memory. She provides the most explicit visualization of the narrative architecture and the pictured site in memory that is haunted by the text of *Beloved,* a remarkable passage that offers a metapicture of the novel:

> Easily she stepped into the told story that lay before her eyes on the path she followed away from the window. There was only one door to the house and to get to it from the back you had to walk all the way around to the front of 124, past the storeroom, past the cold house. And to get to the part of the story she liked best, she had to start way back. (29)

NOTES

A slightly different version of this chapter appears in *Picture Theory* (Chicago: University of Chicago Press, 1994). Reprinted by permission.

1. John Blassingame notes that a "staggering" number of first-person accounts of American slavery survive, not only in the form of full-length autobiographies but also in interviews and transcripts published in the abolitionist press. See his book *Slave Testimony* (Baton Rouge: Louisiana State University Press, 1977), and *Slave Community,* 2d ed. (New York: Oxford University Press, 1979), 378.

2. See Spillers's important essay, "Changing the Letter: The Yokes, the Jokes of Discourse, or, Mrs. Stowe, Mr. Reed," in *Slavery and the Literary Imagination,* ed. Deborah E. McDowell and Arnold Rampersad (Baltimore: Johns Hopkins University Press, 1989), 25–61. Spillers has been principally responsible for the critical redescription of slavery as a heterogeneous "spatio-temporal object" and a *"primarily* discursive" phenomenon that must be "reinvented" by "every generation of . . . readers" (28–99).

3. W. J. T. Mitchell, "Ekphrasis and the Other," *South Atlantic Quarterly* (Summer 1992).

4. The visual emphasis is marked both at the level of inscription ("visible language") and the level of description. The "act of writing," as Charles Davis and Henry Louis Gates note, was "considered the visible sign of reason," and one of the first questions to be asked about a slave narrative was whether it was *written* (as Frederick Douglass advertised his) by the narrator or transcribed by someone else. The ability to decipher visible language, to *read* is of course taken as an even more fundamental sign of freedom and rationality and is often presented in vivid scenes that Davis and Gates identify as "the figure of the talking book," the spectacle of the white master reading aloud. See *The Slave's Narrative,*

ed. Charles T. Davis and Henry Louis Gates, Jr. (Oxford: Oxford University Press, 1985), xxiii, xxvii. Davis and Gates document as well the need for skeptical northern readers to be "ocularly convinced" by eyewitness accounts (9) and the heavy emphasis on visual/visionary rhetoric: "The narrated, descriptive 'eye' was put into service as a literary form to posit both the individual 'I' of the black author, as well as the collective 'I' of the race. . . . The very *face* of the race . . . was contingent upon the recording of the black *voice*" (xxvi).

5. Early reviews of slave narratives testify to this rhetoric of transparency: "Through the well written life of such an individual, we can look in upon the character, condition, and habits of his class with as much clearness and confidence as through a window. . . . [W]e think the reader will not retain, through many pages, a doubt of the perfect accuracy of its picture of slavery. If it is a mirror, it is of the very best plate glass, in which objects appear so clear and 'natural' that the beholder is perpetually mistaking it for an open window without any glass at all" (Anon. review of *The Life and Adventures of a Fugitive Slave,* by Charles Ball, *Quarterly Anti-Slavery Magazine* 1, no. 4 (1836); reprinted in Davis and Gates, *Slave's Narrative,* 6). See also William Andrews, *To Tell a Free Story* (Urbana: University of Illinois Press, 1986), 15, on the "spectacle" of the slave auction as a regular motif in slave narrative. Hortense Spillers also discusses the role of "iconism" and the "image crisis" in "Changing the Letter," 50.

6. Olney, "'I Was Born': Slave Narratives, Their Status as Autobiography and as Literature," in Davis and Gates, *Slave's Narrative,* 148–75. Olney remarks on "the nearly total lack of any 'configurational dimension'" in slave narrative and the lack of self-consciousness about memory, which is "a clear-glass, neutral" faculty that gives "a true picture of slavery as it really is" (150).

7. Davis and Gates, *Slave's Narrative,* 151.

8. William Andrews notes these gaps but traces them to incapacity and lack: "When we find a gap in a slave narrator's objective reportage of the facts of slavery, or a lapse in his prepossessing self-image, we must pay special attention. These deviations may indicate either a loss of narrative control or a deliberate effort by the narrator to grapple with aspects of his or her personality that may have been repressed out of deference to or fear of the dominant culture" (*To Tell a Free Story,* 8). Again, Douglass's *Narrative* indicates a counterpossibility— that silence, or "gaps," in the story may be a sign of resistance. Douglass explains his refusal to tell how he escaped from Maryland as a pragmatic issue (he wants to protect the routes available to other fugitive slaves) and as an act of literary discretion, a refusal of the pleasures of romance and adventure.

9. See Houston Baker on the "extraordinary blankness" (Henry James's phrase) that links white and black American autobiography in the nineteenth century ("Autobiographical Acts and the Voice of the Southern Slave," Davis and Gates, *Slave's Narrative,* 243).

10. Davis and Gates make exactly this point in their introduction to *The Slave's Narrative* (xi). Hortense Spillers testifies with considerable eloquence, however, to her ambivalence to "the spread-eagle tyranny of discursivity across the terrain of what we used to call, with impunity, 'experience'" ("Changing the Letter," 33). This ambivalence is, in my view, traceable to what Spillers shows

to be the heterogeneity of discourse itself, its intersections with representation and iconicity.

11. See William Andrews, *To Tell a Free Story,* chapter 6, on the canonization of Douglass's *Narrative* at the expense of his second autobiography, *My Bondage and My Freedom.* Andrews's own master-narrative of the increasing literary sophistication of slave narrative as a movement toward "free storytelling" (xi) tends to reinforce the notion that the earlier narratives (including Douglass's) are less "readerly."

12. Derrida, "From Restricted to General Economy: A Hegelianism without Reserve," *Writing and Difference,* trans. Alan Bass (Chicago: University of Chicago Press, 1978), 255.

13. "The most obvious distinguishing mark is that it is an extremely mixed production" (Olney, "I Was Born," 151). See also Robert Burns Stepto on slave narrative as "an eclectic narrative form," in "I Rose and Found My Voice: Narration, Authentication and Authorial Control in Four Slave Narratives," Davis and Gates, *Slave's Narrative,* 225–41.

14. Genette, "The Frontiers of Narrative," in *Figures of Literary Discourse,* trans. Alan Sheridan (New York: Columbia University Press, 1984). See also the Yale French Studies special issue "Toward a Theory of Description" (61, no. 13 [Summer 1980]), particularly the essays by Philippe Hamon and Michel Beaujour, which develop in great detail the metalanguage of description, the "figures of literary discourse" that describe for us the function of the descriptive.

15. The precise moment of the historical emergence of the narration-description distinction as an internal frontier of narrative form would be devilishly difficult to locate. Genette's sense that it is modern, or relatively recent, seems generally sound, and I'm tempted to identify it with the rise of the novel, and the emergence of secular subjectivity as a central feature of narrative. Certainly, the "visual/aural" difference that might be linked with the descriptive interpolation can take other forms. Thucydides' division of his *Peloppenesian War* into eyewitness descriptions and orally remembered set-speeches (what he calls "erga" and "logoi") produces this cut in a radically different way, one that is congruent with the diegesis-mimesis distinction. But one would also want to take into account certain powerful precedents such as the tradition of ekphrasis, set-piece descriptions of special objects, works of art, and visual scenes in epic. See Mitchell, "Ekphrasis and the Other."

16. The classic study here is, of course, Frances Yates, *The Art of Memory* (Chicago: University of Chicago Press, 1966). See also Mary Carruthers's excellent study, *The Book of Memory: A Study of Memory in Medieval Culture* (Cambridge: Cambridge University Press, 1990). Carruthers notes the persistence of the key figures of memory (the wax tablet or writing surface, the storage box, and the visual/pictorial impression) well beyond antiquity. She also argues convincingly against the "current opinion that there are radical differences between 'oral culture' (based upon memory) and 'literate culture' (based upon writing)" (16) and corrects the impression left by Frances Yates that "artificial memory" was an "occult" rather than "commonplace" tradition after antiquity (258).

17. See Frances Yates, *The Art of Memory,* for a magisterial account of the ancient memory systems as "imagetexts." The key move in Yates's account is

her noticing that the legendary inventor of the art of memory, Simonides of Ceos, is also credited with originating the *ut pictura poesis* tradition (28).

18. Genette, "Frontiers of Narrative."

19. Genette, "Frontiers of Narrative."

20. The narrative-descriptive hierarchy is, of course, only one of many sites of power difference in the structure of textuality. The distinctions between speech and writing, between telling a story and commenting on it, are perhaps even more obvious thresholds of contention. Frederick Douglass's struggle with the Garrisonian abolitionists was often waged over these textual frontiers. Douglass's decisions to *write* (rather than merely serve the movement as a platform orator) and to be an *editor* (rather than merely serve as a writer for Garrison's publications) are deliberate crossings of thresholds within the literary institution. That this sort of threshold had already been violated from the first time Douglass opened his mouth is indicated in the first reactions to Douglass's oratory: "In those days, whenever Douglass strayed from narrating wrongs to denouncing them, Garrison would gently correct him by whispering, 'Tell your story, Frederick,' and John Collins would remark more directly, 'Give us the facts, . . . we will take of the philosophy'" in Robert Stepto, "Storytelling in Early Afro-American Fiction: Frederick Douglass' 'The Heroic Slave,'" in *Black Literature and Literary Theory*, ed. Henry Louis Gates, Jr. [New York: Methuen, 1984], 175.

21. Derrida, "Economimesis," *Diacritics* 11 (Summer 1981): 3–25.

22. See Carruthers, *Book of Memory*, on memory as a "treasure-hoard" and "money-pouch" (39).

23. Recounted in Yates, *Art of Memory*, chapter 1.

24. James Olney points out that "the narrative lives of the ex-slaves were as much possessed and used by the abolitionists as their actual lives had been by slaveholders" (Davis and Gates, *Slave's Narrative*, 154). Frederick Douglass notes that when he was urged to speak at an antislavery convention in 1841 he felt that "it was a severe cross and [he] took it up reluctantly": "The truth was, I felt myself a slave, and the idea of speaking to white people weighed me down. I spoke but a few moments, when I felt a degree of freedom" (*Narrative*, 119).

25. Davis and Gates, *Slave's Narrative*, xxii.

26. Mauss, *The Gift: The Form and Reason for Exchange in Archaic Societies*, trans. W. D. Halls (New York: Norton, 1990). I'm indebted to Jacques Derrida's lectures collected in *Le Donner le temps* (Given Time) and to a number of conversations with Professor Derrida, for the application of Mauss's work to the question of slavery.

27. Toni Morrison, *Beloved* (New York: Plume Books, 1987).

28. See Mauss, *The Gift*, 49.

29. See note 3.

30. *Jane Eyre* (1847; reprint, Hammondsworth: Penguin Books, 1966), 39.

31. Spillers, "Changing the Letter," 29.

32. Cf. the effacement of visual memory in Art Spiegelman's *Maus*, which "masks" the human bodies of participants in the Holocaust with the features of cartoon animals.

33. As I was finishing the final revisions of this essay, Mae Henderson's

excellent account of the intersection between "public" and "private" memory, specifically psychoanalysis and historiography, in *Beloved* came to my attention. See Henderson, "Toni Morrison's *Beloved:* Re-Membering the Body as Historical Text," in *Comparative American Identities,* ed. Hortense Spillers (New York: Routledge, 1991), 62–86.

34. Quoted in Henderson, "Toni Morrison's Beloved," 65–66.

35. Mae Henderson also notes this ambiguity and is worried about the implications of the most obvious, literal reading of "not a story to pass on": "Must Morrison's story, along with Sethe's past, be put behind?... Clearly such an injunction would threaten to contradict the motive and sense of the entire novel," which is, in Henderson's view, the reconstruction of "public history" (83). As will become evident, I think Morrison intends the negative meaning and is affirming the need not for a "national amnesia" but for a related kind of forgetting we might call "national mourning." Clearly, the vivid "re-membering" of such pictures as Sethe's flayed back is not produced in order to be forgotten. (See Frances Yates, *Art of Memory,* chap. 1, on the technique of *disfiguring* the *imagines agentes,* the figures located in memory places, by splashing red paint on them to make them more vivid and memorable.) The disfigured bodies are re-membered, as Simonides's task reminds us, in order to be identified and given a proper reburial, a public ceremony of commemoration. The alternative to this twofold project of disinterment and reburial is the haunting of national memory by the unquiet dead, the ghosts of slaves whose experiences and memories are not to be passed on. *Beloved* is utopian and comic in its faith that this nation might be able to make the transition from haunting to mourning, from amnesia to public commemoration.

36. I'm using the concept of the "classic public sphere" here in Jürgen Habermas's sense, as a formation associated with the rise of bourgeois social structures in the eighteenth century. See *The Structural Transformation of the Public Sphere* (Cambridge: MIT Press, 1989).

37. See my essay "Influence, Autobiography, and Literary History: Rousseau's *Confessions* and Wordsworth's *The Prelude,*" *ELH* 57, no. 3 (Fall 1990): 643–64.

38. Gayatri Chakravorty Spivak, "Three Women's Texts and a Critique of Imperialism," *Critical Inquiry* 12, no. 1 (Autumn 1985): 243–61.

39. Hortense Spillers's conjunction of history and farce, "yokes" (of slavery) and "jokes," in her comparison of Harriet Beecher Stowe and Ishmael Reed is apposite here. See "Changing the Letter."

Rhetorics of the Body:
Do You Smell a Fault?

Herbert Blau

Ideology and Zoology: The Transparent Veil

That it was the destiny of ideology to be attached to the body, and its politics, was perhaps to be expected from the early history of the term. When it was introduced at the time of the French Revolution, by Antoine Destutt de Tracy, he developed the elements of the concept on the premise that the study of ideology is part of zoology. As it happens, the historical repertoire of the body's images pays a good deal of attention to the birds and the beasts,[1] which are presumably content with their bodies or don't think twice about them, no less as machines, desiring or otherwise, while the drama of humankind seems constructed on a grid of malaise, indulgence, self-hatred, detestation of the body or short-lived ecstasies, followed by remorse, as well as the monstrous knowledge of whatever *jouissance* that the prisonhouse of language is constructed on the makeshift and mortal scaffold of insubstantial flesh and bone.

That may be why, with all the body building and rhetorical building up, there are still very few people about whom we're inclined to say they are perfectly at ease with their bodies. And the same might be said of the new regime of preferential bodies chosen today on psychosexual grounds, no less those imagined in the ideological fantasy, with its surrealist imagery, of the libidinal flow of a postoedipal theater. Such imaginings are actually quite useful in the theater and have found their way into the psychophysical exercises to which actors have grown accustomed. In the experimental work of the last generation some actors developed remarkable abilities to think the body's organs as transposable elements in a combinatory set or to initiate sound or movement as if enacting the credo of schizoanalysis or, with an imagined dissolution of organs, the uttermost wish of polysexual desire. But in the multiplicity of body rhetorics now sounded on the stage, within the universal spectacle whose apotheosis is noise, the one inarguable rhetoric is the inexorable force of gravity in the semiurgy of floating objects, the allegoresis of body parts.

It may be that in the reification of image diffused all over the world the exuberant body is happily rent, dismembered, disseminated, and that no human language nor historical event can resist this diffusion, as it occurs through electronic memory with the speed of light. True, in the age of simulacra we have image-producing technologies capable of realizing what no actor can and the theater has only dreamed, a full fluidity of the body or total reconstruction, from the liquid(ating) fantasy of a body without organs to the sci-fi promise of no bodies at all. All of this can be achieved, maybe even in cyberspace, with a semblance of performance, but not so far without its haunted referent: the resistless remembrance of the surpassing body, the body that is past, bringing its laden knowledge to performance. (The same was true, we might remember, with the referent in art, the overdetermined object or figure with a history, which was extruded for a time, then returned through the body by means of performance.) In the dematerialized imagery of the spectacle (or in conceptual art) the body may appear to give itself over to its utter dissemination or, like Ibsen's Peer Gynt, to the scenarios of liberation fashioned by desire, in which performance forsakes the structures of drama for the hegemony of a purer play. But the knowledge it returns with is what we always knew, attending upon the absence of an empty stage, which in the ironies of aesthetics is the emblem of that knowledge: we are born astride of a grave and return to it in the end. This is not a mere effect of language, power, desire, or appearance, as Beckett tried to make clear through a burst of rage from the blinded Pozzo, shattering in the instant the ideology of play. It could be said, rather, that language, power, desire, and appearance are themselves the effects, the incorporeal materiality of the grave truth of material being, around which the idea of theater has consolidated itself. There have been in the theater, as we've seen, extraordinary imaginings of a countergravity, as in the lyrical drama of Yeats or the puppet theater of Kleist, though even such imaginings are haunted by the grave, like the mannequins of Tadeusz Kantor in his Theater of the Dead. Or to return again to zoology, we are fastened to a dying animal (as Yeats well knew on the way to Byzantium), which inevitably makes an absurdity of any ideology of desire.

With Destutt de Tracy, who might have rejected countergravity as a manifestation of religious thought, ideology was from the outset kept separate from both metaphysics and desire. If not exactly destiny, biology is the basis of human psychology, and the materialism of the science of ideas was intended, through definition of the laws of human nature and sociability, to theorize the grounds of republican citizenship.[2] As it happened, though, the grounds of republican citizenship had already been enunciated in the carceral theater at the cutting edge of the Terror, as Büchner understood, before Foucault, in *Danton's Death:* "The guillotine makes good Republicans!"[3] With his quite precocious historical understanding Büchner picks up from the chop-logic of the revolution—at the lethal limit of its most utopian thought—the loose ends of the philosophy of the Enlightenment. "The Revolution must end and the Republic begin," says Hérault-Séchelles at the beginning of *Danton's Death.* And with a libidinal impulse to the libertarian vision derived from the Enlightenment, by way, it seems, of William Blake, Camille Desmoulins declares with a kind of rapture against the threat of a renewed puritanism: "The Constitution must be a transparent veil that clings close to the body of the people. Through it we must see the pulsing of every vein, the flexing of every muscle, the quiver of every sinew" (1.1, p. 5).

What we have in Desmoulins's conception of the Constitution is an erotic apprehension of the future in the instant, a premonitory image of Love's Body—what was to become, in the polymorphous perversity of the theatricalized sixties, the transcendent figure of totalizing desire. This was the constitution of the body politics of the Living Theater, literally demanding the future in the instant in the production of *Frankenstein* or reaching for its apotheosis in *Paradise Now,* spelled out by the actual bodies of the performers: *PARADISE.* I am often struck by the degree to which, over a generation later, that writing is still inscribed, with the notion of decentering play, in the transgressive rhetoric of recent theory, as in the desiring bodies of various subject positions or the "phantasmaphysics" of Deleuze, not only the flexing of every muscle but also "the epidermic play of perversity . . . without any trace of representation."[4] But as Nietzsche perceived when he spoke of all value as judgments of the muscles, these judgments are caught up, with the vicissitudes of desire, in the will to power—as well as the insidious depredations of the body itself, subject as it is to the cancerous sedimentations of the indeterminacy of time. So it is in Büchner's characterization of Danton himself, with his fastidious awareness of the body's stink and, with each minute crushing the vanities of desire, his equivocal resistance to the assumption of power.

God-Kissing Carrion: The Social Text

I have written elsewhere on this aspect of *Danton's Death*,[5] which is also, along with Büchner's *Woyzeck*, a virtual index to the issues of postmodern performance as it consolidates itself around the phenomenology and instrumentality of the body, that clinical object with a fantasy life: house of pleasure or prisonhouse; interpellated subject or subject of entropic decay; elusive other of the living word or indeterminate antecedent of the sign; inescapable image of itself or, in the negative theology of poststructuralist thought, the memory bank of after-image, its allegorical ground—in the spectacle of a culture whose symbolic is in ruins. Mere currency, passing strange, the body may be too unstable in the economy of exchange to be the last instance or material base—or, as it was with the valorized body of the antiverbal sixties, the tactile court of last resort. "I had things to say," said Jane Comfort, explaining why, not for the first time in dance, language was reintroduced, "I absolutely didn't know how to do with my body."[6]

While discourse on the body is as avid as ever, this is a significant departure from the assumption of body language as a repository of truth, or the notion of an unaccommodated body, the poor bare forked unmediated thing itself. It should be said, however, that in the performative space between these two possibilities there is a good deal of conceptual sweat and methodological wrangling about the precise relation of the body to language. It is an ideological problem of no minor importance. The problem arises from the seeming inseparability of signifier and signified in the performing body itself, which appears to conflate sign and meaning in its very breath and gesture. Once more Yeats has defined the issue in a talismanic question: "How can we know the dancer from the dance?" The line is usually read as a testament to the inseparability, but there is something in performance that also abrades against it, resists the rhetorical assertion. It is this resistance that Paul de Man reflects or shadows in his *Allegories of Reading:* "There can be no dance without a dancer, no sign without a referent. On the other hand, the authority of the meaning engendered by the grammatical structure is fully obscured by the duplicity of a figure that cries out for the differentiation it conceals."[7] One can say, of course, like Dr. Johnson refuting Bishop Berkeley, that the callous or the shin splint knows the dancer from the dance, though the perceptual issue may be more complicated for us by the dancer's covering that up or forgetting it in performance. As the performer approaches a state of being that would, for Nietzsche, be outside of ideology, the condition of that forgetfulness is another complication.

There is still some carryover of Nietzsche in the move to a cultural politics, but this is not the sort of complication that current readings of the body are really prepared for, or concerned with. The condition of forgetfulness seems to throw the dancer again, inseparably, into the vertigo of the dance, which may be thought of as the dance of high modernism, or a form of indeterminacy through which, paradoxically, the body may assert itself as presence. That is, as we know, discomfiting to critical theory. What we are asked to be particularly conscious of now is based on this assumption: prior representations of the body merely disguise the fact that there is no pure phenomenological body or—without the inscriptions of social production—a natural human body as such. To our watchful semiotics such an idea would seem to be as bathetic as the Ghost's anguished outcry in *Hamlet* for the unscarred smoothness of his royal body. In this play so mordantly conscious of the body as machine or, with a residue of desire, god-kissing carrion, the body is with the king, but the king is not with the body. Which is to say that it is not really the body we are talking about any longer but, rather, a corporeal abstraction, the more or less emblooded projection of bodiless thought coursing through the (represented) body, derealized as it is by the wild and whirling words. Whatever the mysterious substance that flowed through "the natural gates and alleys of the body," leaving it "barked about / Most lazarlike, with vile and loathsome crust" (1.5.71–72), we tend to look at the crust now as mere dubious evidence of a bodily absence, to be read as a social text.

So, too, the body is now seen as a social formation or system of relations, discursive, material, and psychosexual, the distinct outgrowth of historical modes of production or, the body entangled with language, as the inscription of a personal history. "Which body?" asked Roland Barthes, whose body existed for him, he said, only in two general forms, migraine and sensuality, "theatrical to itself only to a mild degree," and certainly not as the old heroic body of myth, which has passed through the overexposures of history and the dramaturgy of the unconscious into ideology. Nevertheless, he was "captivated to the point of fascination by the socialized body, the mythological body, the artificial body (the body of Japanese costumes), and the prostituted body (of the actor)."[8] With more or less fascination and (despite a view of language as body) rare displays of sensuality, all of this has come to be taken for granted by critical theorists. But like anything taken for granted, the question remains whether, as counterideology, it is too much so. With a grievous sense of the body as socially produced, the theater has always been—even in the classical world, certainly with Euripides—obsessed with the question, as it struggles with the notion that the body is marked, written, overdetermined, nothing more than a text. Or "tattooed with all the signs of cultural excess on its surface, encoded from within by the language of desire, broken into at will by the ideological interpellation of the subject," something like a "power grid."[9]

As a power grid, then, the body has its political history, its "nature," circumscribed by a set of historical practices and discourses. It is neither hypostatized object nor transcendental signified, nor is it the invariant datum of the Lacanian Real, what in its carnal knowledge takes the position of the one presumed to know by merely remaining mute. The body is, rather, site, instrument, machine, process, or—as Menenius suggests in *Coriolanus* with the parable of the Belly—a kind of ecosystem, invested by the regimen of power and indentifiable as the body of specific historical thought. Thus, we speak now of the atomistic body, the Cartesian body, or the body of organicism that has come to be bureaucratized, the body of use-value, the surreptitiously tortured or polluted body, the body under surveillance, appropriated and pliable, bent to the purposes of an industrial order; or the disaffected bodies of that order: black body, woman's body, gay body, the body in its becoming, with the imagined body of androgyny poised against the unimaginable hybrids of genetic engineering and recombinant DNA.

It is more commonplace now to see upon the material body the inscriptions of ideology and investments of power, without imagining behind it all some prior or elemental body, like an untouched Rosetta Stone, smooth but porous, awaiting the first metonymic marks of the stylus of power. There is more attention now, in cultural critique, to the abject bodies of persecution and repression, but, as we think of the body in its dispossession, the persistent question remains whether there is something about the body that is ontologically dispossessed.

(Do You Smell a Fault?)

At a time when invocation of the Holocaust, that mass site of the dismembered body, seems like a rhetorical device in the discourse of transgression—either its most loaded image or an irony of oppression—there isn't much talk of the Jewish body, once the honorific figure of modernist alienation. Not within that discourse. Or within the developing annals of alienated bodies. That's mainly because of, at least in the United States, the political power of Jews, associated now with bourgeois imperialism, and unswerving support of Israel, despite its distressing status as an oppressor in the Middle East. There is still, however, a Jew in the canonical literature that has been among the chosen figures of the new historicism, though largely for the way in which he exposes the structural contradictions of Shakespeare's time, and of Shakespeare's drama itself, contradictions that persist through the tradition of bourgeois humanism: "If you prick us, do we not bleed?" (*MV* 3.1.66–67). Even before entry into the symbolic, no doubt. There is in Shylock's notorious question not only a reversed pun of phallic aggression but also, amid the current insistence on historically constructed, encoded, or textualized bodies, a reassertion of a universalism of the body, the essential body, which has become in theory something of a historical taboo. A little bit of essentialism doesn't hurt, some say, but when it does it would seem, perhaps, a little closer to history, which has also been defined as the thing that hurts. While there is a quite understandable historical expediency in modalities of performance that deny it, forget it, or deflect attention from it, the deepest conceivable performance still occurs in the order of that body, the essential body, over the unnerving prospect of an ontological fault.

This was, is, and remains the irreducible space of theater. We are reminded of that in the sexual banter that prefaces both the body's mutilations and the political divisions of *King Lear* ("Do you smell a fault?" [1.1.15]). It is also what Beckett seemed to know, in his aporetic way, even before he turned to the stage, a prescience that turns up again, along with the mutilations, in one of his later pieces of prose, what even in the imagining has to be performed: "No mind. Where none. That at least. A place. Where none. For the body to be in."[10] That at least, a place, intimating the fault. (*Pause.*) That pause may be more subjective, more specifically a figure of an ontological break, than the pregnant moment of a Brechtian *gestus,* but it is also a moment of arrested being in which we can hardly ignore the political economy of the body that also enters into performance. Nor the power relations that have "an immediate hold upon it," as Foucault observed, and that, like Pozzo abusing Lucky, "invest it, mark it, train it, torture it, force it to carry out tasks, to perform ceremonies, to emit signs"—and, one might add, to double over those signs in cultural production, of which the theater demonstrates more than any other form that the body, its own major instrument or technology, "becomes a useful force only if it is both a productive body and a subjected body."[11] If institutions and state apparatuses have recourse to the body through diverse procedures, methods, demands, so does the apparatus of theater, each acting method or performance technique constituting, ideologically, another set of demands and verifying by reproduction both a particular image of the body, its capacities and possibilities of freedom, and its systemic constraints.

The systemic constraints of the naturalistic actor are revealed, for instance, by the earlier Brechtian Roland Barthes, in a comparison of the "lovable body" of the Bunraku puppet to the disarticulating mimesis, "the abjectness of its inertia," in the Western marionette. There is, for Barthes, no countergravity in this marionette. Reflecting instead the "inertia of matter" that Kleist attributed to the human body, it is "a caricature of 'life,'" affirming "precisely thereby life's *moral* limits" and serving "to confine beauty, truth and emotion in the living body of the actor—he who nevertheless makes of that body a lie."[12] Since it is still quite arguable whether the constraints of any system produce any more than the approximation of a partial truth, we may be talking, as Nietzsche believed, of degrees of (inevitable) fraudulence, or misrepresentation, like the illusion of truth in the lie of naturalism or, for that matter, in any claim of demystification, the residuum of illusion. As I've suggested elsewhere, the measure of any method is the extent to which it remains convincing about the future of its illusions, or, in the ideological extensions and curvature of time, the way in which the constraints in a system open themselves again, unexpectedly, to history.

With the Bunraku, as Barthes perceives its "lesson in writing," we have another view of performance as a regimen of signs, purified perhaps beyond anything in Brecht. It is not a matter of the puppet aping the human actor, who hardly performs—that animal body impeded by (the forgery of) a "soul"—with anything like the subtlety of the manipulated doll. The dance of the chief operator (his face "visible, smooth, clear, impassive, cold like 'a white onion freshly washed'" [170]) and his two black-hooded assistants rids us of the physiology of the actor and "the alibi of an organic unity," which is, for all its claim of a visceral truth, the simulation of a body that is specifically bourgeois. The Bunraku puppet is neither this unctuous simulation nor, like the marionette, a mere facsimile of bodily gestures, the little phallic thing, a "genital swathe, . . . fallen from the body to become a fetish" (172). What it is, for Barthes, is a concrete abstraction, not a body fetish, with its corporal illusion, but, rather, the versatile instrument of a performative text "in which the codes of expression are detached from each other, pulled free

from the sticky organism in which they are held by Western theater"
(175).

The stickiness of the organism remains an issue in performance
wherever live bodies are still alive (some are not), even through abstraction, like Warda below her blood-red chignon—or, rather, the actor
below the signs of Warda—who is in the psychogenesis of acting an
impertinence of signs. Within the mechanisms or paraphernelia of any
performance, or beyond the nude uncharactered body itself, it is that
impertinent presence that constitutes the expressiveness of codes or the
apparent life force, or vitality, of signs. This is so whether the apparency
of the body is robed, masked, geometrized, armored with doubt or
distanced, or removed from the stage entirely, and, instead of its naked
sonorous streaming realization (as desired by Artaud), there is nothing
but an electronic memory, as in the punctuation of Beckett's *Breath,* the
mere taped vagitus of a cry. It is there that we may feel the cost, the
tragic cost, of emptying the body to all appearances, pulling it free of its
sticky organism, and thinking of it in its absence as a fetishized illusion
that is better deployed in performance as *no more* than a sign.

And this is not only true of the forms of Western theater, since the
organism sticks to all forms, however encoded, like the ritualistic appearances in the dance/drama of the East. There are other, perhaps
worse, things sticking to such appearances, as Brecht observed of the
"magic" of Chinese acting, though he didn't hesitate to borrow its techniques. There are the social structures not only built upon a fault but
which, through the depredations of history or scandals of power or
perversions of faith amounting to a plague, also smell a little or stink to
high heaven—even through such a performance as Mei Lan-Fang's,
which Brecht saw in Moscow. If this is often forgotten amid the new
sentiments about the performance of otherness in cultures remote or
strange, the pull of the organism—its full gravity, the power of the
fault—is a somewhat displaced issue on the postmodern scene, in the
marketplace of culture and the political economy of signs.

The Irreducible Measure

With an inordinately playful consciousness of signs, and a mellower,
cooled-down version of the ecstatic becomings and prospective pleasures
of the body without end, the performance artist Laurie Anderson has
taken a cue, perhaps, from the opening of Dante's *Comedy,* where in the
middle of the journey of life, the dark wood is entered and the straight

way lost. Since she also shares, however, deconstruction's resistance to closure, the errancy in Anderson is accelerated and the body is like a freeway: "I . . . I AM IN MY BODY . . . I AM IN MY BODY THE WAY . . . I AM IN MY BODY THE WAY MOST PEOPLE DRIVE . . . I AM IN MY BODY THE WAY MOST PEOPLE DRIVE THEIR CARS." The song is from *Americans on the Move,* in which she elaborates the parable of lost direction into a landscape of rain and ceaseless traffic and driving through the night to a place you've never been with everything unfamiliar, so that you pull "into the next station and you feel so awkward saying, 'Excuse me, can you tell me where I am?' "[13]

With more or less anxiety or existential angst, or as with Anderson a certain hip levity on the postmodern freeway, I suppose we've all been lost in the body just about that way. There is, however, a sort of countermovement in which, as we think of the aging body, the body is lost in us. (I am not talking here of an ideological category. Excuse me, can you tell me where it went?) Which is to say that it remains in its unceasing disappearance (much too subtle to see) the irreducible measure of our biological existence, what remains in theater its inexhaustible sign, what makes it theater even when, in the always failing scrutiny of the gaze, it claims to be something else: either nonmimetic *performance* without hidden recesses or the *after-image* that, for want of a better word, we think of as *life*—as in the myths of ideology the life spontaneously lived. This is the mortal measure of performance as it occurs in a tactile state, however phantasmatic or dispersed it may appear to be, as with the partial objects of dream, which are instances or relations or states of the body or the refracted appearances of floating body parts. I am in my body the way that is simply inescapable, not to be deferred or lost as on the freeway in the metonymic appearances of a referential chain nor reconstituted in the eternity of ideology as a linguistic subject, though I am that, too, to all appearances, which keep us tautologically in the double bind.

"We are all frail," says Angelo in *Measure for Measure* (2.4.121), taking the plaintive measure of the former piety of his words into the libidinal fallout of his biological existence. What he is saying may be, depending on the acting, as hypocritical as anything he said before—the better the acting, the more impermeable, as if all that went before were nothing but theater, with no guarantee at all that the rest of it won't be. Such an interpretation may arise, it's true, from the paranoia of theater believing its own hype and passing off on us, with a certain pathos, its own ambivalent vision of the omnipresence of appearance. We are all frail. If that's easily verifiable in the psychopathology of everyday life, theater remains the form most dependent upon, fascinated with, drawn, quartered by, and fixated upon the body, its vulnerabilities, pain, and disappearance. The body art of recent years tried, in objectifying the body or treating it impersonally, as an experimental object, to abstract the pain or play with disappearance to keep the pathos at a distance. But what was particularly striking in the focus on the body in the emergence of conceptual art—even the "theatricality" that instrumentalized the body—was that it couldn't quite escape the inheritance of theater, the grievous subtext of all performance: there in the flesh, the attrition of appearance upon appearance.

There might be meditative events in resolute stasis or "movement at any cost," as Charles Olson once wrote, "violence, knives / anything to get the body in,"[14] but once it's in, conceptually in, it's hard to escape certain archetypal images at the extremity of thought. Some of these were almost literalized with violence, knives, at the conceptual end of body art: Prometheus nailed to the rock, before either time (or the theater) began, or the rotting carcass of Ajax, impaled on Hector's sword, there like a grisly sundial at the meridian of ancient theater, as the unendurable measure of the brutality of human time. And what must have been or seemed forbidden: the access to knowledge, the specifically Promethean impulse that, even in the empiricism of certain forms of body art, must have felt in a hallucinatory moment like knowledge of the divine.

The Subject of Knowledge: Extremity of the Actual

"Knowledge does not slowly detach itself from its empirical roots, the initial needs from which it arose," wrote Foucault, "to become pure speculation subject only to the demands of reason; its development is not tied to the constitution and affirmation of a free subject; rather, it creates a progressive enslavement to its instinctive violence. Where religions once demanded the sacrifice of bodies, knowledge calls for experimentation on ourselves, calls us to the sacrifice of the subject of knowledge" (*LCP* 163). Body art, as an ideological and existential manifestation of conceptualism, wanted to have it both ways: to be the subject of knowledge and yet a free subject. The artist who submits his or her body to the stringencies of form—and much body art was intensely formalistic—is on the political level resisting appropriation and refusing to be alienated as labor in the process of the work (and, at least before documentation, the products as well). With less symbolist expressivity than the dancer and the dance, the body artist in performance *is* the work, which doesn't exist outside the performance. Which, of course, is what we say about all performance, though little of what we see causes us to feel that singularity with anything like the same degree of either psychic or physical risk, nor as a decisive intervention in cultural politics.

As a praxis, body art no longer has the ideological purchase or aesthetic currency it had in the 1970s, but it remains at the existential level the nuclear model of all performance, in which the art act is a war of nerves, with the body as a buffer between the artist and a corrupting economy. There are varieties of body art, alluded to before, that are relatively warm-hearted, inviting, and not overtly political, but even when seductive its independence depends on a certain anxiety and, at its most powerful, a form of terror: one resists alienation by demanding complicity. And both the terror and the complicity are not merely the strategies of a self-renunciating modernism but have their antecedents in the practices of the ancient theater, figured most controversially in the notion of catharsis, which has long been at the center of arguments about the politics of form. To the degree that it was political, body art was not, however, seeking a cathartic response, as an alleviation of feeling, nor could it count upon it in a period of anesthetized feeling.

There are kinds of body art that recognize, no holds barred, that they must work at extremities to have any impact at all. At the psychic level what is taken as an objective is the illusion of mental health. The psychological and social order, which has been unceasingly questioned through the whole history of the modern, has either been so nauseated by the questioning or so desensitized that it has to be confronted with actual rather than surrogate risk. In the days of existential anguish, after the war, we could exhort ourselves to accept the moral tightrope, which very soon became merely metaphorical. Body art produced metaphors, too, but with the literalization of danger at the extremity of the actual. As with Philipe Petit on the tightrope between the twin towers of the World Trade Center, there was a perilous distance in the extremity that could turn it into a figure with real symbolic force.

As an offshoot of conceptual art, much of this was theorized, here and abroad. There was, for instance, a high theoretical impetus in the sadomasochistic performances of the Viennese Action group: Nitsch, Muehl, Brus, and Schwarzkogler. The events they conceived were more orgiastic in their concerted extremity, as political manifestations, than almost anything we encountered in the United States, including the performances of the Living Theater, which for all its outrageousness had nothing like Brus's swallowing of urine or Nitsch's disembowelings of animals or the saturation of the performance space with excrement and blood or the self-desecrating violence of Schwarzkogler, who has been mythicized for, quite literally, killing himself in his art. In France there were somewhat similar manifestations, if not quite so repellent, in Situationist occurrences or the revival of surrealism in the form of happenings, by Jean-Jacques Lebel (who in the May Revolution of 1968 also made a performance of the takeover of the Odéon from an older avant-garde figure, Jean-Louis Barrault). As with Joseph Beuys in Germany, there were pedagogical, mythicizing, and solipsistic tendencies too, sometimes picking up impulses from the aestheticized domesticity of Fluxus and turning it all into a political statement: thus, Michel Journiac's *Mass for a Body* (1969), a reflection on (dis)affiliation and solitude, in which he drew his own blood to make a pudding to be offered in communion.

These provocations—for that's what they embody—are counter-images of an ideological order, in which the body insists (or is made to insist) on its *substance* as the most sacred of taboos, what was not meant to be violated, yet is nevertheless manipulated, mutilated, castrated, consumed by all ideology. There is in these self-inflicted lacerations a remorseless refusal of all restriction by repressive authority, including the traces of authority inscribed in the body itself, as an inheritance of senselessly self-depriving privative being. As with Journiac's mass, the performer literally inserts himself as a communicant between the desire for thoroughly unobstructed being and the degraded system that would, with impunity, deny it. That there were Catholic themes and rhetoric in the body language of this sacrificial art was surely to be expected, but the religious figuration could be eclectic, as in Linda Montano's *Mitchell's Death* (1978), in which the sound from an Indian *sruti* box (Hindu) and a Japanese bowl gong (Buddhist) were amplified three times over, while a video monitor showed Montano applying acupuncture needles to her face in mourning for her dead husband. This event was not meant as a provocation but, rather, as a ritual of mourning, crossing the boundaries between art and life.

But to return from this communion to the empirical roots of the subject of knowledge, the heuristic passion of body art: Chris Burden's risks were no less that for the precautions he took to research how the body might withstand crawling over broken glass or the precise point on the palm where a nail might be driven so he might be crucified on a

Volkswagen without irreparable harm. What he was seeking, however, in this sacrificial image was not so much participation in a ritual but a certain kind of knowledge and decisive awareness, in himself, in the viewer, of something more in the body politic than the limited contingency of pain—rather, its suffusion in social fact and history. As with Gina Pane, the submission of the body is a forensic act refusing the reality of pain in human affairs as a tragic and irreversible condition. The performers inflicted pain on themselves so that whoever took notice by being at the event was *on* notice that the only intolerable pain was that gratuitously or compulsively exercised by the social order upon the body. Here the body is conceived of as a final conscience. One can see how the body art of Stelarc—who suspended himself like a bird with fishhooks through his flesh—might have been derived from this, with the notion of the obsolete body as a form of higher morality.

Pane, like Burden, prepared herself over a period of months for the extreme discomforts to which she submitted. There was an empirical regimen through which she learned, like fire-walkers or contortionists, to withstand the ordeal: swallowing rotten meat, walking up a ladder whose rungs have sharp cutting edges, barefooted, or crushing glass in her mouth. When performed the activity was relentless, unmitigated, with no relief for the viewer from its implications, either the mask of indifference or, by censuring the risk taken, moral outrage at the event. If you watched it, you were complicit, and complicit, moreover, with more than the suffering there. (With Burden, it should be said, there were morally dubious events, in one case at least, when his own body wasn't at stake, justifying perhaps more than outrage. That was the event in which he fired at a plane taking off at the Los Angeles airport.)[15] There was always the risk, as with any aestheticized violence, that it might be desensitizing too, or possibly lurid, as with some spectators who, if given a chance, will try to outdo the performer in inflicting pain, less likely upon themselves than upon the performer, as some did once with Marina Abramovic; she did, however, present the temptation: a totally passive body with razor blades beside it. What impressed me, however, in such events—for all the behavior that could be almost unbearable to watch—was the almost Platonic insistence on the purity of thought, the integrity of conception and analysis, and a mastery of the body not unlike that in the spiritual disciplines, sometimes drawing specifically on those disciplines, or based on research of an almost scholarly kind.

In such performance the apparent pain is displaced into a sort of corporeal discourse on other issues: sexuality, power, authority, the family, freedom, terrorism, and torture, and in the material duration of real time, the ordeal or transcendence of time itself. It is this discourse, aroused by the bodily sacrifice of the subject of knowledge, that connects these avant-garde experiments to certain figures of the ancient theater, dominantly the impaled Prometheus, who initiated discourse as the subject of violence, itself subjected, which is why those imaged atrocities, more or less mutated or sublimated in subsequent forms of drama, or— as the charge was eventually made—exhausted as *images,* are still unpurged in the mind.

At the same time they raise the kind of question that was prompted by Brecht in his critique of tragedy: Is it ideologically regressive, even barbaric, to think of (or with) the body thus? Or if—through the mirror stage of Lacan or the endgame of Beckett or the deadends of deconstruction or the reflections of Benjamin on the corpselike body in the ruins of time—we are constrained to reassess the idea of tragedy: Is it ideologically stupid to think we should ever forget? Or do we ever forget? Or is it that we've had along with talk of the death of tragedy a twisted version of an active forgetting: the invention of aesthetic strategies that would, indeed, either anesthetize us against emotions we found intolerable or, as eventually in body art, confront us in such a way that they could be absorbed or experienced again? I am not saying that was the intention of those artists who made performances of their bodies, but it seems to me of historical consequence that their work had something of that effect, corresponding with the (impasse of) theory that would lead, as with Derrida on the cruelty of Artaud, to rethinking tragedy, its fatal representation and suspect cause and effect.

It was the intimidating prospect of that causation, the apparency of an appalling closure, that yielded to another cruelty in the history of modernism: the techniques of anatomy—cutting, tearing, rending, fracture—until we came to take dismemberment for granted, with discontinuity and indeterminacy, as the critical feature of postmodern forms. If it seemed at first like a revolutionary break, it is by no means conclusive that we have superseded the painful syntax of the tragic condition, its visceral realism. Of the disposition to believe that we have—as the psychoaesthetic ground of an alternative to the bourgeois order, with a disjunct politics of the expressive body, autistic, schizoid, postoedipal, whatever—we may say what Brecht himself did about the libertarian sentiments and vertigo of an older expressionism by which some felt themselves carried away: "It was very soon evident that such people had merely freed themselves from grammar, not *capitalism.*"[16] That the realism of the remark seems like a prophecy confirmed by current events is perhaps not so surprising as the fact that, with the severest strains upon it, by artists, mass culture, the whole transgressive agenda of cultural critique, the grammar is still intact, and with it the issues we thought to deal with in the languages of performance. That includes, of course, the language invented by Brecht for the unresolved issue of tragic drama, which he thought inimical to social change. Like the unpurged image of Mother Courage revolving alone on the empty stage, moving as if in possession through the grip of *necessity,* the question remains: *Is it?* and is it, really, *dis*empowering?

NOTES

This essay is, with a few minor changes, part of a chapter from *To All Appearances: Ideology and Performance* (New York and London: Routledge, 1992). Reprinted by permission.

1. See Michael Gill, *Images of the Body* (London: Bodley Head, 1989).

2. See George Lichtheim, *The Concept of Ideology and Other Essays* (New York: Vintage, 1967), 7–8.

3. Georg Büchner, *Danton's Death, Complete Plays and Prose,* intro. and trans. Carl Richard Mueller (New York: Hill and Wang, 1963), 47, act 3, scene 3 (hereafter cited in the text).

4. The phantasmaphysics of Deleuze, its multiple, polyscenic, liberated theater, is described by Michel Foucault in "Theatrum Philosophicum," trans. Donald F. Bouchard and Sherry Simon, in *Language, Counter-Memory, Practice: Selected Essays and Interviews,* ed. and intro. Donald F. Bouchard (Ithaca: Cornell University Press, 1977), 171 (hereafter abbreviated in the text as *LCP*).

5. See *The Audience* (Baltimore: Johns Hopkins University Press, 1990), 280–88.

6. Jane Comfort, quoted in Deborah Jowitt, "Talk to Me," *Village Voice,* 19 April 1989 (Dance Special), 9.

7. Paul de Man, *Allegories of Reading: Figural Language in Rousseau, Nietzsche, Rilke, and Proust* (New Haven: Yale University Press, 1979), 11–12.

8. Roland Barthes, *Roland Barthes by Roland Barthes,* trans. Richard Howard (New York: Hill and Wang, 1977), 60–61.

9. Arthur Kroker and David Cook, *The Postmodern Scene: Excremental Culture and Hyper-Aesthetics* (New York: St. Martin's, 1986), 26.

10. Samuel Beckett, *Worstward Ho* (New York: Grove, 1983), 7.

11. Michel Foucault, *The Foucault Reader,* ed. Paul Rabinow (New York: Pantheon, 1988), 173.

12. Roland Barthes, "Lesson in Writing," *Image-Music-Text,* trans. Stephen Heath (New York: Hill and Wang, 1977), 171; hereafter the volume will be abbreviated as *I-M-T.*

13. Laurie Anderson, "From *Americans on the Move*," *October* 8 (1979): 54–55.

14. Charles Olson, *"Additional Prose": A Bibliography on America Propriocep-tion, and Other Notes and Essays,* ed. George F. Butterick (Bolinas, Calif.: Four Seasons, 1974), 17.

15. For an intelligently skeptical view of various aspects of body art, from its ephemerality to its morality, particularly that of Chris Burden, see Max Kozloff, "Pygmalion Reversed," *Artforum* 15 (1975): 30–37.

16. Bertolt Brecht, "On the Formalistic Character of the Theory of Realism," in *Aesthetics and Politics,* ed. Ronald Taylor (London: Verso/NLB, 1977), 73.

Contributors

Houston A. Baker, Jr. is Professor of English and Director, Center for the Study of Black Literature and Culture, University of Pennsylvania. His most recent book is *Workings of the Spirit: The Poetics of Afro-American Women's Writing*.

Herbert Blau is Distinguished Professor of English and Comparative Literature, University of Wisconsin–Milwaukee. His most recent book is *To All Appearances: Ideology and Performance*.

Morris Eaves is Professor of English, University of Rochester. His most recent book is *The Counter–Arts Conspiracy: Art and Industry in the Age of Blake*.

Margaret J. M. Ezell is Professor of English, Texas A&M University. Her most recent book is *Writing Women's Literary History*.

Hamlin Hill is Ralph R. Thomas Distinguished Professor, Texas A&M University. His most recent book is *Essays on American Humor: Blair through the Ages*.

Jeanne Holland is Assistant Professor of English, University of Wyoming. She is completing a book on Emily Dickinson.

J. Paul Hunter is Chester D. Tripp Professor of Humanities, University of Chicago. His most recent book is *Before Novels: The Cultural Contexts of Eighteenth-Century English Fiction*.

Howard Marchitello is Assistant Professor of English, Texas A&M University. He is completing a book on Renaissance narratology.

Jerome J. McGann is Commonwealth Professor of English, University of Virginia. His most recent book is *Black Riders: The Visible Language of Modernism*.

W. J. T. Mitchell is Gaylor Donnelly Distinguished Service Professor in the Humanities, University of Chicago, and Editor of *Critical Inquiry*. His most recent book is *Art and the Public Sphere*.

Katherine O'Brien O'Keeffe is Professor of English, University of Notre Dame. Her most recent book is *Visible Song: Transitional Literacy in Old English Verse*.

Index

Page numbers in italics refer to figures.